BULL RUN
Its Strategy and Tactics

BULL RUN
Its Strategy and Tactics

BY

R. M. JOHNSTON

Author of The Roman Theocracy and the Republic, etc., etc.

JOHN KALLMANN, PUBLISHERS
701 West North St. • Carlisle, PA 17013

TO

INTRODUCTION

Bull Run, the first major land battle of the U.S. Civil War, what better illustration of the need for military preparedness could there be? So asserts R. M. Johnston in this thought-provoking text. Johnston concentrates on the military conduct of this battle and leaves the study of the underlying political motivations, not insubstantial, to others. Public opinion, stimulated by a critical press, was pressuring official Washington to strike at the rebels. Now these rebels were approaching Manassas Junction, a strategic rail point just under thirty miles from Washington, D.C. The popular hope was that the enthusiastic volunteers could squash the rebellious Confederates and promptly move on to Richmond, the relocated seat of the Confederate Government freshly removed from Montgomery, Alabama.

Following the first battle of Bull Run, Confederate General Joseph E. Johnston wrote, "If the tactics of the Federals had been equal to their strategy, we should have been beaten." R. M. Johnston concludes in this book, "The military problem was one for the experts, and not to be solved by a handful of improperly organized three months' volunteers." Elsewhere in the text, the author decries the rout at Bull Run as, "a lamentable illustration of the awful calamities invariably attending nations that lack or neglect an army." The problem of effective Federal leadership would continue to haunt the administration in Washington and bring hope to Richmond for several years until the struggle at Gettysburg and the surrender at Vicksburg.

Since the founding of the country, military preparedness has always been a controversial issue in the American democratic tradition. The tendency has been to raise armies as required when national exigencies arise and not to keep a large standing army as might be the case in some European countries of the day. At the time of secession and the first shots of Fort Sumter, the U.S. standing army numbered only 17,000 men and 600 officers. On April 15, 1861, President Lincoln issued a proclamation to raise 75,000 militia for three months' service. As Johnston points out here, those who signed up right away would earn their time served and be discharged nearly a week before Bull Run. Of those troops present at Bull Run, many were of the three months' variety. The president again called for more troops on May 3, 1861, this time 500,000, but too late to be effectively trained and ready for Bull Run. Johnston concludes, "Had the country possessed even 50,000 men, a regular division would have been in the field at Bull Run, and few who read this account will doubt that the result of the battle would have been reversed, and the whole course of the war thereby altered."

Robert Matteson Johnston, 1867–1920, was born in Paris where his parents resided. The son of William Edward, a physician, and Bertha (née Matteson) Johnston, the father was formerly a New York *Times* correspondent in the Crimean War. The father's interest in military affairs was to have a formative effect on the son's later academic and writing career. Educated at Pembroke College, Cambridge, Johnston received an A.B. degree in 1889. Later, he received a law degree but never practiced, he engaged in private study in Cambridge and then published the first of many historical books, *The Roman Theocracy and the*

Republic in 1901. After a brief stay in Naples, the author came to the United States where he taught at Harvard, Mount Holyoke and Bryn Mawr. A distinguished lecturer and prolific author, R. M. Johnston was particularly well-known as a proponent of military preparedness as a key to a nation's survival and strength, a theme underscored in this book.

May 15, 1996   John Kallmann, Publishers

PREFACE

HALF a century after the event, the campaigns of the Civil War may well pass out of the domain of reminiscence to enter that of military history. As that term is now understood in other countries, it means the dispassionate, minute, and technical investigation of every form of military activity, from the organization of a mule train to the psychology of a general-in-chief; it cares little for eloquence, the picturesque, and the glorification or depreciation of individual heroes.

From the point of view of the military art one can mark off, in the history of the Civil War, three periods. In the first, we find little but crudeness; in the second, crudeness is flanked by great daring and brilliancy; in the third, brilliancy sobers down to a ripe and masterly exposition of military science; first was Bull Run, then came the Second Manassas, and last of all the terrific struggle from the Wilderness to Appomattox. That is why one is tempted to begin at the beginning, to examine the conditions under which was fought the first conflict of the Civil War. By investigating its crudities, we shall understand better the brilliancy and the maturity that followed.

Bull Run was a lamentable illustration of the awful

calamities invariably attending nations that lack or neglect an army. Fortunate it was for us that our brother,
not our enemy, smote us. Yet Bull Run was just as inevitable in 1861 as something similar would be to-day had
we to face a military power in the field. With our form
and traditions of government, it is futile to lay at the door
of those who for the moment held office, the fact that the
United States had no army, that there were no means
for repressing sedition before it could be organized into
revolt, that no armed force could be raised after the crisis
had arisen save by the devious and wasteful arts of political persuasion. Had President Lincoln at the outset
known so much of military affairs and so little of public
opinion as to demand not 75,000 three months' volunteers
but 300,000 regulars, he would instantly have lost all his
hold on the country; and it is disheartening to reflect that
no other politician could have acted very differently in
his place. Some will answer that, this is the price that
this country has paid and will continue to pay willingly
to escape from the burden of such military establishments
as those under which European countries groan. It is
really the price of ignorance, — ignorance of our national needs, of what constitutes an efficient army, of
what stability an army insures; ignorance of our long
record of inefficiency, disaster, and disgrace; ignorance
of the state of the world, of where it is moving, of how
our interests are involved; ignorance of how we might

suffer attack and of how we might repel it. What we need above all is to get away from glittering generalities, from empty and ignorant sentimentalism, to become businesslike, to add up profit and loss, to estimate what the lack of an army cost us in 1861, to take enough pains to investigate the facts that surround us at the present day.

In narrating the events of the Bull Run campaign I have said little of the political conditions that underlay the struggle of the contending armies. Yet in one sense the foundations of strategy are always to be sought for in such conditions;—von Clausewitz is perhaps sounder on this point than some more modern theorists. I have not thought it worth while to demonstrate at length that the advance of McDowell's army on Manassas might be a mistake as a purely military step, but inevitable as a political one; and that war is a phase of politics. And had McDowell won, which, in view of the composition of the Confederate army, was always possible, Lincoln and the political argument would have appeared justified. It seemed better to indicate in a few brief references only the salient facts of the political situation that led Scott, McDowell, and their Southern opponents to take measures not always in accord with the strict canons of the military art. For there was danger of being led away at inordinate length into non-military considerations, and it is true to say that a book might well be written on the topic of the political organization of the American Republic in relation to military problems. The best course seemed to be to leave this aspect of things, so far as it was not absolutely relevant, for special treatment by others.

To Captain A. L. Conger, U.S.A., a profound student of military history and theory, I owe an unusually heavy debt of gratitude for reading the book in proof. His vigorous and independent views have influenced what I have had to say to an extent which I gratefully acknowledge. Where I have not been able to accept his opinions it has been with reluctance and misgiving; and I have tried, so far as the form would permit, to convey to the reader in footnotes and otherwise that a divergent view might well be taken. Perhaps we were furthest apart in our estimate of General Scott, in whom, as I understand, Captain Conger will admit no weakening. The unevenness or petulance of his dispatches to Patterson would mark nothing more than natural impatience with an incompetent subordinate; the suggested concentration at Leesburg would be defensible on military grounds, and was promptly abandoned not because it was an ill-considered move, as I believe, but because Scott's subordinates were disinclined for it, which, of course, was the case. This is not the place to put before the reader lengthy explanations of events that will be set forth in their proper order. Scott's correspondence

and actions, viewed as a whole, give me the impression
of a man for the most part able and vigorous, but too old
to maintain his strength and clearness of view consistently.
The convergent march on Leesburg and the advance
thence to the Manassas Railroad appear to me far more
dangerous and time-consuming than the advance from
Alexandria; while the possible retreat to Point of Rocks,
where there were no fortifications, might have been in-
finitely more disastrous than the one in which McDowell
was actually involved.

The operations in the Shenandoah Valley have been
treated as subsidiary to the main theme, and the details
for this part of the work have been cut down as far as
possible.

A point of some interest, perhaps, to special students
of the epoch, is that the newspapers are of little value
as historical evidence in connection with military affairs.
For the political side, Mr. Rhodes has demonstrated in
his History what use may be made of newspaper sources.
For the military side, I have found them consistently
inaccurate.

The book is based mainly on the evidence given before
the Committee on the Conduct of the War and on the
Official Records of the War of the Rebellion (cited
O. R.). I have tried not to overload my pages with footnotes, and therefore here emphasize that almost every
paragraph goes back to many places in these two pri-

mary sources. (For Bibliography, see Appendix A.) I have further had the good fortune to study the battleground in the company of several distinguished field officers of our army, among whom I may mention General Crozier, General Liggett, and Colonel Hasbrouck. To my friend, Major J. W. McAndrew, Instructor at the Army War College, I am under special obligations.

I have further to thank for various services the Trustees of the Confederate Museum, Miss McKenney, of Richmond, Miss Martin, of the Virginia State Library, and the librarians of Harvard University, the Massachusetts Society of Military History, the Loyal Legion, and other institutions.

CONTENTS

MAPS

(A Bibliography of contemporary and other maps will be found at page 282.)

BULL RUN

ITS STRATEGY AND TACTICS

I

MILITARY AND POLITICAL CONDITIONS AT THE OUTBREAK OF THE CIVIL WAR

THIS book is concerned with a campaign only, and not with the struggle that broke out between North and South in the year 1861. That campaign was, however, the first in a protracted conflict, and for this reason it will not be possible to draw a rigid line excluding from consideration preliminary matters that really belong to the Civil War viewed as a whole. And it must first of all be pointed out that it was the military feebleness of the United States that made this atrocious war inevitable and so extraordinary a military operation as that of Bull Run possible. Had the country possessed a regular force of no more than 150,000 men, the Southern cities would have been at once occupied and no rising could have occurred. Had the country possessed even 50,000 men, a regular division would have been in the field at Bull Run, and few who read this account will doubt that the result of that battle would have been reversed, and the whole course of the war thereby altered.

At that epoch the army of the United States was a force of less than 17,000 men, mostly distributed in small detachments over the Far West, an immense tract as yet unpierced by railroads. There were about 600 commissioned officers, and a good many graduates of West Point in civil life who might be expected to re-enter the service in a national emergency.[1] This force, of which little was immediately available, might fairly be described as non-existent for the purpose in hand when it is considered that its commander-in-chief, when the crisis arose, advised his Government that the Northern States would have to raise some 300,000 men to put down the South, — a very conservative estimate as it proved. The Government was not disposed, however, to follow the advice of competent authority on a matter in which journalists and politicians have too often had more to say than professional soldiers. Yet it was from the outset admitted that for all practical purposes a new army would have to be cut out of whole cloth. In the South there was a similar situation. The old army, however, was to supply some valuable leadership for the two new armies, Federal and Confederate.

[1] Of those in active service 279, almost one half, followed their States when they seceded.

The corps of officers was very well grounded in the rudiments of the military art, an intelligent, efficient, select group of men; but it was without experience in staff work and in handling masses. The technical services were of good quality, though very small in numbers. When the crisis came the body of officers split into two unequal halves, but the South was more fortunate than the North, as it secured among its recruits General J. E. Johnston, quartermaster-general of the army, Colonel R. E. Lee, and Colonel A. S. Johnston, reputed the three best soldiers in the service after the veteran commander-in-chief, Winfield Scott. The regular troops, however, did not follow this example, but stuck to their colors. They suffered a great weakening by the sudden resignation of so many of their officers and by the detaching of many others to assist in forming new battalions both of regulars and of volunteers. Even so weakened they were steady and valuable troops, much superior to volunteers at the outbreak of the war. But the regulars were mostly in the Far West, and by the end of the month of June, 1861, only one provisional battalion of infantry had been brought together at Washington; it was made up of companies drawn from the 2d, 3d, and 8th Infantry. There were in addition a battalion of 300 marine recruits mustered in on the 1st of July, and a provisional regiment of horse drawn from the 1st and 2d Cavalry, with a squadron of dragoons. The artillery was stronger, amounting, when the first campaign opened, to nine batteries.[1] These troops, less than 2500 in all, actually made up the whole regular contingent that took part in the first campaign of the war.

Failing regulars, volunteers had to be employed, and on the Northern side political, not military, considerations dictated the Government's policy. A call was made on the 15th of April for 75,000 volunteers to serve for three months;[2] and it may be remarked that the men who enrolled that very day actually earned their discharge nearly a week before Bull Run was fought, on the 21st of July. In May, 40,000 more volunteers were called for, and at the same time an increase of 40,000 men in the personnel of the army and navy was ordered. These two steps, however, had little real bearing on the first campaign of the war, which is all that this book is concerned with, for that was fought almost wholly by insufficiently trained and organized volunteers and against the judgment of the military authorities. The volunteers came largely from the existing militia organizations, which in some cases went to the front in a body. These organizations were not very valuable for real military purposes, except in some parts

---

[1] Batteries: G, I, 1st reg.; A, D, E, G, M, 2d reg.; E, 3d reg.; D, 5th reg.

[2] Some States refused their quota, and less than 45,000 were actually mustered in.

of the South where the fear of a possible negro revolt stimulated them to a higher standard of efficiency than existed in the North.

To equip, arm, drill, organize, make mobile, and place in the field these volunteers in any considerable numbers, was a formidable task; especially with the bulk of the men serving on a three months' time limit; and had this been the Government's reason for rejecting the advice of raising an army of 300,000 men, it might in a way have been defensible. Recruiting produced in many cases wholly undesirable results; in the great Northern cities it was too often colored by politics, so that many regiments, from colonel to drummer boy, suggested ward organizations in uniform; in the South there were too many cases of enlistment of workingmen made practically compulsory owing to the stoppage of employment. It was the North undoubtedly that got the worse results from a military point of view in respect of the armies that fought at Bull Run. The loafer was encouraged to believe he was off for a military picnic; and there is a case on record in which the recruiting officer guaranteed, as a special inducement to the would-be defenders of their country, that they were to be stationed at Washington and would not have to face the privations of the camp.[1] Scarcely more convincing were the fancy uniforms in which several of these corps bedecked themselves. There was little distinction to be drawn between officers and

[1] Cte. de Paris, *Guerre Civile*, I, 314.

men, though here and there a West Pointer, or a civilian of character and convictions, served to leaven the mass. The transition from the arts of political persuasion to the practice of military discipline could not be said to have been entered on before the battle of Bull Run was fought. The colonels and quartermasters sometimes treated the whole business as part of the political game, and set to work to earn their little profits out of the provisioning and outfitting of their men.

Having thus stated the bad side of the picture, — and it was a very bad side, — the good one may be more safely added. Scattered in varying proportion through the ranks were men who had come to serve a cause, who had faith and courage. From the West came a few regiments of farmers' sons, that sturdiest and best of all materials for the fighting line. Through all the ranks coursed the native American virtues, quickness, adaptability, intelligence, self-reliance, resourcefulness, cohesive qualities of the first order when retreat has to be faced and morale is shaken.

The tactical instruction given to these troops need not be viewed in any detail so far as it affects the operations of the Bull Run campaign.[1] The fundamental evolutions were the regimental manœuvre by column of divisions and deployment in line of battle on a depth of three

---

[1] The tactical systems, North and South, were based on the French drill books of 1831 and 1845.

ranks.[1] There were few drillmasters available, and the three months' volunteers had attained very little proficiency even in these fundamental manœuvres when they finally went out to meet the foe. In loading, aiming, and firing properly, they showed little proficiency, either not charging their musket at all, charging it improperly, or charging it over and over again. When, by chance or by application, they succeeded in discharging it, they generally missed the object aimed at; for it is calculated that from 8,000 to 10,000 bullets were fired for every man killed or wounded, which is probably a conservative estimate.[2] Volleys at command were unusual; the troops generally fired at will.

In the North equipment was forthcoming in most of the States, and arms too, and in this matter there was less fault to find. The Springfield percussion cap rifle, calibre 58, was sighted to 1000 yards and was theoretically accurate up to 650. It loaded through the muzzle, however, and was soon to be displaced by the breech-loader which the Prussian army was then already introducing. The Ordnance Department worked with efficiency, as is witnessed by the fact that during the year 1861 it supplied: 1,276,686

[1] Sherman actually marched his brigade from the Carter house to Young's branch according to Guibert's famous principle of the *ordre mixte*, line and column.

[2] Tippitt, *Tactical Use of the Three Arms*, 29. There is nothing surprising in these figures. Archibald Forbes reckoned that at Plevna the Turkish infantry fired 60,000 rounds for every Russian who went into hospital.

firearms; 1926 field and siege guns; 1206 guns of position; and 214,000,000 cartridges. The Southern States were less well off in this respect, for although they started with a considerable stock of arms sent South by Floyd, Secretary of War under Buchanan, they were later under a severe handicap for equipment, munitions and arms, owing to the blockade and to their lack of manufacturing resources. The infantry was at first supplied with the old smoothbore percussion cap musket, calibre 69, and to a certain extent used even old flintlocks. As to the artillery, it is said that during the siege of Richmond the men of the 1st Connecticut Artillery picked up shells of no less than thirty-six different models that the Confederates had fired.

The field artillery at the outbreak of the war was armed with smoothbore six- and twelve-pounder muzzle-loaders, but rifled guns were just coming in. The detail of the artillery used in the Bull Run campaign will be given presently. Here it will suffice to say that the smooth-bores, six's and twelve's, had an effective range of 750 and of 1100 yards,[1] while the rifling about doubled the range. Grapeshot and case might be used at 600 yards, and was effective at 400 yards, while canister ranged from 300 yards down. It may be added that at short ranges, and this covers the case of the fighting on the Henry

[1] This is a minimum figure; some authorities rating their fire effective up to about 400 yards more.

house plateau, the smoothbore six-pounders were perhaps more effective than the rifled, as shells from the latter, owing to their high velocity, were apt to bury themselves in the ground on striking instead of continuing *en ricochet.*

The Engineer Department was not to play any essential part in the Bull Run campaign and hardly requires notice in that limited connection, but the transportation service was of greater importance. The most characteristic quality of a field army is mobility, and while this depends largely on the skill and experience of its staff and even of officers of subordinate rank, the chief factor is of necessity mechanical, — that is, wagons, horses, mules, in short, all means of transport. To keep a large body of troops moving through a country of slight resources at a rapid pace and supplied with all it needs, is therefore a large and complicated operation. Neither in the North nor in the South was there any transport service worth mentioning, nor any experienced transport corps. The transportation problem was a big one. McClellan, in 1862, got 3 days' rations into 1830 wagons ; Grant, in 1864, got 10 days' rations into 4300 wagons. Another line on the problem was the computation that each man required per day 4 pounds of transport and each animal 25 pounds ; at which rate about 2000 wagons might keep supplied an army of 100,000 men at two marches from its base, so long as it made no advance.

These calculations would always vary with the complex factors governing each particular problem ; but enough has been said to show how difficult it might be. It is hardly necessary to add that it takes even more skill and experience to manœuvre hundreds of wagons and cattle than it does to handle troops on the march.

At the outbreak of the Civil War the armies were as far from the point of mobility as could well be imagined. A large part of J. E. Johnston's men in the Shenandoah brought along their trunks, and had neither knapsacks nor wagons ; it would have required the combined efforts of several city express companies to move his army for a day's journey in its then condition. His artillery caissons were for the most part boxes fitted on to the running parts of farm wagons. Johnston and every other general had to improvise a transport service, and few officers had any experience whatever in dealing with this fundamental problem on anything like a large scale.[1]

In the enumeration of these deficiencies no space has yet been found for the greatest one of all, that of the higher organization of the armies. There were no brigade, division, and corps organizations ; there were no officers who had ever handled a brigade, division, or

[1] Exception must be made of Colonel A. S. Johnston, 1st U.S. Cavalry, who had solved a great transportation problem in his march to Salt Lake City.

corps;[1] there was no staff for such bodies, nor officers trained to do such staff work. How lamentably both armies, North and South, broke down at Bull Run for lack of this higher organization will be shown at length presently.

We have already noted where the conditions did not apply equally to North and South. But a few of the points of difference between the two sections deserve emphasis.

The South suffered from certain disadvantages: —

1. Although the officers of the regular army split in about equal numbers and the South secured the services of almost her fair proportion of them, the rank and file, mostly Irish and German, stuck to their colors and their paymaster. There was no nucleus of regular troops in the Southern armies. The real importance in this matter lay in the artillery service.

2. Armament was less good owing largely to the fact that the great manufacturing centres were in the North, and that the blockade operated unfavorably to the South; but this difference did not materially affect the operations of the Bull Run campaign, save again in the matter of the artillery, in which the Federals had a marked superiority.

3. The white population of the Southern States was

---

[1] Except a very few veteran officers who played no real part, and the commander-in-chief, Winfield Scott.

roughly only about a quarter of that of the Northern States. This disadvantage was in part neutralized by the greater demand that was made on the Southern population.

4. The South could not control the sea; this fact played no appreciable part in the Bull Run campaign.

The advantages of the South were: —

1. The defensive was in many ways easier to sustain than the offensive, over the vast distances involved, and by raw, half-organized armies.

2. The Southern militia was more efficient than the Northern owing to a variety of reasons, among others the constant though latent fear of having to cope with a negro insurrection. The Confederate Government replied to the Northern call of 75,000 men for three months, by calling up 100,000 men for twelve months. If not a sound step, it made, at all events, a better starting-point.

3. The Government, unlike that of the North, was brought together with a rebellion, and therefore a war, as its immediate policy. A soldier, Jefferson Davis, graduate of West Point, Secretary of War under Pierce, chairman of the Senate Committee on Military Affairs, who had seen active service in the rank of colonel, was made chief executive officer, and whatever his mistakes, this undoubtedly helped the Southern States to create a military organization.

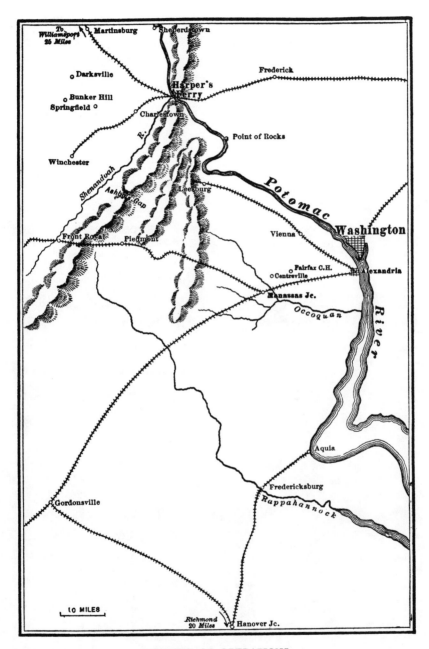

THEATRE OF OPERATIONS

STRATEGIC CONSIDERATIONS

The strategical situation, as it appeared during the first few weeks of the war, before either side had as yet armies fit for field operations, may be summed up as follows : —

NORTH. Washington, the Federal capital, lay on the north bank of the Potomac. Across that river was Virginia, greatest and most important of the seceding States. From the heights of Arlington on the Virginia side, the Capitol itself lay within long cannon range. There was therefore urgent need for the North to carry hostilities into Virginia at this point, if only for the sake of preserving the Federal capital.

About one hundred miles away, almost due south, lay Richmond, capital of Virginia and of the Confederate States, and for that and other reasons one of the chief cities of the South. If it was urgently necessary for the North to invade Virginia, then Richmond, almost inevitably, became the objective of an invading force, and consequently any army formed by the Confederacy to protect Richmond. The main line of shock between North and South clearly lay between these two cities.

Fifty miles to the west of this main line of shock lay a subsidiary line, where, beyond the Blue Ridge, the Shenandoah River flowed northwards through a broad and fertile valley to Harper's Ferry, there to join the Potomac.

Harper's Ferry, on the Virginia side of the Potomac, was an arsenal of the United States, valuable for its stock of arms and for its factory and repair shops. Its importance was heightened by the fact that the Baltimore and Ohio Railroad, the great link between Washington and the West, here passed to the south of the river. As a military position, however, it was weak, for it was dominated from the north bank by Maryland Heights, and from the south by Loudoun Heights, each within less than a mile, and rising five hundred feet above the town. To hold both the town and heights would require a very large garrison, perhaps 15,000 to 20,000 men; and, apart from immobilizing these troops, the step was of doubtful value. Harper's Ferry, however, was supposed to have political importance ; for Maryland, north of the Potomac, sympathized with the South. At the moment when the first volunteers were enrolled, it seemed as though Maryland would join the Southern States, prevent the passage of the newly raised troops, cut off Washington, and thereby throw the national capital into Southern hands. The troops coming down from Pennsylvania, New York, Massachusetts, had prevented this, had got Baltimore under control, and had begun to mass into an army at Washington, closing intercourse between Maryland and Virginia at that point. This left Harper's Ferry as the next point of contact to the west between disaffected Maryland and seceding

Virginia; if the South held it, communication between the two states would be protected.

There were other directions besides the two just noted in which North and South were to come into conflict: the sea, the southern coast-line, Western Virginia, the Ohio and Mississippi Valleys; but to consider the strategical issues involved at all and each of these points would only confuse the narrower one involved in a study of the Bull Run campaign. For that, the general outlook on the Northern side may be summed up as follows. An offensive move from Washington into Virginia towards Richmond was from the first moment clearly indicated, flanked by a subsidiary movement to seize Harper's Ferry, and thence possibly to operate south along the valley of the Shenandoah, or southeast across the Blue Ridge to the valley of the Rappahannock, in direct support of the main advance. We shall see later, in closer detail, how these movements might be effected.

SOUTH. The Southern outlook was defensive, for the Southern States claimed merely to remain outside the Union; they had no policy of repression, that is of invasion or the offensive. The general view of the situation was thereby simplified, but in a strategic sense fundamentally weakened. The threatened advance of the North must be resisted. The banks of the Potomac opposite Washington must be guarded. Harper's Ferry must be protected. But no attack was to be planned against the enemy.

At a very early stage the pressure of the armed force at Washington became too great to be withstood by the scattered detachments of Virginia troops along the Potomac, and they were withdrawn some twenty miles within the border to positions protecting Manassas Junction, a point of considerable strategic importance, the situation of which will be described presently. Southern strategy during the early weeks of the war concentrated its efforts on forwarding enough troops to Manassas and Harper's Ferry, to render these two points secure from attack.

II

EARLY MOVEMENTS AND PLANS

THE FEDERALS CROSS THE POTOMAC

IN Washington, Abraham Lincoln was President, and Simon Cameron, Secretary of War ; neither of them had any competence in military matters. Under the President, Lieutenant-General Winfield Scott ranked as commander-in-chief. The Adjutant-General, Colonel Samuel Cooper, and the Quartermaster-General, Brigadier-General Joseph E. Johnston, had both resigned and thrown in their lot with the Confederate States. Colonel Lorenzo Thomas, a capable officer, had succeeded the former, and Major Sibley, and later General Meigs, an excellent quartermaster, had taken Johnston's place. Colonel Ripley was an efficient Chief of Ordnance. Colonel E. D. Townsend, Colonel Baird, Major McDowell all held the rank of A.A.G. [1]

Scott was afflicted with years. His eyesight had become defective ; he could not get into the saddle ; and even in walking he was glad of the assistance of an aide on either side. His determination of character had suffered, and at times his judgment failed. Yet with all

[1] For a full list of officers on the staff see O. R. Ser. III, vol. I, 964.

these drawbacks, obvious to any person of military
training who came into contact with him, Scott was the
only man at Washington competent to give sound advice on the larger military questions. He had proved
himself a great soldier in the Mexican war, and he remained undoubtedly a master of the craft. He could read
large geographical, political, and military problems in
technical terms of the soldier's art, — a rare accomplish-
ment. It was through his competent channel that the
incompetent policy of the Government was to find expression.

The call for volunteers was clearly a political step ;
the merest tyro in the art of war could not have described
it as a military measure in any serious sense. It was a
plank in a popular platform, and unfortunately entailed
a second plank to follow. Having got the three months'
volunteers, they must be made to complete the announced
programme of putting down the Confederacy. But how ?
Scott, replying in military terms, declared there was no
answer, that the thing could not be done at all, that it
required 300,000 men and three years at the minimum.
The President, retorting in political terms, declared that
it must be done by the 75,000 or less men, and within
three months from the 15th of April. Scott bowed his
head, accepted the impossible, and with great courage
and some skill, though not without making mistakes,
attempted to carry the hopeless burden thus thrust on

his aged shoulders. Quite apart from this conflict of views, almost inevitable in a country so loosely organized as the United States, the course of events served to bring about the first great conflict of the war.

Until about the middle of May the situation in Maryland engrossed the attention of the Cabinet and military authorities. From that date it was well in hand, Baltimore being occupied in strength. Troops then began to accumulate in Washington, and, on the 24th of May, Scott decided to transfer a considerable body to Arlington Heights and to Alexandria, on the farther bank of the Potomac.

The troops in Washington were under the immediate command of Brigadier-General Mansfield, and it was his inspector-general, Colonel Heintzelman, who took charge of the movement. General Sandford, New York militia, commanded the force, which consisted of nine volunteer regiments and some details, about 8000 men in all. There was no opposition ; but a shot fired from a window in Alexandria killed Colonel Ellsworth of the 11th New York (zouaves). Three days later Major McDowell, who was promoted to the rank of brigadier-general, was appointed to command the department of Northeastern Virginia.

McDowell was forty-three, a man of remarkably robust physique, square and heavy, with a strong, round head, a short beard, blue eyes, short nose, large cheeks and jaw.

His manner was simple, frank, agreeable.[1] As a boy he had the advantage of some schooling in France, and returning home, entered West Point in 1830, the same year as Beauregard. He graduated much lower, twenty-third, than his future opponent of Bull Run. His first opportunity in the army came with the Mexican War, in which he won the brevet rank of captain at Buena Vista, and proved himself a good staff officer. In 1856 he received the brevet of major, and was continued on staff duty. Although army opinion placed him little, if any, higher than his West Point instructors had, he was selected for the thankless task of leading the three months' volunteers to the fray. As a general he proved faithful to his duty, courageous, painstaking ; but it cannot be said that his abilities extended further.

McDowell's appointment came in the wrong way, for it did not have the approval of the commander-in-chief. Scott was requested, notwithstanding his reluctance, to choose between Mansfield and McDowell, and selected the latter. But he suggested to McDowell that he should find some way of declining the responsibility, which suggestion the latter met with a refusal. A marked coolness resulted, which did not tend to promote cooperation between the two generals.[2] The action of McDowell was purely patriotic; he did not see his way to declining a

---

[1] Russell, *Diary*, I, 137.
[2] *Rep. Cond. War*, II, 37; Fry, *McDowell and Tyler*, 9.

duty, which he appeared as well qualified to bear as any one. A favorable view of his course is strengthened by the fact that at about the same time he appears to have declined the proposal of Cameron to promote him to the rank of major-general.[1] Mansfield, who outranked McDowell, was apparently nettled at not getting the appointment, with the result that friction ensued, and that when the time came for the advance McDowell had much difficulty in getting troops and transport moved over the river to him.[2]

The troops already across the Potomac were distributed along the line of hills immediately overlooking the river opposite the capital at Arlington, and at the little city of Alexandria, four miles downstream, the starting point of the only line of rail that ran southwards from Washington. This was the Orange and Alexandria Railroad that led westerly twenty-five miles to Manassas Junction, and thence another sixty-five miles southwest across the Rappahannock to Gordonsville, from which Richmond could be reached by rail. This was the only connection between the Federal and the Confederate capitals. From Manassas another line, the Manassas Gap Railroad, ran fifty miles to Front Royal in the Shenandoah Valley, a point about forty miles south of Harper's Ferry. A third line, the Loudoun and Hampshire Railroad, ran from

[1] Fry, *McDowell and Tyler*, 9.
[2] Fry, *McDowell and Tyler*, 10.

Alexandria parallel to the Potomac westwards to just beyond Leesburg, about forty miles.

Fortification was the order of the day;[1] although McDowell stated later that in his view an immediate advance against Manassas should have been attempted.[2] Alexandria, the rail-head, Arlington Heights, dominating the capital, and the Long Bridge, connecting Washington with Virginia, must be protected. McDowell at once turned his attention to this and related problems. Finding a great lack of organization among the regiments in his command, even in the matter of obtaining their daily rations, he formed them into brigades, to the number of three. As the Virginia troops had dismantled the railway, removing rolling stock and breaking down bridges, he directed an engineer officer, Colonel Stone, to report on means for placing the Manassas line in working order. He further made an urgent request for staff officers, of whom he was much in need for supervising the manifold details of organization that faced him; several competent engineer officers were promptly sent to him.

Arlington belonged to Robert E. Lee; and it is not without interest to quote the letter which General McDowell wrote to Mrs. Lee on placing his headquarters at her house.

[1] For the detail of the fortifications of Washington constructed in 1861 and 1862 see the general map at end of volume.
[2] *Rep. Cond. War*, I, 134.

ARLINGTON, May 30, 1861.

MRS. R. E. LEE.

MADAM, — Having been ordered by the Government to relieve Major-General Sandford in command of this Department, I had the honor to receive this morning your letter of to-day, addressed to him at this place.

With respect to the occupation of Arlington by the United States troops, I beg to say it has been done by my predecessor with every regard to the preservation of the place. I am here temporarily in camp on the grounds, preferring this to sleeping in the house under the circumstances in which the painful state of the country places me with respect to its proprietors.

I assure you it has been and will be my earnest endeavor to have all things so ordered that on your return you will find things as little disturbed as possible. In this I have the hearty concurrence of the courteous, kind-hearted gentleman in the immediate command of the troops quartered here and who lives in the lower part of the house to insure its being respected.

Everything has been done as you desired with respect to your servants, and your wishes, as far as they are known or could be anticipated, have been complied with. When you desire to return, every facility will be given you for so doing.

I trust, madam, you will not consider it an intrusion if I say I have the most sincere sympathy for your distress, and that, as far as it is compatible with my duty, I shall always be ready to do whatever may alleviate it.

I have the honor to be,
Very respectfully,
Your most obedient servant,
IRVIN McDOWELL.[1]

Meanwhile the city of Washington was seething with excitement. On the 13th of May General Butler had taken military possession of Baltimore, thus making

[1] O. R. Ser. I, vol. II, 655.

secure the communications between Washington and the North. But this was not enough to allay the anxiety of the capital, nor was the presence of ever increasing numbers of troops. Little was known as to what the Southern States were doing, and a constant crop of rumors did duty for news. Among these rumors few were more thrilling and frequent than those reporting a Southern advance to reoccupy the Virginian soil at Alexandria and Arlington, thence doubtless to menace the capital itself.

STRATEGIC CONSIDERATIONS, JUNE 3 TO 15

NORTH. Within a week of McDowell's taking command of the troops beyond the Potomac, he received the following letter : —

> HEADQUARTERS, June 3, 1861.
>
> GENERAL MCDOWELL,
>   Commanding, etc., Arlington:
> General Scott desires you to submit an estimate of the number and composition of a column to be pushed towards Manassas Junction, and perhaps the Gap, say in four or five days, to favor Patterson's attack on Harper's Ferry.
> The rumor is that Arlington Heights will be attacked to-night.
>
> E. D. TOWNSEND, A.A.G.[1]

To this communication McDowell replied at some length on the following day, in part as follows : —

In view of the number of the enemy supposed to be at Manassas Junction, at Centreville, Fairfax Station, Fairfax Court House, and

[1] O. R. Ser. I, vol. II, 662.

at places beyond Manassas . . . and of the possibility of troops coming from the Valley . . . I think the actual entire force at the head of the column should, for the purpose of carrying the position at Manassas . . . be as much as 12,000 infantry, two batteries of regular artillery, and from six to eight companies of cavalry, with an available reserve ready to move forward from Alexandria by rail of 5000 infantry and one heavy field battery, rifled if possible, these numbers to be increased or diminished as events may indicate. . . . I do not propose to have a supply train of wagons for the main body, but to use the railroad. . . . In relation to the number of troops to be used, I have only to say . . . that in proportion to the numbers used will be the lives saved. . . . Might it not be well to overwhelm and conquer as much by the show of force as by the use of it? [1]

From this exchange of dispatches it is a simple matter to reconstruct the views held at this moment, June the 3d and 4th, at the War Department and at General McDowell's headquarters. First, then, it is clear that General Scott was not for the moment contemplating a real offensive against the Confederacy. The main operation was to be an attack on Harper's Ferry by an army moving to the west of Washington, and the capture of that point itself, the importance of which has already been indicated. "To favor Patterson's attack on Harper's Ferry," it was intended to make what was viewed as a subordinate attack at Manassas Junction, which, even if not successful, would at all events engage the enemy's attention and prevent the sending of reinforcements to Harper's Ferry. It was a perfectly clear strategic idea, and of closely restricted scope.

[1] O. R. Ser. I, vol. II, 664.

We turn now to McDowell's part in it, and note in his dispatch of the 4th the following points : —

1. His calculation of numbers was reasonable and by no means exaggerated as is apt to be the case under such circumstances ; and it may be inferred that he had fairly accurate information of what lay in his immediate front, as will further appear when we turn to the Southern side. He did not, however, overlook the obvious fact that the position of the Confederates at the junction of two railroads gave them opportunity for rapidly increasing their numbers. This should have, and perhaps did, suggest to him that rapidity was of the essence of the contemplated movement; but this is not brought out.

2. The proposal to leave behind 5000 men, nearly one third of the troops, as a reserve advancing in the rear, but apparently not within immediate supporting distance of the first column, is noticeable. Assuming great caution to be warranted, and the protection of Alexandria to be a paramount consideration, there was no need to hold back so large a body of troops at that point during the few decisive hours of the advance and battle; for Alexandria might be defended from hills rising some two hundred feet that lay two miles back of it, and where a comparatively narrow intrenched front was rapidly being developed. However vulnerable the Long bridge and railroad might be, it seems hard to justify the holding back of a really large force which, as the

event showed, could not be expected to reach the field in time to play an effective part if used as a reserve.

The fact appears to be, judging his conduct as a whole through June and July, either that in his scheme of a reserve at Alexandria advancing along the railroad he was merely echoing a more or less definite instruction of Winfield Scott, or that he had evolved the idea himself though an exaggerated sense of the difficulty presented in supplying his army. Even allowing for the fact that he had as yet little transport, the march before him was of less than thirty miles, and through a good farming country that would offer some resources in case of an emergency. There is no direct evidence to tell us whether this was Scott's or McDowell's idea; it appears more probable that it was the latter's.

McDowell apparently viewed a reserve at Alexandria as a force placed on a railroad junction that might rapidly be thrown to his left should his movements require support on the direct line of rail to Manassas, or to his right by the Hampshire and Loudoun Railroad to Vienna, should the Confederates, operating from the Shenandoah through Leesburg, — a remote and unlikely contingency, — threaten his right flank and rear.[1] In any case, as McDowell expected to be short of transport and intended to get on to the Manassas Railroad at the earliest possible

---

[1] The moving of the 1st and 2d New Jersey Regiments by rail from Alexandria to Vienna on the 20th of July serves to support this view.

moment, he attached importance to having a considerable body of troops operating along that railroad and
guarding all its vulnerable points. Prudent, cautious, and
disinclined for the offensive, McDowell felt all the difficulties of the task set him, and tried to parry every one
of them instead of concentrating his efforts on the fundamental difficulty, that of destroying the enemy's army.
His plan, such as it was, could not be described as sat-
isfying the conditions of the successful offensive: the
throwing of every available man to the decisive point,
and rapidity of action.

At Washington, attention was chiefly fixed on Harper's Ferry, and this was the natural outcome of a situation in which Maryland appeared the most pressing
problem. Scott was making great efforts to supply
General Patterson, who was slowly pushing down from
Pennsylvania towards the Potomac with a considerable
mass of infantry and a few guns. On the 8th, writing to
that general, he said : " I do not distinctly foresee that
we shall be able to make any diversion in your behalf on
the other side of the Potomac beyond repairing the lower
part of the railroad leading from Alexandria towards the
Manassas Gap." [1] By which Scott meant that for the present he did not see his way to furnishing McDowell with
the 17,000 men that general required to operate against

---

[1] O. R. Ser. i, vol. ii, 671. — It was at this same date that Scott took
over control of the telegraph lines.

Manassas Junction, or if he did, he judged the risk of an attack at that point too great to be run. For the moment, therefore, the advance of McDowell's army remained a mere possibility, depending largely on what might happen farther to the west.

PATTERSON'S ADVANCE. Meanwhile Patterson had been steadily, but very slowly, moving down across western Maryland towards the valley of the Shenandoah with 8000 or 10,000 volunteers, mostly from Pennsylvania. As he neared the Potomac his progress became less rapid and his assurances of success less emphatic. He proposed following the easiest route, that which crossed the Potomac at Williamsport, some distance above Harper's Ferry, thence leading to Winchester, the great junction of roads, twenty-five miles south of Harper's Ferry and sixty miles west of Manassas. To protect the Baltimore and Ohio Railroad and to connect with Patterson, Scott sent a small detached column under Colonel Stone direct from Washington along the Potomac to Point of Rocks, thence to link up with Patterson's left when he should get possession of Harper's Ferry, and, as that general continued his advance into Virginia, to march on Leesburg. The occupation of Leesburg might eventually facilitate the shifting of Patterson's army towards McDowell's by means of the Loudoun and Hampshire Railroad should that operation become advisable.

These plans probably assumed for their basis a mobility which Patterson's raw army never attained, and a bold, fighting spirit which its commander, a veteran of the war of 1812, prudently sealed up within the four corners of his dispatches. At the end of May, Scott appears to have been confident that in a few days a strong offensive would be developed by Patterson. But it was not until the 14th of June that Patterson got his troops actually to the line of the Potomac, on which day General Joseph E. Johnston, commanding the Confederate forces, withdrew from Harper's Ferry towards Winchester. Patterson had the news in the afternoon of the 15th, but so great was his prudence, so cumbersome his army, that it was not till forty-eight hours later that he actually crossed the Potomac.

On the 13th of June, Patterson had received the following dispatch from headquarters : —

The General-in-Chief directs me to say that on the supposition you will cross the river Monday or Tuesday next (17th or 18th), Brigadier-General McDowell will be instructed to make a demonstration from Alexandria in the direction of Manassas Junction one or two days before. The general does not wish you to hasten, but keep him informed, so that General McDowell may properly time his movement . . .

E. D. TOWNSEND, A.A.G.[1]

Patterson, who was receiving many exaggerated and alarming reports about the enemy, some of these from the commander-in-chief himself, replied that he could

[1] O. R. Ser. I, vol. II, 680.

not cross at the time indicated. On this McDowell was informed, on the 15th of June, that Patterson would not cross until the 19th, and that the expediency of any movement on his part must be determined by events. " General Scott says, whether Harper's Ferry is evacuated or not, General Patterson cannot cross the river before Wednesday next. This in reference to a proposed movement of yours, on the expediency of which events must now decide." [1] This indicates, clearly enough, that a movement against Manassas still occupied a subordinate place as late as the moment when the Confederates evacuated Harper's Ferry.

SOUTH. The first and natural move, when the State of Virginia seceded and placed armed forces in the field, had been to occupy those parts of her soil that lay in immediate proximity to Washington. Alexandria was held by a small body of local volunteers, and pickets were established along Arlington Heights and at the bridges leading to Washington. It did not, however, at any time enter into the views of the State or of the Confederate Government to establish a real line of resistance at that point, much less to take the offensive thence upon Washington; for there were no adequate means to such ends. So early as the 6th of May this is shown by the following dispatch : —

[1] O. R. Ser. I, vol. II, 690.

HEADQUARTERS, VIRGINIA FORCES,
RICHMOND, VA., May 6, 1861.

COLONEL ST. GEORGE COCKE,

 Commanding Virginia Forces, Culpeper Court House, Va.:

 COLONEL:— You are desired to post at Manassas Gap Junction a force sufficient to defend that point against an attack likely to be made against it by troops from Washington. . . .

R. E. LEE

Major-General, Commanding.[1]

Thus from an early moment the Confederate position was well defined : it was defensive, and it recognized the strategic importance of Manassas Junction.

The headquarters organization at this moment was in a state of marked inferiority. At Richmond everything had to be improvised. On the 23d of April, Colonel R. E. Lee was appointed commander-in-chief of the forces of Virginia, and later to the command of the Confederate forces in Virginia, with the rank of major-general. He was virtually commander-in-chief. His adjutant-general was Colonel Cooper, who had resigned from the same post at Washington. Lee is too great a figure in American history to require biographical notice here ; suffice it to say that even all his ability and energy were not equal to creating an army rapidly enough to place the Confederate States in anything like a secure position against attack.

By the 15th of May Cocke had assembled at Culpeper

---

[1] O. R. Ser. I, vol. II, 806.

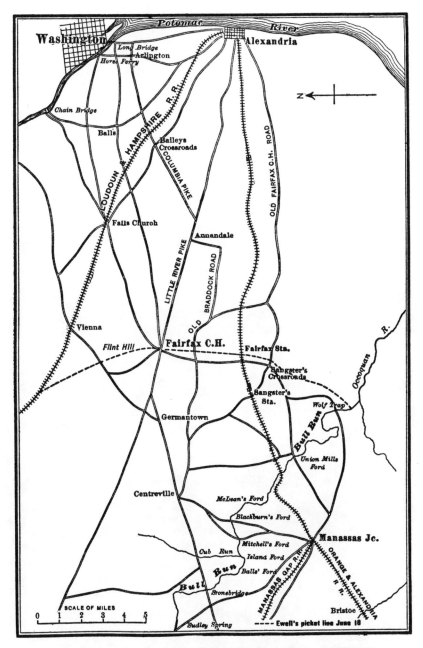

Washington

Potomac River

Long Bridge
Arlington
Horse Ferry

Chain Bridge

Balls

Falls Church

Vienna

Flint Hill

Alexandria

LOUDOUN & HAMPSHIRE R. R.

Balleys Crossroads

COLUMBIA PIKE

OLD FAIRFAX C. H. ROAD

Annandale

LITTLE RIVER PIKE

OLD BRADDOCK ROAD

Fairfax C.H.

Fairfax Sta.

Sangster's Crossroads

Sangster's Sta.

Germantown

Wolf Trap

Occoquan R.

Bull Run

Union Mills Ford

Centreville

McLean's Ford

Blackburn's Ford

Mitchell's Ford

Cub Run

Island Ford

Balls' Ford

Manassas Jc.

MANASSAS GAP R.R.

ORANGE & ALEXANDRIA R. R.

Bull Run

Stonebridge

SCALE OF MILES
0 1 2 3 4 5

Bristoe

Sudley Spring

---- Ewell's picket line June 18

ROADS AND RAILWAYS BETWEEN MANASSAS JUNCTION
AND WASHINGTON

about a thousand men with two field pieces; and on
that day he wrote to Lee:—

With a strong *corps d'armée* at Manassas and at least a division at
Winchester, these two bodies being connected by a continuous railway
through Manassas Gap, there should be kept at all times upon that
road ample means of transportation. These two columns — one at
Manassas and one at Winchester — could readily coöperate and concentrate upon the one point or the other. . . .[1]

This was the strategic idea, fully fledged, that was successfully carried out, ten weeks later, against McDowell
by Johnston and Beauregard on the field of Bull Run.

Cocke was moved up to Manassas a few days later,
and a gradual concentration of reinforcements at that
point took place, of which the detail is unimportant
and the general result will be summarized presently. On
the 24th of May, as we have seen, the Federals occupied
the southern bank of the Potomac for nearly twelve
miles above and below Washington, this move meeting
with no resistance. On the same day Lee, foreseeing the
possible movement on Leesburg which Scott had actually ordered, gave instructions for destroying the Loudoun and Hampshire Railroad. On the 28th, Lee left Richmond for Manassas where he made a rapid inspection
on the following day.

---

[1] O. R. Ser. i, vol. ii, 847. No one, whether at Richmond or at Johnston's or Beauregard's headquarters, assumed the responsibility of carrying out Cocke's sound suggestion; so that when the critical moment
came there was a shortage not only of cars, but, worse still, of engineers.

As a result of Lee's visit a defensive position was selected along the stream of Bull Run, and a cordon of Confederate pickets was formed in front of this line stretching from Wolf Trap Shoal Run through Fairfax Station, Fairfax Court House, and Hunter's Station, towards Draneville, where Colonel Hunton, commanding the small force at Leesburg, continued the line to the latter point. Ewell's brigade, later reinforced by Bonham's, was entrusted with this outpost duty, with headquarters at Fairfax Court House. Lee returned to Richmond, where President Davis installed the Confederate Government on the 31st of May. On the same day they held a conference with General Beauregard who had been selected to command what the Confederates then called the Army of the Potomac. On the 1st of June, at 2 P.M., P. G. T. Beauregard, brigadier-general in the army of the Confederate States, arrived at Manassas Junction and assumed command.

Pierre Gustave Toutant Beauregard was born in Louisiana on the 28th of May, 1818, of Catholic and planter's stock. He entered West Point at sixteen, graduating second of his class in 1838; among his classmates was McDowell. He entered the army as an engineer officer and distinguished himself in the Mexican War; he earned the brevet rank of captain at Contreras and Churubusco, and that of major at Chapultepec; at Garita de Belen he was twice wounded; in 1860 he was appointed Superintendent of West Point, but only held the position a few days.

When the Civil War broke out, Beauregard followed his State, and with his brilliant reputation was at once given high command. He was then a man of attractive personality, and was described by "An English Combatant," who saw him at Manassas, as: —

A small man with a sallow complexion, a heavy black moustache, and closely cut hair. With the left hand in his trowser's pocket, a cigar in his mouth, a buttoned-up coat and small cap, he is the exact type of a French engineer and could not anywhere be mistaken for a civilian. He is jaunty in his gait, dashing in manner, and evidently takes delight in the circumstance of war. It must be confessed his modesty is equal to his merit, he is not imperious or overbearing . . . and is never seen to such advantage as when standing on an earthwork and giving orders, or conversing with animated gesture.[1]

As a general, Beauregard was strong in fortification, and of unquenchable courage, but weak in strategy and wanting in coolness, insight, and method on the battlefield. His dispatches lack clearness, and at times candor; while rhetoric is a pitfall he rarely resists. From his wordy and inaccurate report of the battle of Bull Run, the following lines may well be quoted: —

Oh my country! I would readily have sacrificed my life and those of all the brave men around me to save your honor and to maintain your independence from the degrading yoke which those ruthless invaders had come to impose and render perpetual, and the day's issue has assured me that such emotions must also have animated all under my command.[2]

[1] "An English Combatant," *Battlefields*, 24.   [2] O. R. Ser. I, vol. II, 493.

An even more characteristic effusion was his much-quoted proclamation to the people of Virginia on taking command, from which the following paragraph may be culled : —

A reckless and unprincipled tyrant has invaded your soil. Abraham Lincoln, regardless of all moral, legal, and constitutional restraints, has thrown his abolition hosts among you . . . murdering and imprisoning your citizens. . . . They proclaim by their acts, if not on their banners, that their war-cry is — Beauty and Booty.[1]

The real question that confronted Beauregard at Manassas, and Lee before him, was not so much to find a strong defensive position as to find the best possible defensive position ; for the Confederates were bound to hold the Junction if they could. The line through Fairfax Court House on which Ewell's pickets had been established was too extensive and too easily and variously approachable to serve. But between it and Manassas ran the small stream of Bull Run ; it presented certain advantages which the Confederate leaders decided to utilize.

Manassas Junction itself lay on an open plateau, waterless and exposed, with roads running in all directions, facilitating military movements. By fortifying the Junction an enemy's operations might be retarded, though probably not for long. While it might therefore be advisable to throw up works to protect it, it was necessary

[1] Russell, *Diary*, I, 135.

to place the main line of defence forward, that is, on
Bull Run itself. How to dispose troops to hold Bull Run
depended on a consideration of the lines of advance
open to an army coming from Washington.

Viewing the possible lines of advance of a Federal
army towards Manassas, it was obvious that Alexandria
played a very important part, and must almost inevitably be the real base. Supplies and troops might be
conveniently moved to that point by steamer, and thence
could be readily sent into the interior by means of the
Orange and Alexandria Railroad. The prevailing lack
of means of transportation emphasized these considerations.

Yet it was possible that an attack might be delivered
from further to the southeast, taking Manassas Junction
in right flank and rear by an advance along the valley
of the Occoquan. The Federals controlled the sea, and
could therefore move troops to Accotink or any convenient point whence the valley of the Occoquan might be
reached. But this movement had obvious disadvantages.
It would of necessity be cumbersome and slow and possess none of the advantages of surprise, while it would
uncover Washington. For these and other reasons it was
never seriously considered, nor did the Confederates do
more than keep a close lookout along the valley of the
Occoquan.

Again, to the north of Alexandria lay another possible

line of advance from the Chain Bridge above Washington, through Falls Church and Vienna, towards Fairfax Court House and Centreville. These two lines then, Alexandria–Manassas, and Chain Bridge–Centreville, represented the widest angle within which a Federal advance was likely. As a glance at the map will show, these lines converged on a comparatively short stretch of Bull Run, lying for the most part about three to four miles east and north of Manassas.

Bull Run is a winding stream, in many places quite narrow, nothing more than a glorified ditch. But the banks are cased in, partly precipitous, generally wooded and difficult of access, while its bottom is mud save for an occasional ford. It is a mean, yellow-looking stream, yet it forms a considerable obstacle. From its junction with the Occoquan to Sudley Spring is a distance of about fourteen miles as the crow flies, with Manassas lying midway and a few miles to the southwest. This fourteen miles rather more than covered any probable crossing of an army advancing from Washington along the routes just indicated.

Beauregard wrote of the position to President Davis in the following terms : —

I have reconnoitred closely several of the fords on Bull Run, and one on Occoquan Run (about three miles from here) which offer strong natural features of defence; but they are so numerous and far apart that only a much larger force than I have here at my command (say not less than from ten to fifteen thousand men) could hope to defend them all against a well-organized enemy of about twenty thousand men, who could select his point of attack.[1]

This was a somewhat rough estimate of the situation; and it will be worth while to examine the line of Bull Run a little more closely.

The trend of the roads from Washington and Alexandria, as we have seen, was towards Centreville, whence the direct road to Manassas ran south about six miles, crossing Bull Run at Mitchell's Ford where there was good bottom. For the first two miles from Centreville the road followed a high ridge, then dipped down into low land, and ran for some distance parallel with the river where it was flanked and commanded by the southern bank, which here formed a really strong defence. The line Centreville–Mitchell's Ford–Manassas, may be taken as central; we will now consider what lay downstream, and then upstream from this point.

The next crossing, half a mile downstream, Blackburn's Ford, appeared on the map, or might seem to a wayfarer approaching from Centreville, the obvious route to Manassas. For the road running through that ford, diverging slightly to the east of the Mitchell's Ford road, made a straighter line between the two points. The run was here encased between wooded banks, the northern higher than the southern; but the ford itself was difficult and boggy, and had almost fallen into disuse. Black-

[1] O. R. Ser. I, vol. II, 902; Beauregard to Davis, June I.

burn's Ford and the edge of the Manassas plateau just beyond, were dominated by the Centreville ridge, but partly screened by timber and underbrush.

Farther downstream, at distances of about a mile apart, were McLean's, Union Mills', Gates', and Woodyard's fords. It was here that the line of Bull Run was strongest, because least easy of access. The roads running to these points from the east and northeast were only rough tracks ; the ground was hilly and covered with trees and underbrush through which troops, guns, and transport could be moved only with the greatest difficulty. There were few, if any, positions where batteries could be conveniently planted to command the river and farther bank. The most important point was Union Mills, on the northern side, for here was a convergence of roads from Sangster's crossroads and Centreville, together with the bridge, left standing, by which the Orange and Alexandria Railroad crossed the run. Gates' Ford and Woodyard's Ford were somewhat remote, and hence did not come within the scope of operations.

Upstream from Mitchell's Ford the topography becomes more important. But first it should be noted that the ridge which ran from Blackburn's Ford to Centreville and beyond, afforded an admirable defensive position for the Confederates. Difficult of approach south of Centreville, it must almost inevitably have been attacked directly at the village or by a flanking movement farther north for which an attacking army would have found the roads of little service. Even had the position been outflanked, retirement was not difficult owing to the lines of road running from Centreville west and south to Mitchell's Ford, Ball's Ford, Stone Bridge, and several other crossings. The Confederates, however, did not as yet dispose of sufficient numbers for this purpose, and decided not to hold the ridge, but to come back as far as the stream itself.[1]

From Centreville, the Warrenton turnpike ran four miles almost due west to Stone Bridge, crossing Cub Run about midway. Cub Run ran into Bull Run a little above Mitchell's Ford and below Island Ford, forming a swampy bottom through which no advance was practicable. From the Warrenton turnpike just beyond Cub Run, farm roads diverged to the southwest to Ball's Ford where the crossing was good, and to Lewis' Ford where it was moderate; the south bank at these points was high and dominated the north bank.

Stone Bridge was an important crossing, but, so it appeared, was the extreme point that a Federal advance

[1] The Federal plans were not kept secret and were well known to the Confederates. From an early date the idea was to turn the Confederate right at Union Mills or lower down. The Confederates therefore placed very few troops indeed to the left of Mitchell's Ford. They in fact refused a left which they thought would not be menaced, to concentrate on their centre and right. This they could not have done had they attempted to hold the ridge.

might reach to the northwest. As it turned out, Mc-
Dowell eventually crossed above it, but a consideration
of this part of the field, with the crossings upstream at
Poplar Ford,[1] and at Sudley Spring Ford, will be best
left until later.

The Bull Run position covered the lines of rail that
came together at Manassas. The Orange and Alexandria Railroad ran directly from Manassas Junction to the
southwest, crossing Broad Run at Bristoe, four miles
distant; it was therefore fairly secure. The Manassas
Gap Railroad, however, was more open to attack. For it
ran west and a little north, that is roughly parallel with
Bull Run as far upstream as Stone Bridge, where it began to diverge.

To sum up, then, it might be said that to the right the
Confederate position was strong. At Blackburn's Ford,
owing to the way in which the Centreville ridge dominated the south bank, it was weak; and this weakness
extended to McLean's Ford on one side and Mitchell's
on the other, for a successful move through Blackburn's
Ford would outflank those positions. Frontally, Mitchell's Ford was strong, and there was not much fear for
the fords just south of Stone Bridge. Beyond that point
the Confederates had not considered defensive measures,
and, as will be seen, they were vulnerable.

Let us add here one of the combatants' impressions of

[1] Also called Red House Ford or Locke's Ford.

Manassas and the Bull Run valley at night as viewed from the plateau, not far from the little house in which Beauregard had placed his headquarters: —

Yonder black streak you see rising from the south-south-west, running north and turning off due east, is the timber around Bull Run; 'tis about three or four miles distant from here to any point, and the high grounds you observe rising abruptly beyond the stream — the tableland I mean, northward, and shelving to the east across the track — is Centreville. A small detachment and military telegraph post is stationed there watching the roads from the Upper Potomac and Leesburgh . . . and keeping open communication with General Bonham who holds Fairfax Court House and the railroad station midway between Washington and this place. "See yonder!" said my companion, pointing towards Centreville, "they are working the telegraph! See them repeating the signals on yonder hill!" . . . In a few minutes one of the men sitting around the large fire in front of the general's quarters, seized a long red fagot from the flames, and going to the north end of the house, began swaying it to the right and left, according to directions, now horizontally, again perpendicularly, and seemed to be cutting an imaginary circle at different angles. The signs were instantly repeated from post to post and thus traversed fifteen miles within a very few minutes.[1]

Up to the 15th of June, the Confederate Government had no well-settled plans that looked very much beyond the defence of Manassas Junction and the maintenance of a force in the front of General Patterson as he advanced towards Harper's Ferry. On the 13th of the month, President Davis wrote as follows to General Beauregard: —

If the enemy commences operations by an attack upon Harper's

[1] "English Combatant," *Battlefields*, 21.

Ferry, I do not perceive why General Johnston should be unable, even before overwhelming numbers, to retire behind the positions where the enemy would approach him in reverse. It would seem to me not unreasonable to expect that . . . he could . . . by retiring to the passes on the Manassas Railroad and its adjacent mountains, probably check the progress of the enemy, and prevent him from either taking possession of the Valley or passing to the rear of your position. We hope soon to re-enforce you to an extent equal to the strength you require by the junction of General Johnston, and I cannot doubt but that . . . you would then be better circumstanced to advance upon Alexandria than if General Johnston, by withdrawing from the Valley, had left the enemy the power to pass to our rear, to cut your line of communication, and advance to attack you in reverse while you were engaged with the enemy in front. . . . To your request that a concerted plan of operations should be adopted, I can only reply that the present position and unknown purpose of the enemy require that our plan should have many alterations.[1]

But the generals themselves, as soon as Beauregard assumed command, exchanged letters pledging themselves to mutual support at whichever point the Federal attack should develop.[2]

THE SHENANDOAH VALLEY. Let us now turn to the valley of the Shenandoah. As early as the 27th of April, Colonel T. J. Jackson[3] was assigned to the command of a force of Virginia militia assembling at Harper's Ferry;

---

[1] O. R. Ser. I, vol. II, 922.

[2] Johnston, *Narrative*, 21.

[3] Thomas Jonathan, better known as "Stonewall," Jackson, born January 21st, 1824, at Clarksburg, Virginia; graduated West Point, 1846; lieutenant, 1st Artillery, at Vera Cruz, Cerro Gordo, Churubusco, Molino del Rey, Mexico, 1847, for which he received two brevets; professor of artillery tactics and natural philosophy, Virginia Military Institution, 1851–61.

the numbers of this command gradually rose in the course of a month to about 7000 effectives. Jackson was warned that a movement of Federal troops against that point might be expected, and his attention was called to the possible means of delaying their movements by the breaking down of bridges, railroads, and canals. The details of operations in the Shenandoah Valley do not belong to our subject, however; it is merely the outline of those events that can be given.

For three weeks or so Jackson worked hard raising and arming troops and developing a defensive scheme for Harper's Ferry which he was determined to hold at all costs. The appearance of his camp at this time, as described by Colonel Deas, inspector-general of the Confederate army, is not without interest : —

The troops here are all raw and inexperienced — wanting even in the first elements of the school of the soldier — and there is a great scarcity of proper instructors. Many of the captains are singularly ignorant of their duties. Guard duty is very loosely done; and, indeed, there is apparent on every side the mere elements of men and arms, without the discipline and organization of an army. There is a sad deficiency in clothing and in camp and garrison equipage. . . . To make up, however, for this loose state of things so striking to the professional eye, it must not be forgotten that a fierce spirit animates those rough looking men. . . . This spirit is invincible.[1]

On the 15th of May, General Johnston was appointed to command the troops at Harper's Ferry, and arrived there on the 24th of the month. Joseph Eggleston Johns-

[1] O. R. Ser. I, vol. II, 862; Deas to Garnett.

ton was born on the 3d of February, 1807, at Cherry
Grove, Prince Edward County, Virginia. His father
was a planter and had served in the war of Independence under "Lighthorse" Harry, father of Robert E. Lee.
He entered West Point in 1825, in the same class as Lee,
with whom he formed a steadfast and lifelong friendship.
He graduated high in his class, displayed strength of
character and military aptitude, and formed a marked
habit of reading historical and professional literature.
He had a distinguished career in the army, winning two
brevets in the Mexican War, and receiving three wounds
at the head of his battalion of light infantry on the field
of Chapultepec. Scott said of him: "Johnston is a great
soldier, but he has an unfortunate knack of getting himself shot in nearly every engagement." That knack was
to cling to him throughout the Civil War.

In 1855, Johnston was sent to the 2d Cavalry as lieutenant-colonel under Sumner ; and in 1860 Scott placed him
in a list of four, with C. F. Smith, A. S. Johnston, and
R. E. Lee, for the selection of a quartermaster-general for
the army ; and it was he received the appointment.

Johnston had character, courage, judgment, and prudence, — a useful equipment. He was at times inclined
to be disputatious and over-methodical; but although
not easy to please, his troops always believed in him.
Longstreet wrote, perhaps more enthusiastically than
others might have : —

Johnston was skilled in the art and science of war, gifted in his quick, penetrating mind and soldierly bearing, genial and affectionate in nature, honorable and winning in person, and confiding in his love. He drew the hearts of those about him so close that his comrades felt that they could die for him.[1]

He had, in fact, some qualifications for command, though he entirely lacked the subtlety of Lee, and the hard, brilliant daring of Jackson. Unfortunately for the cause he served, his personal relations with Jefferson Davis were so bad that military operations were more than once seriously affected by them; and he suffered from a chronic inability to make his intentions clear to his subordinates, both in the writing and in the transmitting of his orders.

Up to the moment of Johnston's arrival at Harper's Ferry the prevailing idea had been that that point could and should be held. Jackson had devoted much time and energy to fortifying the heights on both sides of the Potomac with this object in view. But Johnston, immediately on his arrival and much to the chagrin of the Confederate authorities at Richmond, formed an adverse opinion. He found that with little over 5000 men to dispose of he had to watch the Potomac from Williamsport down to Point of Rocks, say thirty miles. The troops had no more than twelve to fifteen rounds of ammunition with as much again in reserve. There was little transport. The soldiers were so undisciplined as to be

[1] Longstreet, *From Manassas to Appomattox*, 100.

unfit for action. But the case will be best stated in Johnston's own words : —

Harper's Ferry is untenable against an army by any force not strong enough to hold the neighboring heights north of the Potomac and east of the Shenandoah, as well as the place itself. It is a triangle formed by the Potomac, Shenandoah, and Furnace Ridge, the latter extending from river to river, a mile and a half above their junction. Artillery on the heights above mentioned . . . could sweep every part of this space. . . . Two main routes lead from Maryland and Pennsylvania into the Valley of Virginia, meeting at Winchester: one passing through Frederick and crossing the Potomac at Harper's Ferry; the other leading through Chambersburg, Williamsport (where it crosses the Potomac), and Martinsburg. These roads are met at Winchester by the principal one from northwestern Virginia into the Valley, and also by a good and direct one from Manassas Junction. . . . Our scouts and friends in Maryland . . . reported that the armies of General Patterson and McClellan were to unite at Winchester. . . . It was necessary of course that the Confederate troops in the Valley should always be ready to meet this invasion as well as to unite quickly with the army at Manassas Junction whenever it might be threatened. . . . At Harper's Ferry they were manifestly out of position for either object. . . . Winchester . . . fulfilled the conditions desired better than any other point.[1]

It is difficult to say to what extent Lee agreed or dis-

---

[1] Johnston, *Narrative*, 17. His official reports are all consistent with this statement. See further his Memorandum, May 26th, and his dispatch to Garnett, O. R. Ser. 1, vol. 11, 880, 881, and Deas' report of inspection, May 23d, *ibid*. 867. I believe Johnston's view was correct, and that his proper position, all factors considered, was a little in front of Winchester. Jackson, a greater soldier, disagreed with his commander. A stand at Harper's Ferry placed Patterson in the possible dilemma either of a direct attack on that place, or of an advance towards Winchester from Williamsport at least as far as Martinsburg, offering his flank to the Confederates. I understand that my friend Captain Conger, who views Johnston's strategy as timid rather than prudent, thinks Jackson was right.

agreed with these views. He knew the ground, and it may well be that Johnston's conclusion appealed to him as sound. But Jefferson Davis fought hard against accepting it. Jackson whole-heartedly believed that Harper's Ferry should be held at all costs ; and in his official correspondence with Johnston, Lee more than once urged upon him the great importance of holding the place, if in Johnston's judgment it possibly could be held. At the same time he acquiesced in that judgment when given adversely; and it may be surmised that he really accepted it as correct, having before this merely echoed the wishes and hopes of his Government.

On the 30th of May, two weeks before Johnston actually abandoned Harper's Ferry, we already find Lee outlining a movement that closely fitted in with Johnston's views and that contained in embryo the decisive operation that carried him to Bull Run two months later. Lee pointed out the possibility that a Federal force might move through Point of Rocks towards Leesburg, the very move Scott had already thought of for Colonel Stone's small column. "In the event of such a movement," he wrote, "should you deem it advisable and should you be unable to hold your position, I would suggest a joint attack by you and General Bonham, commanding at Manassas, for the purpose of cutting them off." [1]

[1] Lee to Johnston, May 30, 1861. O. R. Ser. I, vol. II, 894.

On the 13th of June we find a long dispatch of General Cooper to Johnston. Through it there runs a very perceptible vein of irony provoked by the fact that Johnston had constantly requested the Government to accept his view of the strategic position in express terms. This President Davis had as constantly refused to do, continuing to emphasize the importance of holding Harper's Ferry, without, however, limiting Johnston's discretion. Finally, in the Adjutant-General's dispatch, Johnston obtained what he wanted: —

As you seem to desire . . . that the responsibility of your retirement should be assumed here, and as no reluctance is felt to bear any burden which the public interests require, you will consider yourself authorized, whenever the position of the enemy shall convince you that he is about to turn your position and thus deprive the country of the use of yourself and the troops under your command, to destroy everything at Harper's'Ferry . . . and retire upon . . . Winchester, destroying the road behind you. . . . Whatever . . . would impede your operations in the field it would be well to send without delay to the Manassas road . . . upon some of the passes on which it is hoped you will be able to make an effective stand. . . . Should you move so far as to make a junction with General Beauregard, the enemy would be free immediately to occupy the Valley of Virginia,[1] and to pass to the rear of Manassas Junction. . . . It has been with reluctance that any attempt was made to give you specific instructions, and you will accept assurances of the readiness with which the freest exercise of discretion on your part will be sustained.[2]

[1] The Shenandoah Valley.
[2] O. R. Ser. I, vol. II, 925. When Davis, many years later, wrote his *Rise and Fall of the Confederate Government*, he had apparently modified his judgment and accepted Johnston's position as correct. See pp. 340, 341.

That very day, probably before General Cooper's dispatch reached him, Johnston began his retirement. The immediate cause was the receipt of information that the Federals had reached Romney in western Virginia, whence, even if remotely, they threatened Winchester, the great knot of roads in the Valley. He promptly ordered Colonel A. P. Hill with a couple of regiments to that point, and this merely began a movement that was carried out through the 14th, and completed when his rear guard evacuated Harper's Ferry on the 15th. As Johnston fell back up the Valley towards Winchester, he wrote as follows from Long Meadow to the War Department at Richmond: —

GENERAL COOPER,
      Adj. and Inspector-General, Richmond.
      GENERAL, — I have had the honor to receive your letter of the 13th. I know myself to be a careless writer, and will not, therefore, pretend to have expressed clearly the opinions I wished to have put before the Government. I am confident, however, that nothing in my correspondence with my military superiors makes me obnoxious to the charge of desiring that the responsibility of my official acts should be borne by any other person than myself.
      I had the honor yesterday to report to the President the removal of the troops from Harper's Ferry. . . . [1]

[1] O. R. Ser. I, vol. II, 930.

III

OPERATIONS AND PLANS, JUNE 16 TO JULY 16

NORTH

ON the 27th of April, Major-General Robert Patterson,[1] of the Pennsylvania Militia, a veteran of the War of 1812, had been assigned to the command of the Department of Pennsylvania. For some weeks he devoted his time to organizing his new troops, after which he began to push them down into Maryland and towards the Virginia border. A few detachments of regulars, infantry, cavalry, and guns, were sent to him, which, however slight in numbers, he looked to as the stiffening of his army. By the 1st of June the greater part of Patterson's four brigades was concentrating about Chambersburg, Hagerstown, and Williamsport, practically ready to cross the Potomac at the latter point. He had about 12,000 men and his numbers slowly increased to 14,000 by the 28th of June. On the 15th of that month, the day on which Johnston's rear-guard left Harper's Ferry, Patterson was still at Chambersburg, and had not yet crossed the Potomac.

[1] Captain, lieutenant-colonel, and colonel, 2d Pennsylvania Militia, 1812–13; major-general of Pennsylvania Volunteers, 1846–47.

June 16, 1861 — 11 A.M.

MAJOR-GENERAL PATTERSON . . .

What movement, if any, in pursuit of the enemy, do you propose to make consequent on the evacuation of Harper's Ferry? If no pursuit, and I recommend none specially, send to me at once all the regular troops, horse and foot, with you, and also the Rhode Island regiment.

WINFIELD SCOTT.

To this Patterson replied: "Design no pursuit; cannot make it."[1]

The impatient dispatch of the commander-in-chief, together with its answer, will serve better than anything else to mark the turn which the Federal operations took at this date. Patterson's slowness had discouraged the Government, and Scott was now apparently becoming convinced that a vigorous and effective offensive was hardly to be looked for in that quarter. More important than that, the fact was now being realized by the politicians at Washington that however popular three months' volunteering might be among their electors, it did not seem a very promising method of dealing with the Civil War. Most of the regiments were nearly two months old and still lacking in tactical skill and mobility; while operations were manifestly in nothing more than a preparatory stage. In Patterson's army every regiment but one was on a three months' basis, and he reported that all except the 1st Wisconsin would claim their discharge.[2] It was natural, therefore, that the politicians

[1] O. R. Ser. I, vol. II, 691.

[2] In fourteen regiments, selected at random, the term of service ended

and journalists should begin to abuse somebody for the fiasco that was now threatening. The army was muzzled by discipline and was therefore the natural and inevitable scapegoat for civilian ineptitude ; and in a frenzied effort to make good foolish declarations made to political followers or newspaper subscribers, a fatal cry was raised: "On to Richmond !" From that moment Scott and his devoted staff were to be spurred unmercifully to the finish. Something must be accomplished, whatever the cost, before the three months' army went home again ; that something must be an advance to Manassas, and thence to Richmond.

Scott reluctantly accepted the situation and tried to make the best of it. After all, Manassas was only twenty-five miles from the Potomac, and even a raw army of little mobility might be moved thus far. If the enemy should be outnumbered, a success was within the bounds of possibility. So Scott, while disapproving, and while not committing himself to anything more than the move to Manassas, settled down to reinforcing McDowell and getting him fit to take the field before the end of the three months' army should supervene.

Patterson, meanwhile, clung desperately to his regulars, and Scott sent him several pressing dispatches as follows: one regiment on July the 19th, one on the 20th; one on the 22d; two on the 23d; one each on the 24th, 25th, 27th, and 30th. The battle of Bull Run, it should be remembered, was fought on the 21st of that month.

before he could obtain them. One of these, on the 16th, is interesting, as it shows how Scott viewed the possible effect on the strategic situation of an advance by Patterson up the Valley: —

Why a detachment upon Winchester? If strong enough the detachment would drive the enemy from Winchester to Strasburg and the Manassas Junction. . . . What would be gained? . . . And if your detachment be not strong it would be lost. Hence the detachment, if not bad, would be useless.[1]

From this and other evidence, it is possible to state Scott's general view: There is no hurry now for Patterson to press forward, because McDowell is not yet ready for the advance against Manassas. On the contrary, Patterson's delay near the Potomac will most probably induce the Confederates to keep Johnston's army well to the north, which will delay their concentration at Manassas Junction. If and when, however, Patterson does operate against Johnston, it must be not with detachments but with his whole force, that is, vigorously and in such a way as either to defeat him, or to grip him so closely as to prevent his moving to Manassas in good order as an effective reinforcement for Beauregard.

Things now became more active on the lower Potomac. Reconnaissances were pushed out towards the enemy. On the 16th of June, 400 men under Tyler, starting from the extreme right of the Federals near Chain Bridge, went as far as Vienna, finding no sign of the

[1] O. R. Ser. I, vol. II, 694.

enemy. On the 17th, Scott instructed McDowell to send a strong reconnaissance from Alexandria along the Loudoun and Hampshire Railroad to the same point.

The 1st Ohio Volunteers, Colonel McCook, 697 rank and file, was detailed for this service; General Schenck, the brigade commander, was in charge. The troops left Alexandria by train in the afternoon of the 17th of June. At six miles, Schenck passed the advanced posts and disentrained two companies to guard the line; at ten miles, Falls Church, he disentrained two more companies. He then proceeded at slow speed towards Vienna and, taking no other precaution, was rounding a curve little more than a mile from that place, when two field pieces unexpectedly opened fire on him. Schenck had run into Colonel Gregg's command, the 1st South Carolina Infantry, with a troop of cavalry, and a section of six-pounders under Kemper.[1]

Gregg, too, was on a reconnaissance. From Fairfax Court House he had pushed as far as the Potomac without difficulty. He was now, at 6 P.M., passing through Vienna on his return, when he observed the slow approach of Schenck's locomotive, just in time to take position. The effect of his field pieces on Schenck's train was instantaneous. The men jumped, scattered to the right and left, and promptly took to the woods. The en-

---

[1] The Confederate reconnaissance was properly constituted of the three arms; the contrast with the Federals is striking.

gineer, who was at the rear, detached the now empty platform cars and promptly ran back to Alexandria. Gregg made no attempt at pursuit. Schenck and his men, finding their way back to the railroad, eventually made good their retreat; they had lost 8 killed, 4 wounded, and 1 prisoner. Thus closed an incident trifling in itself, yet which, as far as it went, seemed to indicate better leadership and organization on the Southern side.

Patterson, who had crossed the Potomac at Williamsport on the 17th, became alarmed because of Scott's calling his regulars to Washington, and because of highly exaggerated reports of Johnston's numbers and movements. Although that general was many miles to the south, Patterson promptly decided to retire to the north side of the Potomac, and began a ludicrously cautious approach of the abandoned Confederate position at Harper's Ferry.

On the 20th of June, Scott outlined a plan for bringing in Patterson to coöperate with McDowell against Manassas. Harper's Ferry might be controlled by a single powerful battery placed on Maryland Heights, there being no particular object in occupying the town itself. The bulk of Patterson's forces might then be brought eastwards through Leesburg to coöperate with McDowell.[1]

[1] O. R. Ser. I, vol. II, 709.

There were several valid objections to such a plan. It had been well ascertained by this time that Patterson was not an enterprising general, and that his army was not very mobile. Yet such a move demanded that he should first cross the Blue Ridge and then the Potomac, presumably at Point of Rocks, after which he would have to make a flank march of quite thirty miles with the Potomac on one side of him and the enemy on the other. Johnston, with the Manassas Gap Railroad to help him, would presumably always be able to reach Manassas before Patterson could get to Vienna, and might possibly find a favorable occasion for attacking Patterson in flank before he could effect his junction with Mc-Dowell.

On the 21st, McDowell was requested from Headquarters to frame a scheme of operations for joining hands with Patterson towards Leesburg, "a column co-operating from this end"; and on the 24th, he presented the following plan: —

There is at Manassas Junction, and the places in its front or immediate vicinity, a force of from 23,000 to 25,000 infantry and about 2000 cavalry and a supply of well-provided artillery. . . . How much of a force is beyond Manassas Gap, in the Valley, and could be brought within the operations here contemplated, I have no means of judging. There is nothing to hinder their coming, and unless they are kept engaged by our troops around Harper's Ferry, reinforcements, in case of serious operations from that section, would have to be guarded against, as would also those from places to the south of Manassas on the line of the railroad to Richmond. . . .

We have in this Department good, bad, and indifferent, twenty regiments of infantry, giving an aggregate of less than 14,000; four companies of cavalry giving about 250; one battery of regular artillery of six rifled guns. . . . It seems to me the distance between General Patterson's force and this one is so great and the line of march each has to take is such (a flank exposed), that, in my view, the force to move from each position should be constituted without reference to material support from the other. . . .

What would be our position if a movement is made to the right . . . towards Leesburg? In the first place as we are for any such purpose without means of wagon transportation, we should be obliged to repair and use the railroad; but whether this was done or not, we should march with the left flank of the column exposed to attack from their advanced positions. . . .

Any reverse happening to this raw force . . . with the enemy on the flank and rear and an impassable river on the right would be fatal. I do not think, therefore, it safe to risk anything from this position in the direction of Leesburg farther than Vienna . . . and even to go there the force should be large. . . .[1]

On the whole, it must be concluded that McDowell's views were sounder than Scott's. When one considers the extraordinarily low degree of mobility displayed by the Federals during the whole campaign, it is difficult to view the proposed concentration on Leesburg as anything more than a map problem. It was an important point, it is true, but held only by a weak detachment of a few hundred men; while the operation exposed both Federal armies to flank attacks for no object likely to result in the immediate disadvantage of the enemy. McDowell, however much he may have exaggerated

[1] O. R. Ser. I, vol. II, 718.

the numbers in his front, was surely right in virtually
declining to carry out such a plan.

Scott promptly gave up his Leesburg scheme, on any
large scale, and came back to the old idea of the direct
advance on Manassas. He probably requested Mc-
Dowell to draw up a new statement based on that idea,
for an undated memorandum, which presumably belongs
to the 24th or 25th, was prepared by the latter. From
this document again we must take some long ex-
tracts : —

They have . . . been expecting us to attack their position and have
been preparing for it. When it becomes known positively we are about
to march, and they learn in what strength, they will be obliged to call
in their disposable forces from all quarters, for they will not be able,
if closely pressed, to get away by railroad before we can reach them.
If General J. E. Johnston's force is kept engaged by Major General
Patterson . . . I think they will not be able to bring up more than
10,000 men. So we must calculate on having to do with 35,000 men.

The objective point in our plan is Manassas Junction. . . . The
country lying between the two armies is mostly thickly wooded and
the roads . . . are narrow. . . . This makes it necessary to have the
fewest possible number of carriages of any kind, and our forces, therefore, though the distance is short, will have to move over several lines
of approach in order to get forward in time a sufficient body to operate
with success. . . . The Orange and Alexandria road, which I propose
to look to as the main channel of supply, is now in working order some
seven miles out of Alexandria, and from Manassas Junction to within
fifteen miles of Alexandria. In the intermediate space the road has
been destroyed as effectively as possible, and a long deep cut filled in
with trees and earth. . . .

Leaving small garrisons in the defensive works, I propose to move
against Manassas with a force of 30,000 of all arms, organized into

three columns, with a reserve of 10,000. One column to move from Falls Church or Vienna . . . to go between Fairfax Court House and Centreville, and, in connection with another column moving by the Little River turnpike, cut off or drive in . . . the enemy's advanced posts. The third column to move by the Orange and Alexandria Railroad, and leaving as large a force as may be necessary to aid in rebuilding it, to push on with the remainder to join the first and second columns.

The enemy is said to have batteries in position at several places in his front, and defensive works on Bull Run and Manassas Junction. I do not propose that these batteries be attacked for I think they may all be turned. Bull Run, I am told, is fordable at almost any place. After uniting the columns this side of it, I propose to attack the main position by turning it, if possible, so as to cut off communications by rail with the South, or threaten to do so sufficiently to force the enemy to leave his entrenchments to guard them. . . . Believing the chances are greatly in favor of the enemy's accepting battle between this and the Junction, and that the consequences of that battle will be of the greatest importance to the country as establishing the prestige in this contest on the one side or on the other — the more so as the two sections will be fairly represented by regiments from almost every State — I think it of great consequence that, as for the most part our regiments are exceedingly raw and the best of them, with few exceptions, not over steady in line, they be organized into as many small fixed brigades as the number of regular colonels will admit. . . .[1]

At the moment that McDowell prepared this statement he reported present for duty 13,666 men and 764 officers.[2]

This plan of operations was substantially the one which McDowell attempted to carry out four weeks later, and therefore needs close examination. Let us take it point by point, noting first of all the omissions.

[1] O. R. Ser. I, vol. II, 720, 721.
[2] O. R. Ser. I, vol. II, 726; June 26, 1861.

To begin with, then, it is important to see that Mc-
Dowell, although dealing with a problem that involved
the handling of 30,000 or 40,000 men, still maintains
a certain tone that he had assumed from the start, that of
a subordinate commander and not that of the general-
in-chief of an army. At the moment when he had been
detached from Scott's staff to assume command of the
troops beyond the Potomac, that attitude might in a
way have been justified. He had suddenly been promoted to the rank of a general from that of a major;
General Scott had from the beginning treated him as a
direct subordinate; his orders being often of the most
precise and detailed character, indicating that McDowell was not entrusted with much, if any, initiative.

It had thus unfortunately come about, quite naturally
from the existing circumstances, that, although Mc-
Dowell realized well enough some of the elements of the
strategic problem, he did not always consider it his business to deal with them. For, in fact, the problem before
him was only stated by Scott in part, and he therefore
offered only a part solution. That problem was not
merely how to reach Manassas Junction and how to defeat the Confederate army there, but it was how to deal
with the aggregate of the Confederate forces in the field
that might be brought into action at Manassas. Johnston's army was within sixty miles, and controlled an un-
damaged line of rail for about half of that distance. The

real problem confronting a general marching on Manassas comprised, therefore, both Johnston's and Beauregard's armies. McDowell, while really conscious of the
fact, assumed that his function was limited to carrying out
part only of a larger and quite undetermined operation,
of which the conduct and responsibility rested with Scott.
It is therefore impossible to absolve the commander-in-
chief from some part of the blame due to his failing to
give sufficient scope to the operations and function of
McDowell's army. There was a maladjustment of command, and a failure to seize the essential features of the
situation clearly and logically. McDowell shifted the responsibility for anything that might happen a few miles
to the west of him on Scott; and Scott, while alive to the
danger, did not deal with it completely, in fact drifted, in
a way that will presently be described. McDowell's own
chief of staff declared later that he "was dominated by the
feeling of subordination and deference to General Scott."[1]

On the basis then of McDowell's false assumption
as to Scott's covering his movement against Manassas, the salient features of his scheme may now be
dealt with. And first it may be noted that he was fully
conscious that information passed rapidly from Washington to the Confederate headquarters; that the preparations for such a move as he contemplated could not be
concealed and would give the enemy ample warning;

[1] Fry, *Battles and Leaders*, I, 181.

and that his advance must be relatively slow. In other words, all the conditions would inevitably give the enemy time to effect a heavier concentration in his front unless otherwise prevented. Rapidity of march was therefore essential to his success. The case might even be put on more general grounds, for rapidity is one of the greatest of military virtues ; and judging from the whole record of McDowell, one gets a clear impression that that virtue was not in him.

As against this it might be argued in his favor that his army could not show mobility in its then condition of faulty organization, which he fully realized. He doubtless felt keenly the danger of overmarching such a large body of men, lacking fitness and cohesion. It might be harsh to blame him for leaning towards prudence rather than towards boldness. Yet the offensive has always implied boldness rather than prudence ; and it was an offensive operation he was asked to undertake.

The statement that " we must have the fewest possible number of carriages" requires comment. A sufficient transport train, if it could have been properly managed, would have gone a long way towards making the army mobile, freeing it from the Orange and Alexandria Railroad, and making available the large reserve McDowell contemplated moving along that railroad to establish a line of communications.[1] But this was clearly not what

[1] A railway makes a more efficient line of communications than a road;

McDowell had in mind. His fundamental transport difficulty was one of organization and experience, — the being able to handle transportation; while in one sense he lacked transport, in another he had too much, as appears from Sherman's description of the camps of the volunteer regiments: "They were so loaded down with overcoats, haversacks, knapsacks, tents, and baggage, that it took from twenty-five to fifty wagons to move the camp of a regiment from one place to another, and some of the camps had bakeries and cooking establishments that would have done credit to Delmonico." [1]

The Orange and Alexandria Railroad was broken up at Accotink Creek, about ten miles from Alexandria, and it might be presumed that on retiring the Confederates would destroy the line from that point westward. Under these circumstances the problem of the army's line of communications was not clearly grasped. The Orange and Alexandria could under no imaginable circumstances be the army's line of communication during the period of the actual operation against Manassas Junction, for the reason that it could not be made fit for use within the brief space within which a Confederate concentration could be forestalled. Up to the time when the army should have defeated the enemy and occupied Manassas

but it is more delicate owing to its liability to destruction, and therefore consumes more troops for guarding purposes.

[1] Sherman, *Mems.*, I, 178.

Junction it would have to be supplied by road transportation, and that being the case the railroad line became a subordinate issue until after the moment when McDowell's army should be established at Manassas. After that, the re-establishing, and perhaps the guarding, of the railroad would doubtless become a prime issue. The decision to place a heavy reserve on that railroad, partly to guard and partly to rebuild it, was therefore a grave error. The correct policy was to leave a few posts to cover the line from raiding parties; to move to the front every available man to reinforce the main army; to strike rapidly; and to supply the army by road.[1]

As to the plan for the advance it is less subject to criticism, save in so far as the preceding remarks apply to it. The move towards a front, Centreville – Sangster's Crossroads (the latter point is about a mile south of Fairfax Station), was clearly indicated, and it was fair, in view of defective local knowledge and the uncertainty attending military operations, to leave further movements to be determined later. The general preference for a flanking movement over a frontal attack was natural; but this point will receive further consideration later, as well as the question of the use of artillery. The turning of the Confederate flank was dealt with on the

[1] McDowell's paragraph about the use of his 3d division and reserve on the railroad, when read with his earlier plan, is illogical and contradictory,

basis that Johnston's army need not be considered, and McDowell merely decided to operate on the enemy's line of communications by the flank that left his own line, that is the railroad, as well guarded as possible. He did not consider the effect of this move in possibly compelling Beauregard's retreat towards Johnston, and the resulting accumulation of force against Patterson.

Keenly conscious of the lack of cohesion of his army, McDowell merely repeated a request already made in asking for a brigade organization. It will be more convenient to leave this and similar points to be discussed when we consider the composition and organization of his army at the time the campaign opened.

To sum up: one of the chief criticisms levelled at McDowell's scheme — it might be fairer to treat it as both McDowell's and Scott's — was that it left a loose end of the greatest importance in the matter of Johnston's army. A dispatch of Scott to Patterson of this same date, June the 25th, will reinforce the argument, and show that this problem was not being adequately dealt with. In this, Scott says : —

Remain in front of the enemy while he continues in force between Winchester and the Potomac. If you are in superior or equal force, you may cross and offer him battle. If the enemy should retire upon his resources at Winchester, it is not enjoined that you should pursue him to that distance from your base of operations without a well-grounded confidence in your continued superiority.[1]

[1] O. R. Ser. I, vol. II, 725.

An instruction of this sort to an officer whose caution, not to say timidity, should have been realized, might easily result in giving Johnston a large liberty of action.

The fact appears to have been that Scott was physically unequal to the conduct of the war. It is true that at the outbreak he was the one person at Washington competent to give a sound technical opinion to the Administration. When we contrast his reasoned views with the prevailing ignorance, Scott at once commands our confidence, our admiration, and our sympathy. He could judge what war on such a theatre of operations and with armies of militia meant: Three hundred thousand men might in two or three years destroy the economic resources of the South and bring about a restoration of order, — that was his minimum. It was actually to take nearly ten times that number of men and nearly twice that time; while the Administration had informed the country that one quarter of the men and one tenth of the time would suffice.

But however competent Scott might have been in his general views at the outset, he assumed far too readily that his subordinates were as fit to play the game of war as he was. He was aged and infirm, no longer able to deal with desk work continuously. Headquarters were not sufficiently organized to cope with the heavy and confusing work that the emergency called for; and the politicians made that work even more difficult. Senator Wilson, chairman of the Committee on Military Affairs, for which his qualification was his success in life as a manufacturer of shoes and a manipulator of votes, habitually reviled West Pointers for no better reason than that they were West Pointers. His attitude was typical of that of many other men of the same type who directed the government of the country, for its misfortune.

Scott probably felt little confidence in the abilities of his two army commanders. He limited McDowell's view of his operations so that when that commander knew Johnston had come within them, he declined to act on the information, leaving the responsibility to others. And Scott poured out an unceasing stream of orders and recommendations on Patterson that were not consistent in spirit and that did not tend to stimulate that ineffec-tive commander into efficiency. Thus we find him, two days after the last quoted dispatch, telegraphing to Pat-terson, as follows : "No acknowledgment of mine of the 25th; and letter of the same date. Under the latter I had expected your crossing the river to-day in pursuit of the enemy."[1] Such an expectation was clearly not justified, and the natural effect of Scott's dispatch of the 25th on an officer such as Patterson is that shown in the latter's dispatch to one of his subordinates on the 26th, in which he writes : "If I can get permission to go over into Vir-ginia, I intend to cross the river and offer battle to the

[1] O. R. Ser. I, vol. II, 727; Scott to Patterson, June 27, 1861.

insurgents."[1] The road from Williamsport to Winchester was paved quite solid with Patterson's good intentions!

On the 29th of June a conference was held at the White House to which the President summoned Generals Scott, McDowell, Mansfield, Meigs, Sandford, and Tyler. McDowell read his plan for the attack on Manassas, and after some desultory comment, this was apparently approved by those present.[2] On the following day a meeting of the Cabinet was held at which the retention of Patterson in command was debated; it was decided not to make a change. A week later the same question arose again, but with the same result.[3]

Meanwhile the President had decided that McDowell should march on Manassas in accordance with his plan, and at the earliest possible date, in view of the fact that before another month most of his men would become entitled to be discharged from service. At the moment Scott hoped that the advance might take place in about a week's time, as he informed General Patterson on the following day.[4]

On the 4th of July, Congress assembled. Political questions do not come strictly within our scope, yet it is impossible to pass by some of the demands and state-

[1] O. R. Ser. I, vol. II, 726.
[2] *Rep. Cond. War*, II, 36, 62.
[3] *Rep. Cond. War,* II, 62, 55.
[4] O. R. Ser. I, vol. II, 157; Townsend to Patterson.

ments made by the Administration on that occasion, for they illustrate in a striking degree the grave misfortunes that attend a country that neglects to conduct its military affairs as a matter of business and under competent technical advice. President Lincoln's Message to Congress virtually admitted the uselessness of his previous measures, for he now asked for an army of 400,000 men. But that was almost a confession that McDowell's army was not fit for its purpose, and that the lives of his officers and men were to be deliberately offered up on the sacred altar of political bluff. And the message added insult to injury. Seizing on the fact that so many officers had followed their States and renounced their allegiance, from mistaken loyalty to a cause more than one of them believed hopeless, Lincoln made an odious comparison by declaring: "Not one common soldier or common sailor is known to have deserted his flag." That might be the way to win necessary popular and newspaper approval; it was not the way of facilitating the cruel task he had already loaded on the shoulders of that group of brave and self-denying men at the head of which stood Scott and McDowell. The weightiest historian of the epoch has well characterized Lincoln's message when he says: "No demagogue ever made a more crafty appeal."[1]

Meanwhile Patterson had received some artillery, an arm in which he had been deficient, and finally ven-

[1] Rhodes, *History*, III, 440.

tured across the Potomac. He occupied Martinsburg on
the 3d of July, Confederate detachments retiring before
him. He now informed Scott that he would advance
on the enemy at Winchester, and thence open up communications with McDowell through Charlestown and
Leesburg. This was all fairly satisfactory as seen from
headquarters. It appeared to indicate that energetic
action might be expected from Patterson and that he
would begin pressing in on Johnston a few days before
the moment fixed for McDowell's advance. But in these
same dispatches Patterson announced that he was short
of supplies and must wait to get them up, that Johnston
was in his immediate front, and that he was embarrassed
by the fact that the term of enlistment of his volunteer
regiments had nearly expired. Scott, however, took the
case at its best, and signified his satisfaction to Patterson.
"Having defeated the enemy," he wrote, "if you can
continue the pursuit without too great hazard, advance
via Leesburg . . . towards Alexandria; but . . . move
with great caution." [1] As usual with Patterson, it was the
expression "caution" that fixed his attention and "defeat the enemy" that escaped him. Already on the 5th,
he was giving credit to fantastic reports that Johnston
had been heavily reinforced from Manassas; he showed
the greatest disinclination to advance. He was still at
Martinsburg hurrying all possible reinforcements to that

[1] O. R. Ser. I, vol. II, 157, 159; dispatches of July 3, 4, and 5.

point and clamoring for more troops. His offensive tendencies were not reawakened by a dispatch of the 7th from Washington announcing that owing to the dearth of horses the advance on Manassas could not take place before the 14th.[1]

A long dispatch from Patterson to Colonel Townsend, A.A.G., dated from Martinsburg the 9th of July, reveals that general's state of mind. The last paragraph alone was sufficient to show how little he could be relied on to keep Johnston away from Manassas : —

As I have already stated, I cannot advance far, and if I could I think the movement very imprudent. When you make your attack I expect to advance and offer battle. If the enemy retires I shall not pursue. I am very desirous to know when the general-in-chief wishes me to approach Leesburg. . . .[2]

On the 11th, Scott sent Patterson a report indicating that the Confederates were attempting to lure him as far as Winchester where, by reinforcing Johnston from Manassas, they could strike him at a disadvantage some way from his base. Patterson entirely fell in with this view ; on the 12th, — and McDowell was now almost ready to move, — he asked permission to change his line of operations from Hagerstown–Martinsburg–Winchester, to Harper's Ferry–Charlestown–Winchester, involving a change of base certain, with him, to occupy some days. And yet at that very moment Patterson's in-

[1] O. R. Ser. I, vol. II, 161; Townsend to Patterson, July 7.
[2] O. R. Ser. I, vol. II, 163.

formation, erroneous as it proved, was that Johnston had just fallen back beyond Winchester towards the Manassas Gap Railroad.[1]

On the 13th, news reached Patterson that General McClellan had had a considerable success in western Virginia. He thereupon seized his pen and thus vented his emotions on the general-in-chief: —

MARTINSBURG, July 13, 1861.
COLONEL E. D. TOWNSEND, A.A.G.

McClellan's victory received here with great joy. . . . My column must be preserved to insure to the country the fruits of this and other victories, which we hope will follow. My determination is not changed by this news. I would rather lose the chance of accomplishing something brilliant than, by hazarding this column, to destroy the fruits of the campaign to the country by defeat. If wrong let me be instructed.

R. PATTERSON.[2]

Comment appears to be superfluous. A critique of Patterson's generalship belongs less to the domain of military art than to that of musical comedy.

It is difficult to exonerate Scott from the responsibility of entrusting to such a subordinate so vital and so delicate an operation as the one contemplated; and it is difficult to exonerate him from continuously alternating in his orders recommendations to vigor and to prudence. On the 13th, Scott, for once, is explicit, though it may be questioned whether the following order was closely reasoned out on the facts and capable of execution: —

[1] O. R. Ser. I, vol. II, 165.   [2] O. R. Ser. I, vol. II, 165.

. . . If not strong enough to beat the enemy early next week,[1] make demonstrations so as to detain him in the valley of Winchester; but if he retreats in force towards Manassas, and if it be too hazardous to follow him, then consider the route via Leesburg.[2]

The consistency of this with the general scheme is as evident as its inconsistency with several other dispatches from Scott to Patterson. It may further be noted that it was a pure assumption to suppose that Patterson could get news of a movement by Johnston on the Manassas Gap Railroad in time to act. The contrary assumption would have been nearer the actual fact.

On the 14th Patterson wrote, still from Martinsburg: —

To-morrow I advance. . . . If an opportunity offers I shall attack; but unless I can rout, shall be careful not to set him in full retreat upon Strassburg. . . . Many of the three months' volunteers are restless at the prospect of being retained over their time. . . .[3]

Two days later, after skirmishing so vigorously with the enemy that he claimed to have killed one man, Patterson reached Bunker Hill, twelve miles from Winchester, and announced his movement for the following day, not towards Johnston and the Manassas Gap Railroad, but to his left, towards Charlestown.

The next day, the 17th of July, Patterson moved to his left, to Springfield, midway to Charlestown, and thence reported that eighteen of his regiments would be entitled

[1] That is, about the 16th, the day McDowell actually moved.
[2] O. R. Ser. I, vol. II, 166.
[3] O. R. Ser. I, vol. II, 166.

to their discharge within a week and that he could not
rely on any of them staying with him. "Shall I reoccupy
. . . Harper's Ferry or withdraw entirely?" he asks.[1]
At 9.30 P.M., with the news just in that McDowell was
within five miles of Bull Run, Scott telegraphed as follows: —

I have nothing official from you since Sunday [14th], but am glad
to learn, through Philadelphia papers, that you have advanced. Do
not let the enemy amuse and delay you with a small force in front
whilst he re-enforces his main body at the Junction. McDowell's first
day's work has driven the enemy beyond Fairfax Court House. The
Junction will probably be carried to-morrow.[2]

To this Patterson replied at 1.30 A.M. on the morning of
the 18th that to attack was hazardous, but should he
do so? A few hours later Scott answered: —

I have certainly been expecting you to beat the enemy. If not, to
hear that you had felt him strongly. . . . You have been at least his
equal, and, I suppose, superior in numbers. Has he not stolen a march
and sent re-enforcements toward Manassas Junction? . . . You must
not retreat. . . . If necessary, when abandoned by the short term
volunteers, intrench somewhere and wait for re-enforcements.[3]

This reproach apparently nettled Patterson, for later on
the same day, we find him retorting in highly imagina-
tive if not positively untrue terms, as follows : —

The enemy has stolen no march on me. I have kept him actively
employed and by threats and reconnaissances in force caused him to

[1] O. R. Ser. I, vol. II, 167; *Rep. Cond. War*, II, 57.
[2] O. R. Ser. I, vol. II, 168.
[3] O. R. Ser. I, vol. II, 168.

be re-enforced. I have accomplished in this respect more than the General-in-Chief asked, or could well be expected.[1]

At the time when Patterson wrote those lines Johnston's troops were marching hard for Ashby's Gap, while forty miles further east Longstreet had just flung back Tyler from Blackburn's Ford on Bull Run.

On the 20th, the day before the battle of Bull Run, Patterson telegraphed from Charlestown the far from valuable information that Johnston had moved from Winchester to Millwood on the 18th, with a force of 35,000 men ; the fact being that his total was less than one third of that figure. This information was sent on by Scott to McDowell, and reached him on the field of battle where Johnston's troops were already facing him.

We need not follow the unfortunate Patterson farther, merely adding that an order appointing General Banks to supersede him was dated the 19th of July. A review of his operations will be attempted after first tracing those of his opponent, General Joseph E. Johnston.

THE CONFEDERATES IN THE SHENANDOAH

Following his withdrawal from Harper's Ferry, Johnston took position at Bunker Hill, twelve miles north of Winchester, on the 16th of June. He expected that Patterson would cross the Potomac that day and advance southward. He believed that the Federals out-

[1] O. R. Ser. I, vol. II, 168.

numbered him by about three to one, though in fact the
proportion was only about three to two, and his sole
expectation for the moment was to retard their advance.
He had increased his supply of ammunition to about
thirty rounds.

On the following day, Johnston decided to move back
eight miles nearer to Winchester. There he found a
position at Aittler's Run which he decided to fortify, to
arm with a few heavy guns, and to hold. Strategically
the move was sound, for he could now more easily repel
any advance from western Virginia, or else reach Beauregard at Manassas, while he was almost as well placed for
stopping Patterson, and in a stronger position. Colonel
Stuart with the cavalry, about 300 sabres, was pushed
out towards Patterson beyond Martinsburg, and Jackson's brigade was moved to the latter place, in support,
a few days later. These advanced troops found no enemy
in their front, as Patterson had now recrossed the Potomac.

This was the moment of McDowell's reconnaissances
towards Vienna, and the interpretation of these movements at Confederate headquarters appears from a dispatch of Jefferson Davis to Johnston on the 22d: —

. . . If the enemy has withdrawn from your front . . . it may be
that an attempt will be made to advance from Leesburg to seize the
Manassas road and to turn Beauregard's position. The recent effort
to repair the railroad from Alexandria to Leesburg may have been
with such intent. In that event, if your scouts give you accurate and

timely information, an opportunity will be offered you by the roads through the mountain passes to make a flank attack. . . .[1]

On the 2d of July, as we have already seen, Patterson for the second time crossed the Potomac, and moved on Martinsburg, fighting a heavy skirmish with Jackson and Stuart on the way. On the news coming in, and with a view to imposing on the enemy and stopping his advance, Johnston moved at once towards Martinsburg, taking up his position on the 3d at Darkesville, six miles from Martinsburg, where he was joined by Jackson and Stuart. For four days Johnston remained at Darkesville, prepared to fight if necessary; and then, as Patterson would not advance and as he was not willing to risk the offensive against superior numbers, he fell back towards Winchester again, leaving his cavalry to observe the enemy's movements.

Johnston's advance had had its moral effect, and Patterson showed extreme reluctance to push on beyond Martinsburg. On the 15th, however, he advanced as far as Bunker Hill where he remained on the 16th, and on the next day began to move away towards his left and rear in the direction of Charlestown. This, according to Johnston's report, "created the impression that he . . . was merely holding us in check while General Beauregard should be attacked at Manassas by General Scott."[2] At one o'clock in the morning of the 18th, at the very

[1] O. R. Ser. I, vol. II, 945.   [2] O. R. Ser. I, vol. II, 473.

moment when Patterson was relaxing such slight pressure as he had been exerting, Johnston received from Richmond the following telegram : —

General Beauregard is attacked. To strike the enemy a decisive blow a junction of all your effective force will be needed. If practicable, make the movement, sending your sick and wounded to Culpeper Court House, either by railroad or by Warrenton. In all the arrangements exercise your discretion.

S. Cooper,
Adjutant and Inspector-General.[1]

To this Johnston replied : —

. . . General Patterson . . . seems to have moved yesterday to Charlestown. . . . Unless he prevents it we shall move toward General Beauregard to-day. . . . There are wagons enough to carry but four days' provisions, but the urgency of the case seems to me to justify a risk of hunger. I am delayed by provision for the care of the sick. . . .[2]

A few hours later Johnston's columns were headed for Ashby's Gap en route for Piedmont on the Manassas Gap Railroad.

CRITIQUE OF THE VALLEY OPERATIONS

The operations of the Confederates in the Valley were much better managed than those of the Federals. Johnston received few instructions, and of the widest scope; with Patterson it was the opposite. The former did not hesitate, by abandoning Harper's Ferry, to follow his judgment against the wishes of his Government, while his opponent was always visibly leaning on his superiors

---

[1] O. R. Ser. i, vol. ii, 478.   [2] O. R. Ser. i, vol. ii, 982.

and attempting to evade responsibility. Johnston generally formed an approximately accurate estimate of his opponent's forces; Patterson did the reverse. Making allowance for the deficiencies in ammunition and numbers that imposed caution on Johnston, his movements and orders were clean-cut and well adapted to the immediate object in view; Patterson's were uncertain and timid. Johnston made good use of his cavalry, and of Jackson's brigade thrown out in advance; and, although he did not altogether size up his opponent's weakness, he succeeded in imposing on him by a well-timed feint.

Patterson was undoubtedly an incompetent general. And yet, before dismissing his case, it is only fair to sum up such facts as may be pointed to in his favor. Two of these have already been referred to, Scott's excessive control and the expiration of the volunteers' term of service. As to the former there was occasional inconsistency in the spirit of Scott's instructions and a failure to estimate what might be expected from his subordinate. Yet with a more capable lieutenant it is possible that Scott would have given a greater latitude of action and that the situation would have been better met. As to the volunteers and the expiration of their term of service, it is true to say that in this Patterson had a problem that might well have baffled the most resolute commander.[1]

[1] Patterson's evidence before the Committee on the Conduct of the War (II, 6) tells heavily against him. Fitz John Porter, his A.A.G., testified

THE CONFEDERATES AT MANASSAS

Beauregard was busy fortifying, and concentrated his
attention on Manassas itself rather than on the line of
Bull Run. With the help of slave labor supplied by the
neighboring planters, he erected several considerable
earthworks in front of the junction; later he placed these
under the command of Colonel Terrett, who was given
about a thousand local militia to man the works, and
some naval officers to see to the serving of the guns. At
Blackburn's Ford, at Stone Bridge, nothing was done
to prevent the enemy's crossing Bull Run; only at Mitchell's Ford was there any preparation made by digging
trenches. The fact was that at the beginning of the war
far too high an opinion was held of regular fortifications,
while the art of field intrenchment, which played so
great a part later, was little understood. No one failed
more than Beauregard in this particular, and his neglect
to improve the defensive qualities of the line on which
he had made up his mind to fight was one of the gravest errors committed in this far from faultless campaign.

On the 20th of June, we have the first record of a brigade
organization in Beauregard's army; it was as follows:—

before the same committee that Patterson's staff believed from the first
that Johnston would slip away whenever he wanted to (II, 155). Clearly
the best way to cripple him was to engage him and at all events to make
him fire away his ammunition.

First Corps, Army of the Potomac

First Brigade, Brigadier-General M. L. Bonham.[1]
1st South Carolina Volunteers, Colonel Gregg.
7th South Carolina Volunteers, Colonel Bacon.
2d South Carolina Volunteers, Colonel Kershaw.
8th South Carolina Volunteers, Colonel Cash.

Second Brigade, Brigadier-General R. S. Ewell.[2]
6th Alabama Volunteers, Colonel Seibel.
5th Alabama Volunteers, Colonel Rodes.
6th Louisiana Volunteers, Colonel Seymour.

Third Brigade, Brigadier-General D. R. Jones.[3]
5th South Carolina Volunteers, Colonel Jenkins.
17th Mississippi Volunteers, Colonel Featherston.
18th Mississippi Volunteers, Colonel Burt.

Fourth Brigade, Colonel S. H. Terrett.
1st Virginia Volunteers, Colonel Moore.
11th Virginia Volunteers, Colonel Garland.
17th Virginia Volunteers, Colonel Corse.

Fifth Brigade, Colonel P. St. G. Cocke.[4]
19th Virginia Volunteers, Colonel Cocke.
28th Virginia Volunteers, Colonel Preston.
18th Virginia Volunteers, Colonel Withers.

[1] Milledge Luke Bonham; captain of volunteers in Florida, 1836; brevet colonel of volunteers, 1847–48.

[2] Richard Stoddart Ewell: grad. West Point, 1836; brevet captain for Contreras and Churubusco, 1847.

[3] David Rumple Jones; grad. West Point, 1842; brevet first lieutenant for Contreras, 1847; brevet captain, 1853.

[4] Philip St. George Cocke; grad. West Point, 1828; resigned commission, 1834; colonel of Virginia Volunteers, 1861.

Sixth Brigade, Colonel J. A. Early.
   24th Virginia Volunteers, Colonel Early.[1]
   7th Virginia Volunteers, Colonel Kemper.
   4th South Carolina Volunteers, Colonel Sloan.

This statement, derived from the official reports, covers merely the brigading of the infantry at the date given. A complete statement of the organization and numbers of Beauregard, Johnston, and McDowell, will presently be made for the 16th of July, the date at which the operations of the Bull Run campaign really began.

Beauregard was now strengthening his advanced line especially at Fairfax Court House, Fairfax Station, and Sangster's Crossroads; Bonham's headquarters were at Fairfax Court House; Ewell was at Sangster's and Cocke had established himself at Centreville. The cavalry scouted towards Vienna, Falls Church, and Alexandria, and a post of one battalion of infantry and two troops of cavalry was thrown out as far as the Loudon and Hampshire Railroad to the west of Vienna, whence it could keep in touch through Dranesville with a small Confederate force at Leesburg. Sloan's South Carolina regiment was detached from Early's brigade to reinforce Colonel Hunton at the latter point. It may further be noted that at this moment, the end of June, Beauregard, like Johnston, was short of ammunition. He had about

---

[1] Jubal Anderson Early; grad. West Point, 1833; resigned commission, 1838.

twenty rounds per man, and was asking for forty, with sixty more in immediate reserve.

There is nothing of special note to mention on the Confederate side until McDowell's movement began to take shape. Washington was largely in sympathy with the Confederates and important news leaked through with surprising rapidity. Scott's first expectation to advance early in the second week of July, and the obvious preparations for such a move, were quickly known at Manassas. On the 9th, Beauregard telegraphed to Richmond that the enemy "will soon attack with very superior numbers. No time should be lost in reinforcing me here with at least ten thousand men. . . ." [1] On the 11th, he informed Jefferson Davis that he hoped McDowell would attack him at Mitchell's Ford, but feared he might attempt a flanking movement beyond Stone Bridge. [2] And on the 13th, he followed this up by sending to Richmond Colonel Chesnut of his staff to submit a plan of operations to the Government.

Beauregard's idea was this : —

I proposed that General Johnston should unite as soon as possible the bulk of the Army of the Shenandoah with that of the Potomac . . . leaving only sufficient forces to garrison his strong works at Winchester and to guard the five defensive passes of the Blue Ridge and thus hold General Patterson in check . . . General Holmes . . . to

[1] O. R. Ser. I, vol. II, 969.

[2] Roman, *Beauregard*, 83. If the move was really foreseen, then the lack of preparation to meet it deserves the greater blame.

march hither with all of his command not essential for the defence of
. . . Aquia Creek. These junctions having been effected at Manassas,
an immediate impetuous attack of our combined armies upon General
McDowell was to follow as soon as he approached . . . Fairfax Court
House, with the inevitable result, as I submitted, of his complete
defeat and the destruction or capture of his army. This accomplished
the Army of the Shenandoah . . . increased with a part of my forces
. . . was to march back rapidly into the Valley, fall upon and crush
Patterson with a superior force wheresoever he might be found. . . .
Patterson having been virtually destroyed, then General Johnston
would reinforce General Garnett sufficiently to make him superior to
his opponent, General McClellan, and able to defeat that officer. . . .[1]

This plan of Beauregard's confirms the not very high
estimate formed of him; he was a competent engineer, a
good fighter, but no strategist. His plan was worse than
sketchy; it was almost down to the level of newspaper
strategy. Its fundamental weaknesses were that it assumed a degree of mobility for the Confederate armies
which they did not possess, and, even more important,
that it gave to Johnston's long contemplated march from
the valley westwards an offensive instead of a defensive
character. Beauregard and Johnston together could not
have any marked numerical advantage, while from Fairfax Court House to the line of Federal forts and intrenchments that covered Arlington Heights was only a few
miles. The offensive move of the Confederates proposed
by Beauregard, unless it happened to coincide precisely
with an offensive movement on the part of McDowell,

[1] O. R. Ser. I, vol. II, 485; Beauregard's report.

was in fact bound to resolve itself into an effort to carry
the Federal works, against superior artillery, an unthink-
able proposition that requires no serious consideration.
There is no evidence that President Davis ever received
Beauregard's plan in a written form,[1] although there was
a conference attended by Colonel Chesnut, President
Davis, General Lee, General Cooper, and Colonel Preston. Whatever Chesnut may have said, the precise shape
of Beauregard's idea was probably lost in course of conversation, Chesnut's strategic notions being of the crud-
est.[2] The authorities at Richmond, and this means chiefly
President Davis and General Lee, remained throughout
apparently of one mind. They hoped, though with no
confidence, that Johnston could keep himself sufficiently
disengaged from Patterson in the Valley to secure free-
dom of action, and therefore to reach Beauregard at
short notice of his urgent need. When the latter was
attacked they proposed in any case to rush every available man to his support. This meant a small brigade
under General Holmes from Fredericksburg, several new
regiments from Richmond, and, if possible, Johnston
from the Valley. Should Johnston be able to reach the
field, they hoped to do more than merely repel McDowell,
by dealing him an effective counterstroke. Above all,

[1] See Davis' statement, O. R. Ser. I, vol. II, 504, and Chesnut to
Beauregard, *ibid.*, 506.

[2] O. R. Ser. I, vol. II, 506; Chesnut to Beauregard.

Lee certainly realized,[1] and it is probable that Davis did, the immense difficulty of timing Johnston's movement accurately, not moving him till it was certain Beauregard would be attacked, yet moving him in time to play his part.

It was in the afternoon of the 16th of July that the Federal columns left their camps and began their long expected movement towards Manassas. Early on the 17th, Beauregard had the information and telegraphed it on to Richmond. Within a few hours he was informed that considerable reinforcements would join him from the Confederate capital; he was instructed to detain the 6th North Carolina Regiment, on its way by rail to the Valley, and to repeat the instruction already sent to Johnston to move to Manassas if practicable; Holmes, at Fredericksburg, was directed to march on Manassas with three battalions and one battery. Later on the 17th, as news came in that McDowell was pressing on, Beauregard telegraphed: " I believe this proposed movement of General Johnston is too late. Enemy will attack me in force to-morrow morning." [2]

And yet the Confederate general, who had neglected to fortify the line of Bull Run while the opportunity was his, who depended for success on the ordered reinforcements reaching him in time, made no effort of any sort

[1] O. R. Ser. I, vol. II, 515; Lee to Davis.
[2] O. R. Ser. I, vol. II, 980.

to delay the march of the enemy, but ordered his brigades at Fairfax and Centreville to abandon the intrenchments they had dug there, and to retire to Bull Run. This course was not without reason ; it was probably a big risk to fight a rear-guard action against a superior force and take the chances of a brigade or two becoming stampeded and the whole army demoralized. Yet it is difficult to resist the conclusion that in a general sense Beauregard had not a very close grasp of the facts of the situation.

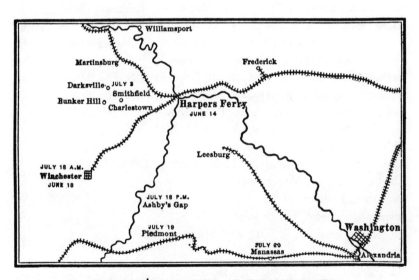

JOHNSTON'S POSITIONS AT VARIOUS DATES

IV

ORGANIZATION OF THE ARMIES [1]

NORTH

BEFORE going further we must now take up the organization of the armies that met at Bull Run, and we will begin with that of McDowell.

Army of Northeastern Virginia

Commander-in-Chief, Irvin McDowell, Brigadier-General.

Aides-de-camp, Lieutenant H. W. Kingsbury, Lieutenant G. V. Henry, Major C. S. Brown, New York Volunteers; Major J. S. Wadsworth, New York Volunteers.

Acting Assistant Adjutant-General, Captain J. B. Fry.

Acting Assistant Quartermaster, Captain O. H. Tillinghast.

Chief Commissary, Captain H. F. Clarke.

Signal Officers, Major Myer, Major M. McDowell.

Chief Engineer, Major Barnard.

Assistants, Captain Whipple, Lieutenants Abbot and Putnam.

Chief of Artillery, Major Barry.

Ordnance, Lieutenant Strong.

Inspector-General, Major Wood.

Medical officers, W. S. King and Magruder.

---

[1] The statements in the following section have been laboriously compiled from a cross-examination of all available reports and other documents, many of them conflicting, not only in the official Records, but elsewhere. Footnotes would have been endlessly complicated and not very profitable; they have therefore been omitted save where they seemed directly in point.

First Division, Daniel Tyler,[1] Brigadier-General.
Acting Assistant Adjutant-General, Captain Baird.
Acting Assistant Quartermaster, Captain Merrill.
Chief Engineer, Captain Alexander.
A.D.C. and other duties: Lieutenants Houston, Abbot, Upton, O'Rorke and Audenried.

First Brigade, Colonel E. D. Keyes.[2]
Acting Assistant Adjutant-General, Lieutenant Hascall.
Acting Assistant Quartermaster, Lieutenant Hodge.
Commissary, Lieutenant Ely.
A.D.C. and other duties: Lieutenants Walter, Gordon.
2d Maine, Colonel Jameson.
1st Connecticut, Colonel Speidel.
2d Connecticut, Colonel Terry.
3d Connecticut, Colonel Chatfield.

Second Brigade, Brigadier-General R. C. Schenck.
1st Ohio, Colonel McCook.
2d Ohio, Colonel Mason.
2d New York, Colonel Tompkins.
Battery E, 2d U.S. Artillery, Captain Carlyle.
1 Parrott thirty-pounder gun, Lieutenant Hains (Battery G, 1st U.S. Artillery).

Third Brigade, Colonel W. T. Sherman.[3]
Acting Assistant Adjutant-General, Lieutenant Piper.
Acting Assistant Quartermaster, Lieutenant McQuesten.

[1] Daniel Tyler; grad. West Point, 1816; resigned as lieutenant, 1834; brigadier-General of Connecticut Volunteers, 1861.

[2] Erasmus Darwin Keyes; grad. West Point, 1828; captain, 1838; major, 1858; lieutenant-colonel and military secretary to General Scott, 1861; colonel 11th Infantry, 1861; brigadier-general of volunteers, 1861.

[3] William Tecumseh Sherman ; grad. West Point, 1840; resigned commission, 1853; president Louisiana Military Institute, 1860.

A.D.C. and other duties: Colonel Coon, Wisconsin, Lieutenant
  Bagley.
13th New York, Colonel Quinby.
69th New York (Irish), Colonel Corcoran.
79th New York (Highlanders), Colonel Cameron.[1]
2d Wisconsin, Colonel Peck.
Battery E, 3d U.S. Artillery, Captain Ayres.

Fourth Brigade, Colonel I. B. Richardson.[2]
  Assistant Adjutant-General, Lieutenant Eastman.
  Assistant Quartermaster, Lieutenant Brightly.
  Chief Engineer, Lieutenant Prime.
  A.D.C., Cadet Meigs.
Light Infantry Battalion, Captain Brethschneider.[3]
3d Michigan, Colonel McConnell.
1st Massachusetts, Colonel Cowdin.
12th New York (Militia), Colonel Walreth.
2d Michigan (Colonel I. B. Richardson).
                Major Williams.
Battery G, 2d U.S. Artillery, Lieutenant Edwards.
Battery M, 2d U.S. Artillery, Major Hunt.
1 Squadron 2d U.S. Cavalry, Captain Brackett.

Second Division, Colonel David Hunter.[4]
Assistant Adjutant-General, Captain W. D. Whipple.
Chief Engineer, Captain Woodbury.
A.D.C. and other duties: Lieutenant Cross, Lieutenant Flagler,
  Lieutenant S. W. Stockton, Hon. J. W. Arnold.

[1] This regiment wore the kilt as a full-dress uniform, but fought at Bull
Run in trousers.

[2] Israel Bush Richardson, grad. West Point, 1836; brevet captain,
Contreras and Churubusco, 1847; brevet major, Chapultepec, 1847; resigned commission, 1855; colonel 2d Michigan Vols., 1861.

[3] One company was detailed from each regiment of the brigade to form
this light battalion.

[4] David Hunter, grad. West Point, 1818; captain, 1833; major, 1842;
colonel 3d Cavalry, 1861.

First Brigade, Colonel Andrew Porter.[1]

> Acting Assistant Adjutant-General, Lieutenant W. W. Averell.
> Acting Assistant Quartermaster, Lieutenant J. B. Howard.
> A.D.C. and other duties: Lieutenants Trowbridge and Bache.
> 1 Battalion U.S. Marines, Major Reynolds.
> 1 Battalion U.S. Infantry, Major Sykes.
> 1 Battalion U.S. Cavalry,[2] Major Palmer.
> 27th New York, Colonel H. W. Slocum.
> 14th (84th) New York (Brooklyn), Colonel Wood.
> 8th New York (Militia), Colonel Lyons.
> Battery D, 5th U.S. Artillery, Captain Griffin.

Second Brigade, Colonel A. E. Burnside.[3]

> Acting Assistant Adjutant-General, Lieutenant Merriman.
> Acting Assistant Quartermaster, Captain Anson.
> Commissary, Captain Goodhue.
> A.D.C. and other duties: Captain Woodbury, Lieutenant Beaumont.[4]
> 1st Rhode Island, Major Balch.
> 2d Rhode Island, Colonel Slocum.
> 71st New York (Militia), Colonel Martin.
> 2d New Hampshire, Colonel Fiske.
> Rhode Island Battery, Colonel Monroe.
> Two howitzers, 71st New York.

Third Division, Colonel Heintzelman. [5]

Acting Assistant Adjutant-General, Captain McKeever.

[1] Andrew Porter, West Point, 1836–37; lieutenant and captain of Mounted Rifles, 1846–47; brevet major, Contreras, 1847; brevet lieutenant-colonel, Churubusco, 1847; brigadier-general of volunteers, 1861.

[2] Two squadrons 2d Dragoons, four squadrons 1st Cavalry, eight squadrons 2d Cavalry; two squadrons to one company.

[3] Ambrose Everett Burnside, grad. West Point, 1843; resigned commission, 1853; colonel 1st Rhode Island Vols., 1861.

[4] Governor Sprague of Rhode Island was present at Bull Run and apparently performed some of Burnside's duties himself.

[5] Samuel Peter Heintzelman; grad. West Point, 1822; captain, 1838; major, 1855; colonel 14th Infantry, 1861.

Chief Engineer, Captain H. Wright.

A.D.C. and other duties: Lieutenants Snyder, Farquhar, Sweet, and Fairbanks.

First Brigade, Colonel W. B. Franklin.[1]

Acting Assistant Adjutant-General, Captain Jenkins.

Acting Assistant Quartermaster, Lieutenant Gibson.

A.D.C. and other duties: Lieutenant Baker, Colonel Hartranft.[2]

5th Massachusetts, Colonel Lawrence.

11th Massachusetts, Colonel Clark.

4th Pennsylvania,[3] Colonel Hartranft.

1st Minnesota, Colonel Gorman.

Battery I, 1st U.S. Artillery, Captain Ricketts.

Second Brigade, Colonel O. B. Willcox.

Assistant Adjutant-General, Lieutenant Woodruff.

A.D.C. and other duties: Lieutenants Parker and Edie.

1st Michigan, Major Bidwell.

4th Michigan,[4] Colonel Willcox.

11th New York (Zouaves), Colonel Farnham.

38th New York (Scott Life Guard), Colonel Ward.

Battery D, 2d U.S. Artillery, Captain Arnold.

Third Brigade, Colonel O. O. Howard.[5]

Acting Assistant Adjutant-General, Captain Burt.

Acting Assistant Quartermaster, Lieutenant Burt.

---

[1] William Buel Franklin; grad. West Point, 1839 (first); captain, 1857; colonel 12th Infantry, 1861.

[2] His regiment refused to advance on the 21st, claiming that their time was up. Their colonel joined the staff.

[3] Turned back from Centreville the morning of the battle on expiration of service.

[4] Was detached and left behind at Fairfax Court House.

[5] Oliver Otis Howard; grad. West Point, 1850; colonel 3d Maine Volunteers, 1861.

A.D.C. and other duties: Lieutenants Buel and Mordecai, Charles H. Howard.

2d Vermont, Colonel Whiting.

3d Maine, Major Staples.

4th Maine, Colonel Barry.

5th Maine, Colonel Dunnell.

Fifth Division, Colonel D. S. Miles.[1]

Acting Assistant Adjutant-General, Captain Vincent.

Assistant Quartermaster, Lieutenant Hawkins.

Chief Engineer, Lieutenant Prime.

A.D.C. and other duties: Major Ritchie, Lieutenants M'Millan, Mendell, Cushing.

First Brigade, Colonel L. Blenker.

8th New York (Volunteers), Colonel Stahel.

29th New York, Colonel Steinwehr.

39th New York (Garibaldi Guard), Colonel Utassy.

27th Pennsylvania, Colonel Einstein.

Battery A, 2d U.S. Artillery, Captain Tidball.

Battery, 8th New York Militia [2] (Varian's), Captain Bookwood.

Second Brigade, Colonel Thomas A. Davies.[3]

Acting Assistant Adjutant-General, Lieutenant Cowdrey.

Acting Assistant Quartermaster, Lieutenant Hopkins.

Commissary, Lieutenant Bradford.

A.D.C. and other duties: Lieutenant Howland.

16th New York, Colonel Marsh.

---

[1] Dixon Stanbury Miles; grad. West Point, 1819; captain, 1836; major, 1847; two brevets for expedition to Mexico, 1847; lieutenant-colonel, 1851; colonel 2d Infantry, 1855.

[2] Abandoned by its own men at Centreville, it was manned by volunteers commanded by Captain Bookwood.

[3] Thomas Alfred Davies; grad. West Point, 1825; resigned commission, 1831; colonel 16th New York Volunteers, 1861.

18th New York, Colonel Jackson.
31st New York, Colonel Pratt.
32d New York, Colonel Matheson.
Battery G, 1st U.S. Artillery, Lieutenant Benjamin.

Register of Volunteer and Militia Regiments

	Div.	Brig.		Div.	Brig.
1st Connecticut	I	1	13th New York	I	3
2d Connecticut	I	1	14th New York	II	1
3d Connecticut	I	1	16th New York	V	2
2d Maine	I	1	18th New York	V	2
3d Maine	III	3	27th New York	II	1
4th Maine	III	3	29th New York	V	1
5th Maine	III	3	31st New York	V	2
1st Massachusetts	I	4	32d New York	V	2
5th Massachusetts	III	1	38th New York	III	2
11th Massachusetts	III	1	39th New York	V	1
1st Michigan	III	2	69th New York	I	3
2d Michigan	I	4	71st New York	II	2
3d Michigan	I	4	79th New York	I	3
4th Michigan	III	2	1st Ohio	I	2
1st Minnesota	III	1	2d Ohio	I	2
2d New Hampshire	II	2	4th Pennsylvania	III	1
2d New York	I	2	27th Pennsylvania	V	1
8th New York (Militia)	II	1	1st Rhode Island	II	2
8th New York (Vols.)	V	1	2d Rhode Island	II	2
11th New York	III	2	2d Vermont	III	3
12th New York	I	4	2d Wisconsin	I	3

General Runyon's division was left behind at Alexandria, and its only direct participation in the operations
was a movement of the 1st and 2d New Jersey to Vienna
and thence to Centreville on the 21st; they did not come
into contact with the enemy, and played no part.

The above statement of McDowell's organization is
subject to the two following corrections: the staff returns
are in some cases probably incomplete and inaccurate,
and the numerous civilians who rendered more or less

staff service are not wholly listed; then again there is room for variation in the statement of the regiments present; some deserted—that is, claimed their discharge—while on the march and before any fighting had occurred; others, less prudent, did not abandon the army until the very morning of the battle, like the 4th Pennsylvania; the former have been excluded from the enumeration, the latter included. This again shows the difficulty of giving an accurate estimate of the numbers involved, which must be our next endeavor. First of all we may take McDowell's own showing for the 16th of July when he opened his march.

	Present for duty		
	Officers	Men	Total
First (Tyler's) Division.............	569	12,226	12,795
Second (Hunter's) Division.........	121	2,364	2,485
Third (Heintzelman's) Division......	382	8,680	9,062
Fifth (Miles') Division.............	289	5,884	6,173
Total	1,361	29,154	30,515

The figures just given represent an estimate more than facts, for divisional and brigade commanders exercised a more or less wide discretion in selecting regiments to go to the front or to stay behind in the Alexandria–Arlington lines up to the very last minute. McDowell's original document, from which the above is largely deduced, is a curious arithmetical puzzle which the reader may attempt to make sense from if he chooses.[1]

On the whole, and looking at the matter roughly, one may conclude that McDowell expected to arrive at Centreville with not more than 30,000 men, leaving some 6000 men behind in his works.[2]

The number of guns is easier to ascertain.

1st U.S. Artillery, Battery G, 2, 20-lb. rifled; 1, 30-lb. rifled.
1st "   "   "   I, 6, 10-lb. rifled.
2d   "   "   "   A, 2, 6-lb. smooth; 2, 12-lb. howitzers.
2d   "   "   "   D, 2, 6-lb. smooth; 2, 13-lb. rifled.
2d   "   "   "   E, 2, 6-lb. smooth; 2, 13-lb. rifled.

[1] "Abstract from the returns of the Department of Northeastern Virginia, commanded by Brigadier-General McDowell, U.S.A., for July 16 and 17, 1861.

Commands	Present			
	For duty		Total	Aggregate
	Officers	Men		
General Staff.........................	19			21
First (Tyler's) Division*.................	569	12,226	9,494	9,936
Second (Hunter's) Division.............	121	2,364	2,525	2,648
Third (Heintzelman's) Division........	382	8,680	9,385	9,777
Fourth (Runyon's) Division...........	247	5,201	5,502	5,752
Fifth (Miles') Division................	289	5,884	5,917	6,207
21st New York Volunteers.............	37	684	707	745
25th New York Militia................	34	519	534	573
2d U.S. Cavalry, Company E..........	4	56	63	73
Total..........................	1702	35,614	34,127	35,732

* "The total and aggregate present in the Fourth Brigade of this division is not carried out on the original return. Hence the anomaly of a smaller total and aggregate 'Present' than 'Present for duty' in the division." O. R. Ser. I, vol. II, 309.

[2] We shall later give a more precise estimate of the numbers he actually had in the battle, and also of those seriously engaged.

2d U.S. Artillery, Battery G, 4, 10-lb. rifled.

2d   "   "   "   M, 4, 12-lb. smooth.

3d   "   "   "   E, 2, 10-lb. rifled; 2, 6-lb. smooth; 2, 12-lb. howitzers.

5th   "   "   "   D, 4, 10-lb. rifled; 2, 12-lb. howitzers.

2d Rhode Island Volunteers,   6, 13-lb. rifled.

71st New York Militia,   2 small howitzers.

8th New York Militia Battery,   6, 6-lb. smooth.[1]

The total was therefore fifty-five guns, mostly of the regular army, and divisible as follows : —

	Rifled	Smoothbore
30-pounders,	1	
20-pounders,	2	
13-pounders,	10	
12-pounders,		10
10-pounders,	16	
6-pounders,		14
Small howitzers,		2

This gave McDowell a strength in artillery of almost two guns per thousand men and it will be observed that more than half of his pieces were rifled ten-pounders or better.

The cavalry of the army was insignificant in numbers,[2] which was a source of weakness as will be seen later.

---

[1] The 8th New York went home on the morning of the battle, but left their guns to be served by volunteers. If a few had been drumhead court-martialled and shot for cowardice in presence of the enemy the effect would doubtless have been healthy; unfortunately they were voters, and therefore sacred.

[2] The country about Bull Run was not well suited to this arm.

The transport and artillery swallowed up all available horses.

STAFF AND COMMAND. McDowell's infantry was properly distributed into brigades and divisions; but his organization was so hasty, and those entrusted with its working were so inexperienced, that it broke down in many ways when brought to the test. The strength of the army lay in the number and quality of its guns, and in the training and discipline of the artillery corps, which was almost wholly of the regular army. But the organization of this arm was faulty, unsuited to the problem in hand, and unlikely to produce good results. The batteries were merely distributed more or less haphazard among the different brigades, changes being made while actually on the march and on the field. Some brigades were without guns, others had two batteries. Now it is clear that such raw infantry as McDowell's required artillery support at every point where the enemy's fire would have to be faced. On the other hand it was essential to concentrate the fire of as many guns as possible at the decisive point, and not to take the chance that a battery would fail to get there merely because the brigade to which it was attached was not engaged. It would seem therefore as though a divisional grouping would have been best, each division commander controlling his batteries through a chief of artillery. But there were no such officers in theory or in fact. Major Barry did not join McDowell until the 17th, and his functions as chief of artillery were largely nominal. When it came down to practice, the organization was so bad that some battery commanders received orders from brigade and division commanders, the chief of artillery, and the commander-in-chief in person.

The higher command and staff organization were too hastily improvised to be effective. Turning to the divisional and brigade commanders first of all, it may be said that at this point there was least ground for criticism under the circumstances. They were mostly regular officers of considerable rank: Keyes was colonel of the 11th Infantry, Sherman of the 13th, Hunter of the 3d Cavalry, Porter of the 16th Infantry, Heintzelman of the 17th, Franklin of the 18th, and Miles of the 2d; Tyler, though long in civil life, was a West-Pointer, as were one or two of the others. On the whole, it might be said that all that was possible had been done in the way of selection.

The staffs of these generals and of the commander-in-chief were small, and made up of young and inexperienced officers; they were, however, almost wholly regulars, except for a considerable number of civilian aides-de-camp, and showed courage, ability, and driving power when put to the test. Though of the generals only Sherman was destined to rise beyond mediocrity, there were among the staff officers mere boys, almost straight from West Point, like Upton, who had the makings of first-rate soldiers in them.

Neither these staff officers nor their commanders had experience or instruction enough to control any army, leave alone a raw one, in field operations. There was no well-defined system of command. Some of the brigades were constituted within a few hours only of the advance. Practically none of the brigadiers had ever held, or even seen, a brigade drill. When they reached the field, the capable and energetic, from McDowell down, gave such orders as seemed best, without much regard for the methods of systematized command. They energized in one direction while they added to the confusion in another.

The transport service was in the charge of Captain H. F. Clarke, chief commissary, and worked better than was anticipated. The teams and teamsters were green, wagons and horses were few, notwithstanding which 160,000 rations were conveyed to Centreville by the 18th and there distributed, though in disorderly and wasteful fashion. Had McDowell taken, say, another 3000 men of Runyon's division from Alexandria for active operations, there seems little doubt but that the victualling problem could have been solved. Some account of the work of the transport service will be given in its proper place.

The officering of the volunteer regiments was very defective. Political considerations outweighed military, and instead of making a large draft of junior officers of the regular army for the command and organization of the volunteers, the regiments were mostly given to prominent politicians. Very few, indeed, of these officers were fit for their post, and some were hopelessly unfit. In one case Sherman found a way out of the difficulty by promoting the colonel to his staff, leaving the regiment to be led by a junior but more efficient officer.

If the colonels were poor, the regimental officers were on the whole poorer, usually elected by their men, currying their favor by winking at slackness and insubordination, and ignorant of all that pertained to military affairs. The results of all this will presently appear; but we must first turn to the Confederate army.

SOUTH

Army of the Potomac

First Corps, Brigadier-General G. T. Beauregard.
Acting Assistant Adjutant-General, Colonel T. Jordan, Capt. Clifton H. Smith.
Acting Assistant Quartermaster, Major Cabell.
Chief Commissary, Colonel R. B. Lee.
Chief of Artillery, Colonel S. Jones.
Chief Engineer, Colonel Williamson.
Chief Signal Officer, Captain E. P. Alexander.
Chief Surgeon, R. L. Brodie.
A.D.C., Colonels Preston, Manning, Chesnut, Miles, Rice, Hayward, and Chisolm, Captains D. B. Harris and W. H. Stevens, Lieutenants W. Ferguson, H. E. Peyton.

First Brigade, Brigadier-General M. L. Bonham.

    Acting Assistant Adjutant-General, Colonel Lay.

    Acting Assistant Quartermaster, Colonel Kemper, Lieutenant Washington.

    Chief Commissary, Major Kennedy.

    Military Secretary, Major Walton.

    A.D.C. and other duties: Generals Hagood and McGowan, Colonels Aldrich, Simpson and Lipscomb, Majors Davies, Tompkins, Butler, and M. B. Lipscomb, Captains Stevens, Venable, Nyles, Alfred Moss.

    11th North Carolina, Colonel Kirkland.

    2d South Carolina (Palmettos), Colonel Kershaw.

    3d South Carolina, Colonel Williams.

    7th South Carolina, Colonel Bacon.

    8th South Carolina, Colonel Cash.

    30th Virginia Cavalry, Colonel Radford.

    Alexandria Light Artillery, Captain Kemper.

Second Brigade, Brigadier-General R. S. Ewell.

    Acting Assistant Adjutant-General, Captain Fitzhugh Lee.

    5th Alabama, Colonel Rodes.

    6th Alabama, Colonel Seibel.

    6th Louisiana, Colonel Seymour.

    1 Battery Washington Artillery, Captain Rosser.

    A half battalion of cavalry, Colonel Jenifer.

Third Brigade, Brigadier-General D. R. Jones.

    Acting Assistant Adjutant-General, Lieutenant Latham.

    Acting Assistant Quartermaster and other duties: Captains Coward, Ford, Taylor, Curfell, Lieutenant McLemore.

    17th Mississippi, Colonel Featherston.

    18th Mississippi, Colonel Burt.

    5th South Carolina, Colonel Jenkins.

    A troop of cavalry, Captain Flood.

    1 section Washington Artillery, Captain Miller.

Fourth Brigade, Brigadier-General J. Longstreet.[1]

Acting Assistant Adjutant-General, Lieutenant Armistead.

Acting Assistant Quartermaster, Lieutenant Manning.

A.D.C. and other duties: Colonels Terry, Lubbock, and Riddick, Captains Sorrel, Goree, Chichester, Thompson, and Walton.

1st Virginia, Colonel Moore.

11th Virginia, Colonel Garland.

17th Virginia, Colonel Corse.

24th Virginia, Colonel Hairston.

5th North Carolina, Colonel McCrae.

1 section Washington Artillery, Captain Garnett.

1 troop cavalry, Captain Whitehead.

Fifth Brigade, Colonel P. St. George Cocke.

Chief Engineer, Captain Harris.

8th Virginia, Colonel Hunton.

18th Virginia, Colonel Withers.

19th Virginia, Colonel P. St. G. Cocke.

28th Virginia, Colonel Preston.

49th Virginia, Colonel W. Smith.

1 Battery, Loudoun Artillery, Captain Latham.

1 company cavalry, Captain Langhorne.

Sixth Brigade, Colonel Jubal A. Early.

Acting Assistant Adjutant-General, Captain Gardner.

A.D.C., Lieutenant Willis.

7th Virginia, Colonel Kemper.

7th Louisiana, Colonel Hays.

13th Mississippi, Colonel Barksdale.

1 Battery Washington Artillery, Lieutenant Squires.

[1] James Longstreet; grad. West Point, 1842; brevet captain for Contreras and Churubusco; brevet major for Molino del Rey.

Seventh Brigade, Brigadier-General Nathan G. Evans.[1]
  Acting Assistant Adjutant-General, Captain A. L. Evans.
  A.D.C., Captains McCausland and Rogers.
  4th South Carolina, Colonel Sloan.
  1st Louisiana (New Orleans Tigers), Major Wheat.
  1 Squadron Cavalry, Captain Terry.
  1 Section Latham's Artillery, Captain Davidson.
  1 Squadron Campbell Rangers (mounted), Captain Alexander.

Holmes' Brigade, Gen. F. H. Holmes.
  Acting Assistant Adjutant-General, Lieutenant Walker.
  1st Arkansas, Colonel Fagan.
  2d Tennessee, Colonel Bate.
  1 Battery, Captain Walker.

Unbrigaded.
  8th Louisiana, Colonel Kelly.
  Harrison's Battalion of Cavalry (4 companies), Major Julian
    Harrison.

Artillery Reserve, Major Walton.

  A battalion of Virginia militia, Colonel Wilcox (within the de-
    fences at Manassas).

Artillery.
  Washington Artillery, Major Walton.
    4 twelve-pounder howitzers.
    3 six-pounders rifled.
    6 six-pounders smoothbore.
  Alexandria Light Artillery, Captain Kemper.
    4 six-pounders smoothbore.
  Loudoun Artillery, Captain Rogers.
    4 six-pounders smoothbore.
  Walker's Battery, Captain Walker.

---

[1] Nathan George Evans; grad. West Point, 1844; captain, 1856.

4 six-pounders rifled.

Latham's Battery, Captain Latham.

4 six-pounders smoothbore.

A total of 29 guns, of which 18 were smoothbore six-pounders, 9 were six-pounders rifled, and 4 were twelve-pounder howitzers.

Second Corps, General Joseph E. Johnston.[1]

Acting Adjutant-General, Brigadier-General Kirby Smith,[2] Major Rhett.

Acting Assistant Adjutant-General, Captain T. C. Preston.

Acting Assistant Quartermaster, Major McLean.

Chief Engineer, Major Whiting.

Chief of Artillery, Colonel Pendleton.

Chief Commissary, Major Kearsley.

Chief Ordnance Officer, Colonel Thomas.

A.D.C., Captain Fauntleroy, Lieutenant J. B. Washington, Colonels Cole and Duncan, Major Dees, Captain Mason.

First Brigade, Brigadier-General T. J. Jackson.

Acting Assistant Adjutant-General, Colonel F. B. Jones.

Ordnance Officer, Lieutenant A. S. Pendleton.

A.D.C. and other duties: Captain Marshall, Lieutenant T. G. Lee, Cadets Thompson and N. W. Lee.

2d Virginia, Colonel Allen.

4th Virginia, Colonel J. F. Preston.

5th Virginia, Colonel Harper.

27th Virginia, Colonel Echols.

33d Virginia, Colonel Cummings.

1 Battery, Captain Stanard.

---

[1] Promoted to the rank of general, July 4th; notified July 20th; confirmed August 31st.

[2] At the very moment when Johnston was starting for the Valley, Smith was placed in command of the 4th Brigade. Captain Preston filled his place until Johnston's arrival at Manassas, when Major Rhett took over Kirby Smith's functions.

Second Brigade, Colonel F. S. Bartow.

> Staff Officers, General Gist, Colonel Shingler, and Major Stevens.
> 7th Georgia, Colonel Gartrell.
> 8th Georgia, Colonel Gardner.
> 9th Georgia, Colonel Elzey.
> 1st Kentucky, Colonel Duncan.
> 2d Kentucky, Colonel Pope.
> 1 Battery, Captain Alburtis.

Third Brigade, Brigadier-General Bee.[1]

> Acting Assistant Adjutant-General, Captain T. L. Preston.
> 1st Tennessee, Colonel Turney.
> 2d Mississippi, Colonel Falkner.
> 11th Mississippi, Colonel Liddell.
> 4th Alabama, Colonel Jones.
> 1 Battery, Captain Imboden.

Fourth Brigade, Brigadier-General Kirby Smith,[2] Colonel Elzey.[3]

> Acting Assistant Adjutant-General, Lieutenant Chentney.
> Acting Assistant Quartermaster, Lieutenant McDonald.
> A.D.C., Lieutenant Contee, Colonel Buist, Captains Tupper, Hill and Cunningham on General Kirby Smith's staff.
> 1st Maryland, Colonel F. J. Stewart.
> 3d Tennessee, Colonel Vaughan.
> 10th Virginia, Colonel Gibbons.
> 13th Virginia, Colonel A. P. Hill.
> 1 Battery, Captain Grove.

[1] Barnard Elliot Bee; grad. West Point, 1841; brevet first lieutenant, Cerro Gordo, 1847; brevet captain, Chapultepec, 1847.

[2] Edmund Kirby Smith, grad. West Point, 1841; 2 brevets for campaign of Mexico, 1847; major, 1861; assumed command at Piedmont, but was badly wounded at the beginning of the action when Elzey took over the command.

[3] Arnold Elzey; grad. West Point, 1833; brevet captain for Contreras and Churubusco.

Unbrigaded.
6th North Carolina, Colonel Fisher.[1]

Reserve.
1 Battery, Captain Beckham.

Artillery.
5 Batteries of 4 six-pounder smoothbores, Colonel Pendleton.
Total, 20 guns.

Cavalry.
1st Virginia, Colonel J. E. B. Stuart.[2]

The strength of the two Confederate Corps at the date of the battle according to the official returns may be stated as follows : —

First Corps, Brigadier-General Beauregard

Infantry —	Officers and men
First Brigade	4,961
Second Brigade	2,444
Third Brigade	2,121
Fourth Brigade	3,528
Fifth Brigade	3,276
Sixth Brigade	2,620[3]
Seventh Brigade	1,100
Holmes' Brigade	1,355
8th Louisiana	846
Hampton's Legion	654

[1] This regiment was intended for Bee's brigade; it joined Johnston on the battlefield of Bull Run.

[2] Grad. West Point, 1850.

[3] In this total the 4th South Carolina is reckoned.

Cavalry [1] —

Harrison's Battalion	209
Ten troops	583
Artillery	543
Total	24,240

Second Corps,[2] General J. E. Johnston

Infantry —

	Officers and men
First Brigade	2,151
Second Brigade	2,546
Third Brigade	2,790
Fourth Brigade	2,262
6th North Carolina	600

Cavalry —

1st Virginia	334
Artillery	278
Total	10,961 [3]

Register of Confederate Regiments

	Brigade	Corps		Brigade	Corps
4th Alabama	Bee	II	2d Mississippi	Bee	II
5th Alabama	Ewell	I	13th Mississippi	Early	I
6th Alabama	Ewell	I	17th Mississippi	Jones	I
1st Arkansas	Holmes	I	18th Mississippi	Jones	I
7th Georgia	Barton	II	5th North Carolina	Longstreet	I
8th Georgia	Barton	II	11th North Carolina	Bonham	I
9th Georgia	Barton	II	2d South Carolina	Bonham	I
1st Kentucky	Barton	II	3d South Carolina	Bonham	I
2d Kentucky	Barton	II	4th South Carolina	Evans	I
6th Louisiana	Ewell	I	5th South Carolina	Jones	I
7th Louisiana	Evans	I	7th South Carolina	Bonham	I
8th Louisiana	unbrigaded	I	8th South Carolina	Bonham	I
1st Maryland	Ewell	I	1st Tennessee	Bee	II

[1] The 30th Virginia, attached to Bonham's brigade, is counted with it.

[2] The figures given are for the 30th of June. At Bull Run Jackson numbered 2611; the composite brigade under Bee, 2732; Kirby Smith, 2250, of whom he took 1700 into action, leaving 550 men under A. P. Hill at Manassas.

[3] There is a return in the *Report on the Conduct of the War* (II, 249) which contains many inaccuracies, and inspires no confidence. Its total is 29,949 for the two corps.

	Brigade	Corps		Brigade	Corps
2d Tennessee	Holmes	I	13th Virginia	Smith	II
3d Tennessee	Smith	II	17th Virginia	Longstreet	I
1st Virginia	Longstreet	I	18th Virginia	Cocke	I
2d Virginia	Jackson	II	19th Virginia	Cocke	I
4th Virginia	Jackson	II	24th Virginia	Early	I
5th Virginia	Jackson	II	27th Virginia	Jackson	II
7th Virginia	Early	I	28th Virginia	Cocke	I
8th Virginia	Cocke	I	30th Virginia (Cavalry)	Bonham	I
10th Virginia	Smith	II	33d Virginia	Jackson	II
11th Virginia	Longstreet	I	49th Virginia	Cocke	I

STAFF AND COMMAND. In the Confederate army it is noticeable that Johnston's corps was far better organized than Beauregard's. His 10,000 or 11,000 men might well be taken as constituting a division, and it was broken up into four brigades of almost equal size. His artillery command was centralized in Pendleton's hands; and although four of his batteries were distributed among the infantry brigades, the fifth was in reserve under Pendleton's control. The cavalry, small as it was, was not split up into detachments, but kept together under Stuart's able leadership. And when Johnston moved his army from the Shenandoah to Bull Run, Stuart and Pendleton moved together by road, and accentuated, by that march of the combined cavalry and artillery, a degree of organization in Johnston's army higher than in those of McDowell and Beauregard.

In Beauregard's corps, conditions were very different. The creation of two or three divisions was urgently needed, as events were soon to demonstrate. His seven brigades (not counting Holmes') were very uneven in number and quality, and the smaller ones lacked cohesion. The artillery was badly organized, almost one half of it—with three types of guns—belonging to one command, the Washington Artillery (Louisiana). This was broken up irregularly and distributed, with the other three batteries of the corps (four if we include Walker's battery of Holmes' brigade), among the various brigades. In practice, however, Beauregard apparently tended to create an artillery reserve out of some part of the Washington Artillery. The few troops of horse were scattered, save for the 30th Virginia (cavalry), which was attached to Bonham's brigade for patrol and outpost duty.

In the Confederate army the higher command was better in quality, or better selected, than in that of the North. Among the corps and brigade commanders, Johnston, Kirby Smith, Jackson, Longstreet, Ewell, and Early, and among the colonels, A. P. Hill, Wade Hampton, and J. E. B. Stuart, were eventually to prove themselves competent, and one or two of them, brilliant, soldiers.

In the matter of the staff it might be said that there was no great superiority on one side or the other. While the North had more young regular officers, the South had, except in some of Beauregard's smaller brigades, slightly better organization. At Bonham's headquarters might be seen, in an extreme form, the amateur soldiering of politicians and Southern colonels, turned aides-de-camp for the occasion. On the whole, the staff service of McDowell's army was probably rather better performed than that of Beauregard's army and possibly better than that of Johnston's.

The command of regiments was marked by the same features in the Southern as in the Northern army, but on the whole the level of military training seems to have been higher, while the planter politician was perhaps more adaptable to military command than the city politician.

When it came to the control and command of troops in battle, it will be seen presently that, whatever the differences of the two armies, they both broke down badly from lack of organization. And this, after all, is only what might have been expected under the circumstances.

V

McDOWELL'S MARCH TO CENTREVILLE

THE ADVANCE

UNDER the spur of the political and military necessities already discussed, McDowell decided that his advance must begin on the 16th of July. Accordingly the following general order was issued that morning: —

GENERAL ORDERS   HDQRS. DEPT. N.E. VIRGINIA,
   No. 17.   ARLINGTON, July 16, 1861.

The troops will march to the front this afternoon in the following order: —

1. The brigades of the First Division (Tyler's) will leave their camps in light marching order, and go as far as Vienna, the Fourth Brigade taking the road across the Chain Bridge . . . the others by the Georgetown turnpike and Leesburg stone roads. . . .

2. The Second Division (Hunter's) will leave their camps in light marching order, and go on the Columbia turnpike as far as the Little River turnpike, but not to cross it. . . .

3. The Third Division (Heintzelman's) will leave their camps in light marching order, and go on the old Fairfax Court House road . . . as far as the Accotink, or the Pohick, if he finds it convenient. . . .

4. The Fifth Division (Miles') will proceed in light marching order by the Little River turnpike as far as Annandale or to the point where the road leads to the left to go into the old Braddock road. . . .

5. The brigades of the several divisions will be put in march in time to reach their respective destinations by dark.

6. The reserve will be held in readiness to march at the shortest notice. . . .

II. On the morning of the 17th, the troops will resume their march

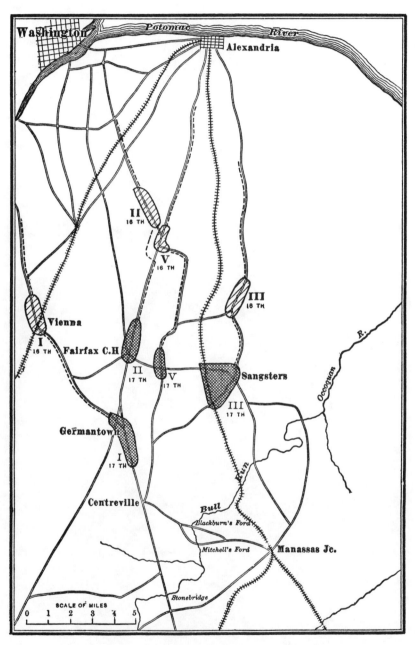

MCDOWELL'S CAMPS, JULY 16TH AND 17TH

after daylight in time to reach Fairfax Court House (the Third Division, Sangster's) by 8 A.M.

1. Brigadier-General Tyler will direct his march so as to intercept the enemy's communication between Fairfax Court House and Centreville. . . .

2. The Second Division (Hunter's) will (after the road shall be cleared of the Fifth Division) move on the direct road to Fairfax Court House by the Little River turnpike.

3. The Fifth Division (Miles') will turn off from the Little River turnpike and gain the old Braddock road, which it will follow to its intersection with the road from Fairfax Court House to Fairfax Station, where it will turn to the right and move on the Court House.

4. The Third Division (Heintzelman's) will move by the best and shortest of the roads to the south of the railroad till he reaches the railroad at Sangster's. He will, according to the indications he may find, turn his Second and Third Brigades to the right, to go to Fairfax Station, or to the front to support his First Brigade. He may find it necessary to guard the road coming up from Wolf Run Shoals and the one leading to Yates' ford.

III. The enemy is represented to be in force at Centreville, Germantown, Fairfax Court House, and Fairfax Station, . . . and on the road towards Wolf Run Shoals. He . . . is believed . . . to have thrown up breastworks and planted cannon. It is therefore probable the movements above ordered may lead to an engagement, and everything must be done with a view to this result.

The three following things will not be pardonable in any commander: 1, to come upon a battery or breastwork without a knowledge of its position; 2, to be surprised; 3, to fall back. Advance guards with vedettes well in front and flankers and vigilance, will guard against the first and second.

The columns are so strong and well provided that, though they may be for a time checked, they should not be overthrown. Each is provided with intrenching tools and axes, and if the country affords facilities for obstructing our march, it also gives equal facilities for sustaining ourselves in any position we obtain. A brigade should sustain itself as long as possible before asking for help from another. It can hardly be necessary to attack a battery in front; in most cases it may be turned. Commanders are enjoined to so conduct their march as to keep their men well closed up. This is of great importance. . . . Wagons will only be taken . . . for ammunition, the medical department, and for intrenching tools. A small baggage train for each brigade . . . will consist of from twelve to fifteen wagons. . . . Department headquarters will be with the Second Division, on the Little River turnpike. Division commanders will communicate with them by every opportunity. . . .

JAMES B. FRY, A.A.G.[1]

McDowell's objective, the Confederate advanced line at Fairfax Court House, was clearly defined; and the march of the four columns was well calculated to give an initial success to the Federals if the Confederates should linger in their advanced positions. It was evidently McDowell's hope that they would, and he undoubtedly expected much from his flanking columns, especially that under Tyler. If, however, the Confederates retired, then an awkward accumulation of troops on the Warrenton pike near Centreville was entailed for no sufficient object. It may further be noted that the short march for the first day tended to reduce the total distance to be traversed by the army before the enemy should be warned of its approach, but on the other hand involved making camp at night, an undesirable thing with green troops.

The order has a peculiarity, which is only the natural

[1] O. R. Ser. I, vol. II, 303.

outcome of the circumstances: its laying down of certain precepts for the guidance of the division commanders. It was not a very practical way of teaching them their business; yet what was McDowell to do? These precepts are not unsound, as far as they go, but it may be pointed out that in one of these elementary lessons in the military art McDowell failed to develop his subject sufficiently. His problem was how to move, with no undue delay, an untrained army under a broiling July sun for a limited distance. It was essential to keep the men as short a time as possible on the road. The way to do this was to avoid delay by pushing out advanced guards, as McDowell in fact indicated. But in practice what happened was that the generals turned their whole divisions into advanced guards, kept deploying and scouting and deploying again, while the main column painfully waited, getting fatigued, demoralized, and undisciplined to no useful purpose. Had McDowell seen to it that each of his divisional generals had a properly constituted advanced guard clearing the way at a sufficient distance from his column until the Confederate position at Fairfax Court House was reached, the advance towards Bull Run would have gained very much in effectiveness.

The sentence, " A brigade should sustain itself as long as possible before asking help from another," suggests that McDowell for the moment forgot that his army was organized into divisions, and that the question of whether one brigade should reinforce another was one for his divisional generals. Still, as matters went in that semi-organized army, this proved of no great consequence. On the whole, it might be said that the general order was as good a one as might reasonably be expected from a general officer wholly untrained for war; it showed on McDowell's part those qualities of painstaking attention to detail which, with his undoubted courage and sense of duty, made up most of his equipment for command.[1]

---

[1] A military correspondent says of McDowell's order, that it "displays all the crudities to be expected in a march order by an officer devoid of experience or training in the handling of a force of 30,000 men.

"Two contingencies were to be looked for: either the Confederates would fight at Fairfax Court House, or they would retreat. This might have been guessed had McDowell stopped to consider the enemy's point of view and to inquire what course of action the enemy's best interests demanded; but Lee, Sherman and Grant were to be the first to solve, in the Civil War, this most interesting and essential personal-psychological factor of success.

"At any rate, had cavalry been sent ahead on the 16th, reports must have been received which would have given an intelligent basis for the issuance of orders for the 17th. But McDowell not only did not wait for information, he did not even seem to desire it. His order providing for two days' marches in advance was ill-suited to either case.

"Had the enemy been found in force at Fairfax Court House, the 1st division (Tyler) had a six-mile march and could march at 5 A.M. The 5th division (Miles) had a nine-mile march over a rough country road, part of which must be passed over before daylight. To ensure the division reaching Fairfax Court House at 8 A.M., it must march at 2 A.M., and even then the column (with the lack of discipline) would have straggled beyond all conception; only half the men would have reached Fairfax Court House that day, and those that did reach there would have been useless for fighting. The 3d division (Heintzelman) was not ordered to Fairfax

The army was still in considerable confusion. Some of the brigades that were marked off for the advance were not completed until the very day when the march opened, several regiments, on that very day, crossing the Potomac to join the army. The staff service was inadequate, and to such an extraordinary degree that the commander-in-chief himself had to drive back from Arlington to the railroad station at Washington, just as his army was opening its march, to attend to a comparatively slight detail: we quote from W. H. Russell's "Diary" for the 16th of July : —

On arriving at the Washington platform the first person I saw was General McDowell alone, looking anxiously into the carriages. He . . . inquired eagerly if I had seen two batteries of artillery — Barry's and another — which he had ordered up and was waiting for, but which had gone astray. . . . The general could hear nothing of his guns; his carriage was waiting and I accepted his offer of a seat to my

Court House and the roads for him to march there would have been blocked by the 5th division.

"Thus in case of a fight, only two of the five divisions could reach Fairfax Court House in any sort of condition for fighting. The lines of march converged from three directions and the routes of the 1st and 5th divisions over narrow, wooded, and hilly country roads made it possible for a small Confederate force to have delayed almost indefinitely either of these columns.

"On the other hand, if the enemy did not hold Fairfax Court House, then the unnecessary night-rising and night-marching is inexcusable. All three divisions are concentrated on the Little-river–Warrenton turnpike, whence they must march in single column to Centreville, by the only practicable wagon supply route, and thus, with the friction due to lack of organization and discipline, complications are bound to arise and all the delays actually experienced become thereafter unavoidable."

lodgings. Although he spoke confidently, he did not seem in good spirits.[1]

Notwithstanding such difficulties as these, McDowell got his army started on its disastrous journey early that afternoon. The day was warm, but clear and not oppressive. The distance to be marched was not too great. Danger was as yet comparatively remote. And so the men went forward in good spirits, and, for the most part, reached the designated points in good time.[2]

Early on the 17th, McDowell's four divisions resumed their march, Hunter's, in the centre, at 5 A.M. He had only seven miles to go, but it took him five hours to make the distance. The long column blocked the road, making little and at times no progress. As the sun rose and the air became very warm, straggling began for water, for blackberries. The leading troops and the cavalry continuously deployed in front of imaginary and untenanted Confederate positions. An onlooker described the artillery as "badly horsed, miserably equipped and . . . the worst set of gunners and drivers which I, who have seen the Turkish field-guns, ever beheld. . . . Their transport is tolerably good, but inadequate ; they have no carriage for reserve ammunition; the commissariat drivers are civilians, under little or no control. . . . "[3]

[1] Russell, *Diary*, I, 157.

[2] Tyler's division was very slow, and could not keep closed up. Richardson's brigade, marching from Chain Bridge, did not reach Vienna till 11 P.M. Cudworth, *Hist. 1st Mass.*   [3] Russell, *Diary*, I, 157.

At about ten o'clock, just before reaching Fairfax Court House, Tyler's column was càught sight of, about two miles away to the northwest, his wagons showing against the skyline as they crossed the top of Flint Hill, on the road from Vienna to Germantown. No opposition was met with at the barricades which the Confederates had placed across the approaches to the village. A few shots were fired by the last pickets; one or two men were wounded, and at that modest price Hunter was in occupation of Fairfax Court House; at 1 P.M., Tyler reached Germantown less than two miles beyond on the Warrenton turnpike; while Miles and Heintzelman, farther to the south, were reaching their respective positions. At every point no greater resistance was met with than at Fairfax Court House. The enemy had evidently fallen back towards Manassas.

A halt was made at Fairfax Court House, of which the first object was to rest the troops and to enable the commanding general to fix the position of his columns. He was soon satisfied as to the whereabouts of Tyler, just west of him, and of Miles who had marched about parallel with Hunter two or three miles to the south. But no word came from beyond the Alexandria and Orange Railroad, where Heintzelman was advancing. Finally, at about 3 P.M., McDowell decided to proceed in that direction in person. Two miles south, at the crossing of the old Braddock road, he found Miles' division at

rest, and ascertained that Wilcox's brigade of Heintzelman's corps was at Fairfax Station, another two miles
south.

It appears probable that McDowell pushed on farther
and saw Willcox at the station, though this is only matter for inference. Whether he did or not, the precise position of Heintzelman's other two brigades does not seem
to have been cleared up until later in the afternoon when
Willcox wrote to McDowell, now back at Fairfax Court
House, that he had just had word from Heintzelman
that he was at Sangster's waiting orders.[1]

Summing up, it may be said that, even if clumsy and
somewhat slow, McDowell's move on the Confederate
advanced positions had turned out well, though he had
failed to engage the enemy and win a preliminary success. But no sooner had he occupied Fairfax Court
House than the machine showed signs of falling to pieces:
the columns did not reach their respective positions as
early as was expected; one, at least, of the divisional
commanders failed to inform headquarters of his whereabouts; and so great was the lassitude, disorder, and
straggling that it appeared hopeless to whip the men up
for a further movement that day. It was for these reasons

[1] O. R. Ser. I, vol. II, 310; Willcox to Fry, July 18. It is difficult to say at
what hour this dispatch was written, but it does not seem probable that
McDowell received it before four o'clock. Sangster's probably meant the
crossroads where Heintzelman held one brigade while he pushed another
on to Sangster's Station.

that McDowell, whose early intention had been to push on another four or five miles to Centreville, finally gave this up as hopeless and decided to start fresh on the 18th. His most advanced body was Richardson's brigade of Tyler's corps which camped along the Warrenton turnpike about three miles east of Centreville.

An account of this day's march would not be complete unless it mentioned the fact that both at Fairfax Court House and at Germantown there was a good deal of pillaging and some burning of houses. This resulted in the indignation both of the generals and of the public, but not in the punishment of the offenders. This disorder was not surprising, however, if the composition of the army and the conditions of its day's march, are considered.

It cannot be doubted that McDowell left Washington with a fixed plan. He intended to risk no frontal attack, but to outflank the enemy ; and the flanking movement was to be made towards the south, his left. In this may be discerned a sound idea, but an unsound state of mind. There is no more advantageous position than on an enemy's flank, and with raw troops the idea has double force ; yet military operations are in their nature full of the unforeseen, while opportunities for flanking are not easy to create, so that few things are more dangerous than to prejudge a situation, or to have rigid ideas ; few things are more fatal than not to seize any opportunity, whatever it may be, that presents itself. But McDowell's mind did not work in the higher plane of strategy; he had little information as to the topography of the country or the positions of the Confederates; he had predetermined that his attack should be a flank attack; while for the moment, that is up to the evening of the 17th of July, this flank movement was to be by his left. His orders for the 18th were framed accordingly: —

GENERAL ORDERS   HDQRS. DEPT. N.E. VIRGINIA,
    No. 19.   FAIRFAX COURT HOUSE, July 18, 1861.

The troops will move to-day as follows: —

Heintzelman's division will go to Little Rocky Run, on the road hence to Centreville. Tyler's division will go beyond Centreville, on the road to Gainesville. Hunter's division will go as near Centreville as he can get water.

The above movements will be made after supplies shall have been received. If the supply trains do not come up in time, division commanders will procure beef from the inhabitants. . . .

The troops should be at the places indicated to-night and they must have two days' cooked rations in their haversacks. . . .

JAMES B. FRY, A.A.G.[1]

There was apparently a separate order to Miles, perhaps verbal, to move directly to Centreville.

These orders are curious. Their effect was to allot one whole day to a movement in which the maximum distance which any body of the troops had to march was no more than six miles. It further provided for an excessive concentration, as all four divisions were to be brought to Centreville or as near there as possible. Whether the

[1] O. R. Ser. I, vol. II.

eventual attack was to be frontal or by a flank, this accumulation of troops would in any case have to be reduced before such a movement could be carried out. The question of supplies did not in fact materially affect the situation and will be dealt with later.[1]

McDowell apparently left Fairfax Court House early on the morning of the 18th and found the road thence to Centreville full of the moving troops of Hunter and Tyler. At a quarter past eight he was with the advance, Richardson's brigade of Tyler's corps, nearing Centreville, and he wrote as follows to General Tyler, who was close behind with the other three brigades of his division:—

> I have information which leads me to believe you will find no force at Centreville, and will meet with no resistance in getting there. Observe well the roads to Bull Run and to Warrenton. Do not bring on an engagement, but keep up the impression that we are moving on Manassas. I go to Heintzelman's to arrange about the plan we have talked over.[2]

This done, the general turned off from the direct road to Centreville and made his way to the road leading from Centreville southeasterly to Sangster's, on which he continued until he reached Sangster's Crossroads about noon, where he had a conversation with Heintzelman. The latter moved on Centreville in the course of the afternoon.[3]

It was just as McDowell turned south that an incident

---

[1] McDowell tries hard to explain his slowness as due to the failure of his transport, but this is little better than an excuse.

[2] O. R. Ser. I, vol. II, 312.   [3] *Rep. Cond. War*, II, 28, 29.

occurred, slight, yet illustrating the haphazard and loose organization of his army. Major Barnard was Mc-Dowell's chief engineer officer; he was with McDowell in the early morning and relates that his chief "was then about going to Sangster's and invited me to attend him. Not understanding his journey to have the character of a reconnaissance, but as simply to communicate with the division of Colonel Heintzelman, I preferred accompanying the division of General Tyler to Centreville."[1] Captain Fry similarly abandoned his general. And, apparently for no better reason, McDowell's reconnaissance had to be conducted without his adjutant-general and his chief engineer.

Accompanied by a small escort, McDowell proceeded for several hours to explore the country to the south, along the line by which he hoped to effect his outflanking movement. It was while thus occupied, and at an hour that may be conjectured as about 3 P.M., that news reached him that an engagement was in progress between Tyler and the enemy along Bull Run. Having already pretty well come to a decision as a result of his reconnaissance, he started at once for Centreville, only to find on his arrival there that an unsuccessful skirmish had been fought at Blackburn's Ford. Before dealing with this, however, it will be better to trace the Confederate movements up to that point.

---

[1] Major Barnard's report, O. R. Ser. I, vol. II, 329.

THE CONFEDERATE RETIREMENT FROM FAIRFAX COURT HOUSE

On the Confederate side there is less to be narrated. As early as the 8th of July, doubtless informed from Washington that McDowell's advance was hourly expected, Beauregard issued his orders for the eventual retirement from the advanced lines to that of Bull Run.[1] The Second Brigade, Ewell's, was to fall back from the railroad about Fairfax Station and Sangster's Crossroads to Union Mills Ford, burning bridges behind them; the First Brigade, Bonham's, was to retire from Fairfax Court House through Centreville to Mitchell's Ford; and the Fifth Brigade, Cocke's, was to follow the Warrenton turnpike to Stone Bridge, leaving behind a detachment to make a stand, if practicable, at Cub Run. Beauregard's chief object was undoubtedly to avoid a conflict on the advanced line where McDowell stood a chance of concentrating superior numbers and winning a partial success.

Beauregard's plans and views at this moment are not easy to unravel ; the only constant factor in them being his pugnacious temperament. We have already seen that Bull Run as a line of defence had weak as well as strong points. Taking Blackburn's and Mitchell's Fords as the centre, it might be said that the Confederate right was a good deal stronger than the left. The river was

[1] Special Order 100, O. R. Ser. I, vol. II, 447.

deeper at this point;[1] the farther bank was densely wooded and rugged; while on the Confederate side the roads and terrain generally facilitated the concentration of troops at any threatened point. Yet here, as at Blackburn's Ford and farther upstream towards Stone Bridge, the river was not a real obstacle. It ran mostly through a deep wooded gully that might serve the purposes of an ambuscade excellently and yet be untenable by infantry against a well-directed artillery fire, if a suitable place for guns could be found. A few trestles, even a single pontoon, would in many places have served to bridge the stream in a very short time; but McDowell's army was not organized to solve this simple problem.

In his order of the 8th of July, Beauregard's not altogether sound appreciation of the defensive value of Bull Run appears in the instructions as to what is to follow the retirement from Fairfax Court House to that stream: —

These brigades, thus in position, will make a desperate stand at the several points hereinbefore designated on the line of Bull Run, and will be supported. . . .

It then goes on: —

Should the enemy march to the attack of Mitchell's Ford via Centreville, the following movements will be made with celerity: —

1. The 4th brigade will march from Blackburn's Ford to attack him on the flank and centre.

2. The 3d brigade will be thrown to the attack of his centre and rear towards Centreville.

[1] The stream is tidal up to Union Mills.

3. The 2d and 6th brigades united will also push forward and attack him in the rear by way of Centreville, protecting their own right flanks and rear from the direction of Fairfax Station and Court House. . . .[1]

The above-quoted order reveals Beauregard's intentions clearly enough. He attached no importance to his outlying position at Fairfax Court House, and merely wished to fight the enemy on his own line. Anticipating that he would be attacked at his strongest point, Mitchell's Ford, simply because that was the best route to Manassas, he intended as soon as such a movement took place to attempt a counterstroke at the enemy's most vulnerable flank. The idea was good. What Beauregard overlooked was that the Federals might not attack at Mitchell's Ford, but somewhere else. He also neglected to take steps by scouting and reconnaissance work to keep in touch with the enemy, by that means learning more of his movements and intentions, and gaining opportunities for action. Thus Bonham, who had with him nearly all the available cavalry at Fairfax Court House,[2] brought it back with him to Mitchell's Ford, where it was of the least possible use. Thrown out on the right flank it could have kept close contact with Heintzelman, and when McDowell had packed his army into Centreville, might have raided successfully in the Federal rear ; on the left

[1] O. R. Ser. I, vol. II, 448.
[2] The 30th Virginia, Colonel Radford, with four independent troops under Captains Wickham, Ball, Powell, and Payne.

flank, if supported from Stone Bridge, the cavalry might have kept watch along the line of Cub Run and given early warning of any Federal movement by their right.

Bonham, Ewell, and Cocke slipped away from their positions on the 17th without any great difficulty and with hardly a shot fired. They had precise instructions as to what to do, and they had ample warning of the Federal approach. Bonham reached Centreville about midday, and there lingered to see whether the Federal movement would develop further. As it did not, he remained until midnight unmolested, and then, on receipt of a positive order from Beauregard, resumed his march and filed into position at Mitchell's Ford in the early hours of the morning of the 18th.

THE SKIRMISH AT BLACKBURN'S FORD, JULY 18

Richardson's advance reached Centreville at nine o'clock on the morning of the 18th. Turning to the left, he came out, as it happened, not on the road leading west towards Stone Bridge and Warrenton, the direction indicated in McDowell's order, but on that leading south to Manassas, coming to a halt about one mile from the village. Tyler soon joined Richardson. The instructions which he had just received from McDowell were sufficiently clear,[1] but he apparently paid little heed to them.

---

[1] That is, the letter of 8.15 A.M., quoted above.

Instead of directing his main column along the Warrenton turnpike, and not risking an engagement, he pushed
Richardson along the Manassas road and brought on
an unfortunate skirmish. The fact was probably that the
road along the Centreville ridge, from which the sur-
rounding country could be easily discovered, was a
tempting line along which to advance, and Tyler could
not resist the temptation.

Taking Richardson and an escort with him, Tyler
pushed along the Centreville ridge about a mile farther
until he reached the point where it dips down to Bull
Run. From this point it was clear that the Confederates
were in position beyond the stream, and probably in
some force. On the rising ground beyond Blackburn's
Ford a section of artillery was in plain sight, and in the
woods and at various points the glint of rifles and bayonets announced the presence of the enemy. Tyler quickly
decided to test their strength and sent back orders for
Ayres' battery of Sherman's brigade, which was close
behind Richardson's, to come to the front. Richardson's
brigade was ordered up in support. Tyler was now
joined by Major Barnard and by Captain Fry, who
freely supplied him with advice in the name of their
absent general.[1]

Ayres' guns were brought up at a gallop and wheeled
to the right. They were rifled ten-pounders, well served,

[1] Barnard's report, O. R. Ser. i, vol. ii, 329.

and got the range at once. The Confederate guns, a
mile away to the south, were much weaker; Longstreet
almost immediately ordered them to be withdrawn.[1] A
section left by Bonham on the north bank also fired a few
shots from the right, and then retired across the run at
Mitchell's Ford. This seemed on the whole encouraging.

The infantry, meanwhile, some light companies and
the 12th New York,[2] had been pushed down in front of
the guns and into the woods where the bank descended
sharply towards Blackburn's Ford, a few Confederate
pickets falling back before them. The enemy did not
appear to be showing fight to any alarming extent and
Tyler now decided to push in on the position. The 1st
Massachusetts was ordered to follow the 12th New York,
while the 2d and 3d Michigan were deployed to the right,
descending to the lowlands in the direction of Mitchell's
Ford.[3] Benjamin's section of rifled twenty-pounders was
placed on the ridge, and Ayres was ordered to send his
section of twelve-pounder howitzers into the gully to support the 1st Massachusetts and 12th New York. It was
now nearly two o'clock.

---

[1] Longstreet, *From Manassas to Appomattox*, 38; which confirms his
official report.

[2] A very poor and insubordinate regiment, of which a part had to be
disarmed on the afternoon of the 21st.

[3] An amusing example of the greenness of the commanding officers was
afforded by Major Williams, of the 2d Michigan, who immediately on
entering the woods ordered his regiment to form square to resist cavalry.
Lyster, "Bull Run," *Paps. Loyal Legion Mich. Command*, 1.

On the Confederate side Longstreet was in position, with the 1st, 11th and 17th Virginia; he had Bonham on his left at Mitchell's Ford, which was never threatened, and Early in reserve behind him. He withdrew his pickets from the farther bank of Bull Run without firing, at some time between twelve and one, and with his infantry as well screened as was possible in the underbrush on the southern bank, awaited the advance of the enemy. The Confederates had no intrenchments.

Longstreet succeeded fairly well in getting his men to reserve their fire. A few straggling shots were exchanged. Presently the 12th New York advanced in deployed order, and was met by a tremendous but ill-aimed volley; the Federals at once broke and fell back.[1] The 1st Massachusetts, with a few regular troopers and the light infantry, took cover and did rather better. For fifteen minutes or more a hot musketry fire was kept up by both sides, neither showing much steadiness at a comparatively close range, and part of the Confederate line in turn broke away.[2] Longstreet called for reinforcements, and Early brought up the 7th Virginia and 7th Louisiana which, formed in a second line, proved almost as dangerous to friend as to foe; at all events, Longstreet

---

[1] Richardson tried to rally the regiment, but could find no officers. Tyler came up, but concluded it was hopeless, and told Richardson to let them go. *Rep. Cond. War*, II, 20.

[2] Longstreet actually sabred his men up to their work. *From Manassas to Appomattox*, 38.

relates that to escape their fire he had to jump off his horse and roll on the ground. Early also brought up five more guns of the Washington Artillery which were massed with Longstreet's two pieces and placed a little to the rear. When the Federals presently withdrew, an artillery engagement was continued for an hour or so until past four o'clock, the Federals having rather the best of it.[1] The casualties were, for the North, 19 killed, 38 wounded, 26 missing; for the South, 15 killed, 53 wounded, 2 missing.[2]

It is clear that Blackburn's Ford was an ill-managed affair. Tyler should not have engaged at all, in view of

[1] In Alexander's excellent account of this affair he gives the following details of the artillery practice: The Federals, with eight guns engaged, fired 415 rounds; the Confederates, with seven guns, fired 310 rounds. The Burton and Archer shell which was used with three of the Confederate guns was badly designed and "tumbled"; another of the Confederate guns became useless through an enlarged vent. It was only owing to their being masked by timber that the Confederate guns stood any chance at all against the heavier metal of their opponents; and they would have been entirely withdrawn at the close of the action if the Federals had fired a few more rounds than they did. Alexander, *Military Memoirs*, 24. It may be suspected, though direct evidence as to the supply of ammunition is scanty, that the Federal batteries had little left in hand at the close of the engagement.

[2] For Blackburn's Ford, see the reports of officers present in O. R., Ser. I, vol. II, particularly those of Tyler, Richardson, Barnard, Beauregard, Longstreet, and Early. Among other accounts those of E. P. Alexander, in his *Military Memoirs*, of Longstreet in his *From Manassas to Appomattox*, and of H. J. Raymond in the New York *Times*, are specially good. The figures for casualties on the Northern side are from Richardson's report, but Cudworth (*Hist. of the 1st Mass.*), who gives 13 killed and 20 wounded for that command, has been read with it.

his precise instructions from McDowell and of the representations made to him by Major Barnard and Captain Fry. Having engaged, he should not have sent the main body of his raw infantry into the woods until he had searched them thoroughly with his guns, which his superiority over the Confederate artillery and dominant position should have facilitated. But having once gone in, Tyler should not have ordered a general retirement to Centreville merely because he had lost a few dozen men and because one of his regiments had become demoralized. He could have safely established himself towards the end of the ridge in such a way as to impede or delay any counterstroke which the Confederates might attempt by crossing Blackburn's and Mitchell's Fords. He could have imposed on the enemy, threatened their centre, and, at the least, maintained the morale of his troops.

The fight should have revealed the weakness of the Confederate position at Blackburn's Ford, yet this was apparently not perceived by the Federals. Longstreet's regiments, as it happened, were nearly dislodged by the ill-directed attack made on them. The little plateau back of them could easily be covered by the fire of the guns from the Centreville ridge, and that plateau gave access to the left flank and rear of Bonham covering Mitchell's Ford. Longstreet displayed cool nerve and some judgment, and his handling of his men had much to do with the success they won.

VI

FROM THE EIGHTEENTH TO THE TWENTY–FIRST OF JULY

McDOWELL

McDOWELL arrived at Centreville late in the afternoon of the 18th, just as Tyler was completing his retirement from Blackburn's Ford. Richardson's and Sherman's brigades were at that moment to the south of the village, Schenck's to the west, Keyes' to the east. There was apparently a good deal of recrimination over what had occurred, Barnard and Fry making the most of the advice they had given Tyler against attacking, McDowell justly annoyed at his divisional commander's disobedience of orders. The scene was unfortunately public, and confirmed the impression of undiscipline already produced by many similar scenes which had taken place on the march among the junior officers.[1]

There is nothing to show that McDowell himself proceeded along the Centreville ridge to view the central line of approach to the Confederate position. He was ap-

---

[1] The rout of the 12th New York and Tyler's retreat undoubtedly had a very demoralizing effect. McDowell believed that it led to the defection of the 4th Pennsylvania and 8th New York Battery on the 20th. Fry says: "After the affair at Blackburn's Ford . . . and Tyler's action in the battle of the 21st, a bitterness between Tyler and McDowell grew up which lasted till they died." *Battles and Leaders*, I, 187.

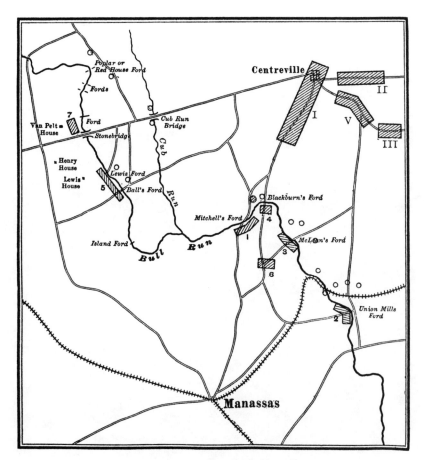

POSITION, JULY 18TH, 8 P.M.

parently wedded to the idea of outflanking it, and as he had earlier in the day decided that to march by his left was impracticable, his mind was now fixed on discovering a means of effecting the same purpose by his right. It never entered his head apparently that by means of the Centreville ridge and his superior artillery he might either force the enemy's centre, or at all events cross Bull Run and keep the enemy under such pressure as to give a flanking movement the best chance of success. The check to Tyler was wrongly accepted at its face value.

For the moment McDowell confined himself to ordering Tyler at once to push a brigade (Richardson's) back along the ridge so as to keep in touch with the enemy and observe their movements. On finding this order neglected, he repeated it sharply at 12.30 A.M. on the 19th. For the rest he decided to let the troops remain at Centreville until he could find out by means of reconnaissances how to turn Beauregard's left.

Let us turn for a moment now to the matter of transportation. In the postscript to his report on Bull Run,[1] McDowell speaks of a day's delay in his transport, "making it necessary to make on Sunday the attack we should have made on Saturday." It is doubtful whether the excuse is a valid one.

The army had started on Tuesday, the 16th, with three

[1] O. R. Ser. I, vol. II, 324.

days' rations carried by the troops. It was the case, however, that what with the undiscipline of the men and the
fatigue caused by the great heat which began on the 17th,
the men wasted or threw away a large proportion of
this supply. These rations consisted in part of coffee,
sugar, beans, and rice, but the transport had been so cut
down that some regiments, if not all, left behind them
their camp-kettles and mess-pans, so that these articles
proved useless.[1] Cooked beef and biscuit was the substantial part of what they carried.

By the night of the 18th, the army was starving, for
the supply trains were not yet up and the rations were
now consumed. For a few hours there was a difficult situation, and it undoubtedly gave McDowell considerable
anxiety.

The general-in-chief's apprehensions were not in fact
well founded, and were soon allayed, for ample supplies
were within immediate reach. Three wagon trains con-
veying nearly 200,000 rations and 225 head of cattle,
equivalent to over 120,000 rations more, had been
started close behind the columns. The first, under Hawkins, reached Fairfax Court House early on the 18th,
and, after detaching 14 wagons to Miles' division on
the old Braddock road, pushed on and reached Centreville the same evening. At the same time the second,
under Curtis, had parked on the Warrenton turnpike be-

---

[1] See the statement in Captain Curtis' report; O. R. Ser. 1, vol. 11, 341.

tween Germantown and Centreville; it was able to dis-
tribute rations at the latter place early on the following
morning. The third, under Bell, reached Fairfax Court
House at 4.45 P.M. on the 18th, left there at 4 A.M. on the
19th, and reached the army four hours later.[1]

There was some wastage by the way; there were unnecessary supplies; there was much confusion and irregu-
larity in their distribution. Apparently the commissariat
officers found it hopeless to get proper receipts, and in
some cases were nearly pillaged by mobs of disorderly
and famished men. Yet Captain Clarke, chief commissary,
who probably is optimistic, estimates that after all de-
ductions 160,000 rations were actually distributed at or
near Centreville on the night of the 18th and morning
of the 19th. Add to these the cattle, and it is no exagger-
ation to say that McDowell's army was largely supplied
and fit to use within a radius of a few miles by ten or
twelve o'clock on the morning of the 19th of July; nor
was it reasonable to delay an advance on Manassas, six
miles from Centreville, for the slaughtering and cooking
of the cattle.[2]

Probably in view of what had happened the day before, McDowell decided on the 19th to remain with his

[1] In the dispatch to Tyler, written at 12.30 A.M. on the 19th, McDowell
says: "The train of subsistence came up long ago." O. R. Ser. I, vol. II,
306. He evidently refers to Hawkins' train.

[2] See generally the reports of Clarke, Hawkins, Curtis, and Bell; O. R.
Ser. I, vol. II, 336–44.

troops at Centreville and to delegate the duty of reconnaissance to his subordinates. Major Barnard and Captain Woodbury of the Engineers were selected for this
duty. They conferred with the commanding general, it
being assumed from the maps [1] and information before
these officers that a flank movement towards the right
must pass either by Stone Bridge, or a few miles farther
north by Sudley Spring. Given the premises, there is
little reason to quarrel with this general proposition, for
the Confederate centre might properly be reckoned as
running to about Island Ford. From this point to Stone
Bridge, which was supposed to be strongly held, their
left wing was marked off. Therefore the question, as Mc-
Dowell and his engineers approached it, really narrowed
down merely to this: How could the position at Stone
Bridge be turned?

Assuming for a moment the soundness of a flanking
movement beyond Stone Bridge, McDowell's mental
working can better be followed. The next important
crossing of Bull Run above the bridge was at Sudley
Spring, whence a road that would facilitate the movement of guns and wagons led south a mile and a half,
where it cut the Warrenton turnpike little more than a
mile beyond Stone Bridge. From this crossroads it was
about six miles farther to Manassas. It was presumable
that the Confederate line did not extend as far as Sudley

[1] See McDowell's map at back.

Spring. How could McDowell, from Centreville, reach the Sudley Spring road? If he could once get on it with a sufficient force, he hoped to be able to roll up the Confederates the whole distance of nearly eight miles that lay between Sudley Spring and Manassas. It was possible, too, that fords might be found between Sudley Spring and Stone Bridge, unguarded by the enemy and shortening the route. There were in fact several such fords, of which Poplar or Red House Ford was the best.

Barnard and Woodbury, accompanied by the ubiquitous Governor Sprague of Rhode Island and a troop of U. S. cavalry, started on their reconnaissance early on the morning of the 19th. The question was largely whether roads could be found on the northern side of Bull Run connecting the Warrenton turnpike with Sudley Spring.

We had information, — says Barnard, — that a road branched from the Warrenton turnpike a short distance beyond Cub Run, by which, opening gates and passing through private grounds, we might reach the fords. . . . I . . . followed up the valley of Cub Run until we reached a point west 10° north and about four miles in an air line from Centreville, near which we struck a road which we believed to lead to the fords. Following it for a short distance we encountered the enemy's patrols. As we were most anxious to avoid attracting the enemy's attention to our designs in this quarter we did not care to pursue the reconnaissance farther. We had seen enough to be convinced of the perfect practicability of the route. To make more certain of the fords, however, Captain Woodbury proposed to return at night, and, with a few Michigan woodmen from Colonel Sherman's brigade, to endeavor to find them. On returning to camp it was determined to send Captain Wright and Lieutenant Snyder, Engineers, with Captain Woodbury.

At the same time the commanding general directed Captain Whipple,
Topographical Engineers, and Lieutenant Prime, Engineers, to make
a night reconnaissance of the run between Warrenton Bridge and Blackburn's Ford. Both these night expeditions failed. It was found the
enemy occupied the woods too strongly on our side of the run to permit the reconnaissances to be accomplished.[1]

From this report it may be seen that McDowell was at
the disadvantage entailed by a surprise attack in that he
could not show his hand, and could therefore obtain only
slight information. Barnard saw a very small part of the
Sudley Spring road, which eventually proved a difficult
route for artillery, and circuitous. He failed to reach Bull
Run itself, and got no information as to Poplar Ford.
McDowell was dissatisfied with the result, and we find
him on the next day contemplating a reconnaissance in
force.[2]

On the night of the 19th, General Tyler was struck by
the sound of locomotives coming from Manassas, as were
many others in the Federal lines. He was an experienced railroad man, and was able to draw inferences.
He was convinced from what he heard that heavy reinforcements, probably parts of Johnston's army, were

[1] O. R. Ser. 1, vol. 11, 330.

[2] McDowell to Townsend; O. R. Ser. 1, vol. 11, 308. If an account in the
New York *World* (July 23) may be trusted, orders were drawn up after
Barnard's return for an advance at 6 A.M. on the 20th; this was found, however, to be much too late an hour at which to start, besides which a shortage in artillery ammunition was discovered, so it was decided to postpone
the advance until the 21st. This order suggests the reconnaissance in
force which might develop into a real attack.

reaching the enemy's camp. He went with his news to McDowell's headquarters at once, only to be met with a very cool reception.[1]

On the 20th nothing was done. In the early morning McDowell was still for a reconnaissance in force. "I wished yesterday," he wrote to Colonel Townsend, "to make a reconnaissance in force, but deferred to the better judgment of others — to try and get it by observation and stealth. To-day I propose to drive in the enemy and get the information required." [2] He was once more, however, persuaded to defer to the opinion of others and not to resort to such a measure. More reconnoitring parties went out, and in the course of the day further information came to eke out Barnard's meagre report of the day before. A rumor also reached McDowell, and a true one as it proved, that Johnston had reached Manassas; it was possibly an echo of what Tyler had said the night before. Under these circumstances he decided to delay no longer, but to attempt on the next day the movement through Sudley Spring.

To carry out this purpose McDowell's first plan was to move his right wing well forward late on the 20th, so as to get it through Centreville and shorten the distance it would have to march the next day. Once more, however, he allowed himself to be persuaded against his better judgment. "I deferred," he says, "to those who

[1] Alexander, *Military Memoirs*, 27.   [2] O. R. Ser. I, vol. II, 308.

had the greatest distance to go, and who preferred starting early in the morning and making but one move." [1]
There are few remarks in McDowell's reports or dispatches that give one a stronger impression of his unfitness for command.

The General Order for the movement of the army,
issued on the evening of the 20th, ran as follows: —

GENERAL ORDERS   HDQRS. DEPT. NORTHEASTERN VIRGINIA,
    No. 22.   CENTREVILLE, July 20, 1861.

The enemy has planted a battery on the Warrenton turnpike to
defend the passage of Bull Run. . . . It is intended to turn the position,
force the enemy from the road, that it may be reopened, and, if possible, destroy the railroad leading from Manassas to the Valley of Virginia, where the enemy has a large force. As this may be resisted by all
the force of the enemy, the troops will be disposed of as follows: —

The First Division (General Tyler's), with the exception of Richardson's brigade, will move at 2.30 A.M. precisely on the Warrenton
turnpike to threaten the passage of the bridge, but will not open fire
until full daybreak.

The Second Division (Hunter's) will move from its camp at 2 A.M.
precisely and . . . will after passing Cub Run turn to the right and pass
the Bull Run stream above the lower ford at Sudley Springs, and then,
turning down to the left, descend the stream and clear away the enemy
who may be guarding the lower ford and bridge. It will then bear off
to the right to make room for the succeeding division.

The Third Division (Heintzelman's) will march at 2.30 A.M. and
follow the road taken by the Second Division (Hunter's) but will cross
at the lower ford, after it has been turned as above, and then, going to
the left, take place between the stream and Second Division.

The Fifth Division (Miles') will take position on the Centreville
Heights. (Richardson's brigade will for the time form part of his division, and will continue in its present position.) One brigade will be in

[1] O. R. Ser. I, vol. II, 317.

the village and one near the present station of Richardson's brigade. This division will threaten Blackburn's Ford and remain in reserve at Centreville. The commander will open fire with artillery only, and will bear in mind that it is a demonstration only he is to make. . . .[1]

Such was the order that took the Federal army to the field of Bull Run, and before leaving that army on the night of the 20th of July, some comment on this order should be made.[2]

Probably the worst feature of McDowell's plans and operations was the persistent way in which Johnston's possible presence at Manassas was left out of account. If Johnston was a likely combatant, then every hour of time might be decisive of failure or success; if he had arrived at Manassas, then it was certainly a question whether it was not better to assume the defensive, or to attempt a combined operation with Patterson. Even on the assumption that Johnston was in the Valley, and making every allowance for McDowell's difficulties, it is not possible to acquit him of having wasted invaluable time.

The flanking movement by Sudley Spring was defensible chiefly because the fortifications of Manassas stood

[1] O. R. Ser. I, vol. II, 326.

[2] I have left it largely to the sequel to show the crudity of the time table and other arrangements of McDowell. It was a mistake to attempt a night march with such troops as he had; his marching arrangements were absurdly bad; he was scattering his army over an enormous front; he was working out a plan whereby his men were nearly sure to be physically exhausted at the decisive moment: — all these matters will appear at considerable length in the course of the narrative.

in the way of the direct advance through Blackburn's
Ford. But the planning of the march was clearly defective, for it involved covering a distance of over ten miles
along a doubtful line of approach. In hot July weather and
for troops such as those, this was a very considerable enterprise, and one that was insufficiently worked out, as appeared when the troops attempted to carry out the order.

With his right once moved as far as Sudley Spring,
it became imperative for McDowell to establish a communication at Stone Bridge, and to resist all possible
counterstrokes against the Centreville ridge, else he
might easily see his army broken at either point or
turned.[1] Even more dangerous than this was the fact
that his turning movement prolonged his line of operations so as to open a wide flank to an enemy's counterstroke; so extended was his right that his left had
actually to be thrown back and to face one of its brigades towards Alexandria, the base. Yet it may be questioned whether there was any other move open; and
some military experts, General Sherman chief among
them, have considered his plan an admirable one. That

[1] A comparison of the reports of Barnard and McDowell suggests that
the latter possibly made a mistake. Barnard reported that the ford below
Stone Bridge, that is Lewis' Ford, was guarded; McDowell may have
understood the ford above Stone Bridge, and therefore decided to swing
far around by Sudley Spring. A long and fatiguing march would have been
avoided had the troops crossed at Poplar Ford, while the army would have
avoided the dispersal that the advance along the Sudley Spring road eventually caused.

opinion it is not possible to share. The soundest feature of the plan was that from Sudley Spring the advance should be by the left; and it was the opposite that actually took place.

McDowell's mental attitude appears to have been that of a subordinate carrying out a defective order from his superiors to the best of his ability. He deliberately dismissed Johnston from his mind, on the supposition that this was a matter that did not concern him. He clung closely to the idea that a frontal attack was hopeless with such troops as he commanded, and that there was nothing to do but to outflank the enemy. If this could not be done by his left, then it must be done by his right, whatever the risk. On the basis of these assumptions, all fundamental and to a certain degree false, the march through Sudley Spring was ordered.

The plan of the next day's operations was carefully explained to the division and brigade commanders who assembled that night at headquarters for the purpose. It may be doubted whether this conference was altogether cheerful. For the army was showing signs of grave demoralization, and that very evening two commands had obtained from the commander-in-chief a release from service because of the expiration of their three months' term. The 4th Pennsylvania and the 8th New York militia battery were making their arrangements to march not on Manassas but on Washington the following morning. The New Yorkers left their guns behind them at Centreville, and there they lay unnoticed and uncared-for during some hours, until General Blenker eventually took them and added them to his brigade. Those abandoned guns might have played a big part in the struggle for the Henry house plateau.[1]

BEAUREGARD

On the 18th of July, while Tyler was unskilfully engaging Richardson's brigade at Blackburn's Ford, word reached Beauregard that Johnston's movement had begun. Whatever his imperfections as a general, Beauregard did not lack the offensive spirit; he seems from the first to have been anxious to avail himself of any opportunity that should present itself of striking back at the enemy across Bull Run. The news of Johnston's approach led to his working out a new scheme.

Beauregard sent his aide, Captain Chisolm, on the evening of the 18th, to propose that Johnston should detach part of his forces to operate through Aldie Gap and

[1] The Hon. Simon Cameron, Secretary of War, was at McDowell's headquarters. He expended some eloquence on the recalcitrant troops, but in vain. It is doubtful whether, even with a free hand, McDowell was the man to order a few of these deserters to be shot as an example; but with his superior present the blame cannot be laid at his door. The undiscipline of the volunteers and the political weakness of the Government went as far in one direction as the ferocity of the disciplinary code of the regular army did in another. In camp at Centreville the volunteers were startled to see two deserters from Sykes' battalion of regulars triced up, receive thirty lashes, and get branded. Slocum, *Hist. of 27th New York.*

take Centreville in reverse. Captain Chisolm reached
Johnston twenty-four hours later, on the evening of the
19th, at Piedmont on the Manassas Gap Railroad, and
placed Beauregard's proposal before him.

I did not agree to the plan, — says Johnston, — because, ordinarily, it
is impracticable to direct the movement of troops so distant from each
other, by roads so far separated, in such a manner as to combine their
action on a field of battle. It would have been impossible, in my
opinion, to calculate when our undisciplined volunteers would reach any
distant point that might be indicated. I preferred the junction of the
two armies at the earliest time possible, as the first measure to secure
success.[1]

While he was figuring out this more or less fantastic
scheme, Beauregard was not neglecting to call other reinforcements to his aid. Colonel Hunton was marching
fast from Leesburg with the 8th Virginia, while General
Holmes, under orders from Richmond, with the 1st
Arkansas, 2d Tennessee, and four rifled six-pounders, was
on the way from Fredericksburg. Hunton arrived on the
19th and took position near the Lewis house. Holmes
arrived on the 20th and was placed in reserve between
Manassas and Union Mills Ford. Meanwhile, as Mc-
Dowell's offensive did not develop further, clearly the
best plan for Beauregard was to await the approaching
reinforcements and to strike the instant they arrived and
before Patterson should have time to reach the scene of
operations; and this was the course he followed.

[1] Johnston, *Narrative*, 38. The controversy concerning this plan of
Beauregard's appears to be negligible.

JOHNSTON

It has already been stated that it was at 1 A.M. of the 18th, while the Federals were camping along the Warrenton turnpike from Fairfax Court House to Germantown, that Johnston received the dispatch from Richmond stating that Beauregard was attacked.[1] He had long foreseen this contingency and apparently made up his mind at once to move to Beauregard's help. He had several important matters to attend to before starting : how to dispose of his sick and wounded ; how to provide for the defence of Winchester. Even more difficult was the problem presented by Patterson. Johnston, not unnaturally, assumed that his opponent's movements were related to those that McDowell was carrying out towards Manassas. The day before, July the 17th, Patterson had marched by his left from Bunker Hill to Smithfield (now Midway) closely shadowed by Stuart's cavalry. On the whole it seemed probable that this move meant either that Patterson was still aiming at Winchester but avoiding the obstacles in his direct route, or that he would continue twelve miles farther south to Berryville where he would be across the direct road from Winchester through Snicker's Gap to Manassas, and within six miles of the

---

[1] For Johnston's movement to Manassas his *Narrative* strongly corroborates the official reports and should be read with them. A comparison of the texts, however, leaves little doubt but that Johnston had copies of his reports before him when he wrote the *Narrative*.

road through Ashby's Gap, farther south. Even if Patterson were thrown back at that point, the mere necessity
of fighting an engagement there would be fatal to any
hope of Johnston's army reaching Beauregard so as
to be of help. The early hours of the 18th were, therefore, anxious ones for the Confederate general, and, while
he employed them in making indispensable preparations,
up till noon he issued no orders for moving his troops. It
was probably at about this time that he received a report
from Stuart stating that up till nine o'clock that morning
there had been no signs of an advance by Patterson towards Berryville. On this Johnston issued his orders of
march.

There were fifty-seven miles to be accomplished by
Johnston's army before it could reach the point where, at
the very moment it was filing out of Winchester, Tyler's
guns were already booming along the banks of Bull Run.
Fifty-seven miles was a formidable distance to carry even
veteran troops on a forced march; and when, after an
hour or two, his green soldiers began to straggle and
his green officers to display their incompetence, Johnston
was seized with something like despair. Could he ever
reach Manassas in time?

Presently he ordered his Chief Engineer, Major
Whiting, to ride forward to Piedmont, a little station on
the Manassas Gap Railroad not quite halfway to Manassas, and to make ready to entrain the troops. In the

late afternoon Jackson, with the leading brigade, reached the Shenandoah beyond Millwood, forded the river, and climbed up the steep ascent beyond, seven hundred feet, into Ashby's Gap, where the troops bivouacked about 8 P.M. At dawn of the 19th they started again, the advance reaching Piedmont Station at 8 A.M., — the very hour at which Major Barnard was pushing his reconnaissance up Cub Run.

The Manassas Gap Railroad was a poor line, far from plentifully equipped with rolling stock; yet at first all seemed to promise well. Trains were waiting sufficient to convey Jackson's brigade which was rapidly sent on its way, reaching Manassas at four o'clock that afternoon. The railroad authorities declared that the whole army would be transported in the course of twenty-four hours.

Nevertheless Johnston decided that the artillery should proceed by road. Stuart had been instructed to keep in close contact with Patterson through the 18th, closing all roads along which information might pass, and then to slip away at nightfall to rejoin the army. This he did, and from Piedmont to Manassas acted as escort for the artillery. It was not till one o'clock in the morning of the 21st that this part of Johnston's army reached Manassas.[1]

Unfortunately for the Confederates the Manassas Gap Railroad broke down almost immediately under the strain thus suddenly placed on it. The chief trouble ap-

[1] Imboden, *Battles and Leaders*, I, 230.

pears to have been that the force of engineers was insufficient. The locomotive hands, much overworked, apparently refused to do any night duty, and the line soon got almost completely tied up. While Johnston and his men, only thirty-four miles from their objective point, grew more and more impatient, hours, almost days, passed with little accomplished.

Bartow's brigade reached Piedmont early in the afternoon of the 19th, and the 7th and 8th Georgia were entrained and sent off at 3 P.M.; but no more troops left that day.

During the night of the 19th–20th, enough cars returned from Manassas for about 1000 men, but the train hands insisted on resting till morning, so that it was not until between 7 and 8 A.M. on the 20th — just when McDowell was wondering whether he should not make a reconnaissance in force over the ground which Barnard had reconnoitred the day before — that the moving of the troops could be continued, the 4th Alabama, 2d Mississippi, and two companies of the 11th Mississippi, all from Bee's brigade, being entrained. With about one half of his infantry, and all his cavalry and artillery thus started, Johnston himself decided to join Beauregard. He left Kirby Smith to replace him at Piedmont, and arrived at Manassas a little before noon.

As to the troops left at Piedmont this much may now be added. The causes of delay worked in increasing

ratio, so that no more troops left on the 20th and it was
not till the next morning that Kirby Smith with four
more regiments could move. A collision near Manassas
early on the 21st added slightly to the delay, but he
reached the battlefield just in time to play an important
part.

Johnston's movement was much criticized at the time,
and chief among the critics was President Davis. There
is no need to renew this old controversy here, for there
was really little in it; the outline must suffice. Davis and
Johnston were not on good terms, and the latter was
punctilious and combative. His trenchant attitude on the
Harper's Ferry question had nettled the Confederate
President, who was wedded to the idea that Harper's
Ferry was a position to be retained at all hazards. But
Johnston insisted on having his way, and thereby had
his army ready for the emergency at Manassas when the
critical moment arrived.

Now it was evidently a question whether, under the
most favorable circumstances, a corps of 10,000 men
could be moved from Winchester to Manassas within a
sufficiently short space of time to render help against an
enemy having so short a distance to traverse as Mc-
Dowell had. It does not appear that the Confederate authorities at Richmond took much more trouble to work
out a plan for making the mutual support of their two
generals effective than did the Federal authorities at

Washington to co-ordinate the movements of Patterson and McDowell. It was left as a generally understood matter under the responsibility of the commanders themselves.

But, in fact, it was most difficult to carry out the proposed combination against an enemy who realized the conditions. For Johnston had to cover more than twice the distance that McDowell had; he was further handicapped by the inevitable loss of time entailed by the transmission of the news of McDowell's start and to a further possible loss of time from pressure by Patterson. A reasonably rapid and resolute advance by the Federals, which took account of these conditions, must have led to the battle being fought before the Confederate forces could effect their junction.

Lee, Davis, and Johnston were all doubtless more or less conscious that the chances might be against them; it was failing a better plan, that they accepted the concentration at Manassas with all its drawbacks. But when it came to carrying out the operation, Davis and Johnston were apparently inclined to throw back on each other the responsibility for its danger and inherent shortcomings. They did their best, however. Davis telegraphed to Johnston the instant word reached him from Beauregard that McDowell was moving. Johnston started from Winchester as quickly as could reasonably be expected in view of the indispensable arrangements he had

to make and of the necessity for learning whether Patterson was advancing or not towards Berryville and the
Confederate line of march. But when, after the first comparatively rapid day's march, while every hour through
the 19th and 20th Beauregard and Davis expected Mc-
Dowell's attack to be delivered and Johnston's army remained in large part unable to pass beyond Piedmont,
impatience, dissatisfaction, and recrimination naturally
arose. A few hours one way or another, a few thousand
men more or less, and the fate of the Confederacy might
be sealed. Johnston knew it as well as Davis, but the
latter scanned the former's conduct closely to prove that
he alone was to blame for the situation.

Davis at the time, and for many years afterwards, maintained the view, with which few agreed, that Johnston's
march might have been more rapid had he strictly
obeyed the orders he received. The questions involved
have no importance for the present purpose. Should
Johnston have sent his sick and wounded to Culpeper,
or was he right in leaving them at Winchester and
thereby saving a certain number of wagons for transport
purposes? What was the precise meaning of the expression "if practicable," applied to Johnston's movement? It will suffice to say that in the period following
the war these matters received undue attention.

On the whole the conclusion must be that the move of
Johnston from the Shenandoah Valley to Manassas was

a doubtful proposition in terms of space and time. Yet it was clearly the best move open to the Confederates. It was effected with as much rapidity as was possible under adverse circumstances. And its success was due mostly to the slowness of McDowell.

Johnston reached Manassas, as we have seen, about noon on the 20th. He had at that moment available Jackson's brigade, about half of Bartow's and about half of Bee's. His artillery and cavalry were still on the road, but his remaining infantry was due in the course of the day or at latest on the morning of the 21st, although as a matter of fact this expectation was not realized. Still it was good work, in forty-eight hours since leaving Winchester, to have come so near transferring his little army to Manassas; and fortunately the enemy continued to show no sign. It was at this moment that Johnston received, in reply to a query he had sent from Winchester, a notification from President Davis that he was appointed to the rank of general, and this made him the senior officer of all the troops at Manassas.

Johnston had had no petty object in view when he asked Davis to settle the question of rank as between himself and Beauregard. He wished to avoid the difficulties and dangers that a contested command might raise rather than to exalt his personal position. He did not wish to hamper or control Beauregard's operations, but he wanted a free hand to assert an individual control, should the necessity for it arise. He seems to have arrived at Manassas bent on taking the offensive at once, for he still credited Patterson with more energy than that officer possessed. Having lost sight of him on the 18th he rightly assumed the worst, — that he should probably next hear of Patterson marching to join McDowell through Leesburg. The thing to do then, was to settle the issue while yet Patterson was out of the game.

He discussed the situation with Beauregard immediately on meeting him, and found that complete agreement existed between them in their general view of the situation. Beauregard produced his maps and showed Johnston the position of his troops between Union Mills and Stone Bridge, and the convergence of the roads from these points on Centreville. He then indicated how an offensive movement could be carried out along those roads.

Here it may be surmised, for there is no evidence to show it, that the Confederate generals may have considered what might be the meaning of McDowell's inactivity since about four o'clock of the afternoon of the 18th. If they did so, there can be but one conclusion, that they decided this inactivity must be due to McDowell's awaiting Patterson's arrival. All the more reason, therefore, for a prompt offensive.

Since one o'clock on the morning of the 18th, Johnston had had scarcely any rest. He was physically exhausted.

Beauregard knew the ground and had made suitable plans. Johnston felt unable to face the problem, and therefore passed over to his subordinate the task of preparing the orders for moving the army. He then turned in to rest.

Johnston apparently expected that Beauregard would make the orders out immediately and send them on to him for approval, so as to inform the brigade commanders that night. But Beauregard failed in promptness. By the time his order was written, the proper number of copies made, and the whole sent to Johnston for approval it was 4.30 A.M. of the 21st.[1] It ran, in part, as follows:—

. . . The following order is published for the information of division and brigade commanders:—[2]

I. Brigadier-General Ewell's brigade, supported by General Holmes' brigade, will march via Union Mills Ford and place itself in position of attack upon the enemy. It will be held in readiness either to support the attack upon Centreville, or to move in the direction of Sangster's Crossroads, according to circumstances.

The order to advance will be given by the commander-in-chief.

II. Brigadier-General Jones' brigade, supported by Colonel Early's brigade, will march via McLean's Ford to place itself in position of attack upon the enemy on or about the Union Mills and Centreville road. It will be held in readiness either to support the attack upon Centreville or to move in the direction of Fairfax Station, accord-

[1] Beauregard's report is obviously unreliable as to the order, the failure of the Confederate attack, and the movement of McDowell's right.

[2] It may be remarked that there was no division organization, and that the whole sentence, especially the phrase "for the information," is bad from the point of view of military orders.

ing to circumstances, with its right flank towards the left of Ewell's command, more or less distant, according to the nature of the country and attack.

The order to advance will be given by the commander-in-chief.

III. Brigadier-General Longstreet's brigade, supported by Brigadier-General Jackson's brigade, will march via McLean's Ford to place itself in position of attack upon the enemy on or about the Union Mills and Centreville road. It will be held in readiness either to support the attack on Centreville or to move in the direction of Fairfax Court House according to circumstances, with its right flank towards the left of Jones' command, more or less distant, according to the nature of the country.

The order to advance will be given by the commander-in-chief.

IV. Brigadier-General Bonham's brigade, supported by Colonel Bartow's brigade, will march via Mitchell's Ford to the attack of Centreville, the right wing to the left of the Third Division (*sic*), more or less distant, according to the nature of the country and of the attack.

The order to advance will be given by the commander-in-chief.

V. Colonel Cocke's brigade, supported by Colonel Elzey's brigade,[1] will march via Stone Bridge and the fords on the right thereof to the attack of Centreville, the right wing to the left of the Fourth Division (*sic*), more or less distant, according to the nature of the country and of the attack.

The order to advance will be given by the commander-in-chief.

VI. Brigadier-General Bee's brigade,[2] supported by Colonel Wilcox's brigade, Colonel Stuart's regiment of cavalry, and the whole of Walton's battery, will form the reserve, and will march via Mitchell's Ford, to be used according to circumstances.

VII. The light batteries will be distributed as follows: . . .

VIII. Colonel Radford, commanding cavalry, will detail . . . as follows: . . .

IX. The Fourth and Fifth Divisions, after the fall of Centreville, will advance to the attack of Fairfax Court House. . . .

[1] On the assumption that Kirby Smith (Elzey) would arrive during the night or early in the morning.

[2] Part of Bee's and part of Bartow's, the whole temporarily under Bee.

The First, Second, and Third Divisions will, if necessary, support the Fourth and Fifth Divisions.

X. In this movement the First, Second, and Third Divisions will form the command of Brigadier-General Holmes; the Fourth and Fifth Divisions that of the second in command. The reserve will move upon the plains between Mitchell's Ford and Stone Bridge, and, together with the Fourth and Fifth Divisions, will be under the immediate direction of General Beauregard.

By command of General Beauregard:

THOMAS JORDAN, A.A.G.[1]

It would be difficult to conceive a worse drawn-up order. To do it full justice it must be reviewed at considerable length : —

First, then, one may note for criticism that now, at the last moment, just before entering into battle, Beauregard realized that the splitting-up of an army of 30,000 men, extended over a line of eight or ten miles, into brigades, most of them numbering two to three thousand men, was a faulty organization. Divisions were clearly necessary, and so, confusedly, they appear in his order. Beginning with brigades, Beauregard presently takes to calling them divisions, which shows how his mind is working. Then at the end of his order he improvises not merely a divisional but a corps arrangement by dividing his own troops between himself and Holmes, — that is, on paper.

It seems unnecessary to point out that a divisional and corps organization could hardly be created in such a way ;

[1] O. R. Ser. I, vol. II, 479. This order was dictated during the night to Major Whiting, of Johnston's staff. Beauregard, *Commentary*, 60.

but even assuming it would work, the order issued did not fit it. If Beauregard's First, Second, and Third Brigades were to be handled together as a division, or as a corps, by General Holmes, the first thing to do was to place that officer in the position of exercising this command effectively by making the necessary staff adjustments, and by notifying the brigadiers to look to him and not to the army commander for their orders. It would then be the case that the disposal of these three brigades would lie with the divisional general, receiving his orders from the commander-in-chief. If, then, General Holmes was to act as a divisional general, the orders to Ewell, Jones, and Longstreet were wrong because misleading and confusing.[1] This, however, was only a part of the difficulty.

Even leaving out of account this vital question of divisional organization, the order could not be expected to produce concerted and effective action among the brigades. Its very tone suggested delay. Some of the officers who read it interpreted it as a preparatory order, not implying action. No hour was mentioned at which the brigades should begin their forward movement. The positions they were to occupy were indicated only in the vaguest manner. And at the end of each instruction came the re-

---

[1] That Holmes never knew anything of the matter appears from his report to Beauregard: "About 9 o'clock on Sunday the 21st, I received a copy of your note to General Ewell directing him to hold himself in readiness to take the offensive at a moment's notice, to be supported by my brigade." O. R. Ser. I, vol. II, 565.

mark: "The order to advance will be given by the commander-in-chief." To advance, whence? From the position occupied on the night before, or from the new one
to be taken up in the morning? If the whole meaning
was, as generally interpreted, that nothing was to be done
until Johnston sent orders, then the order was next to
meaningless except in so far as it involved a waste of
precious time.

The actual disposition of the brigades was very open
to criticism, though largely governed by topographical
considerations and the necessity of attacking at once and
at all hazards. The line of attack was very long. It formed
an arc circling through difficult country about the Centreville ridge, which the enemy occupied in strength. From
the Warrenton turnpike it would be most difficult for
Cocke to keep in touch with Bonham through the woods
and low ground along Cub Run; while on the left the east
front of the Centreville ridge was awkward of access, over-
grown with thickets, a difficult terrain through which Jones,
Ewell, and Longstreet would have to maintain their line.

When, at 4.30 on the morning of the 21st, Johnston was
awakened to approve and countersign this order, he was
apparently surprised and annoyed at the delay and at the
order itself. He had supposed that the troops would march
with the dawn, then just breaking, but apparently for
fear of incurring further delay, he at once signed Beauregard's document and had it sent out.

VII

THE BATTLE; PRELIMINARY MOVEMENTS[1]

NORTH

A NIGHT march is proverbially one of the most delicate of military operations, especially with an inexperienced army. In McDowell's case it was complicated by several facts. The troops had, for a distance of two miles, — that is to a point six hundred yards beyond Cub Run, — to defile along a single road. The leading division, Tyler's, which had to continue along the Warrenton road beyond that point, could not clear it except by advancing over ground not hitherto reconnoitred and that might be held

---

[1] For the account of the battle the official reports and the evidence of commanding officers before the Committee on the Conduct of the War, give the substance of the facts, create a composite picture. The reports must be read critically, as they vary in value; for instance, Beauregard is always flowery and rhetorical, constantly disguising, distorting, or omitting facts, while Johnston is restrained, clear, and definite; it is with such allowances as should be made, and with constant comparison and checking, that these reports, most of them vague and inaccurate, sometimes wilfully misleading, have been used. Wherever a special or controversial point has been made, the specific reference to the report or other authority has been given. But it has not been thought necessary to enter into certain past controversies, as, for instance, whether Kirby Smith's brigade was detrained near the battlefield and marched straight to it, or not; the story, however widespread, reposes on no evidence, and is not worth discussing; Smith's brigade, without any question, detrained at Manassas.

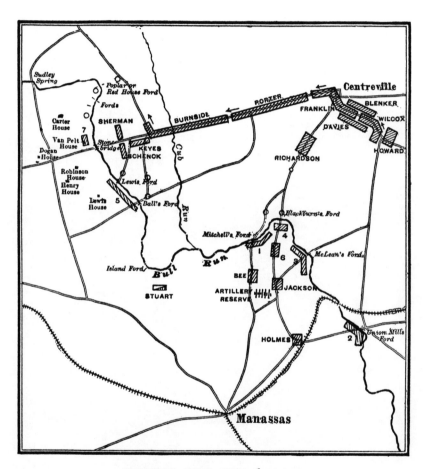

POSITION, JULY 21ST, 6.30 A.M.

by the enemy. This was likely to, and in fact did, cause obstruction and delay. McDowell had already proved his inability to march in daylight; in darkness conditions were bound to be worse. The road leading to Sudley Spring was inadequately known, and, as it proved, difficult for the passage of artillery.

Under these circumstances it was more than likely that McDowell's crude marching arrangements should immediately break down; and they did. Of the troops that were to execute the flanking movement, Hunter's division, camping just east of Centreville, was under arms at 2 A.M., according to orders; but it was not until 4.30 A.M. that its head of column was in Centreville village, and not till 6 A.M. that it had covered the next two miles and turned off from the Warrenton turnpike; and that was the hour at which the commander-in-chief hoped to have his whole force at Sudley Spring.[1] Heintzelman's division formed column at 2.30 A.M., but found itself unable to advance at all until 6 A.M; Hunter's division filling the road at this moment from Centreville to the junction of the Sudley Spring road.

This bad beginning of the day's work was in part due to the slowness and timidity of Tyler's advance. Parading at 2.30 A.M., that general had opened the movement along the Warrenton turnpike. Leaving Richardson on the Centreville ridge to take his' orders from Miles, he

[1] Barnard's report, O. R. Ser. I, vol. II, 331.

pushed his remaining three brigades towards Stone Bridge in the following order: Schenck, Sherman, Keyes.

Schenck's camp was one mile south of Centreville on the ridge, and he anticipated orders by parading at 2 A.M. instead of 2.30. But so great was the confusion in the dark that it was not till 3 A.M. that he actually got started. He very slowly and cautiously advanced to the village and turned into the Warrenton turnpike.

Attached to Schenck's brigade was a thirty-pounder rifled Parrott gun, weighing no less than 6000 pounds,[1] and this piece was hauled along at the head of McDowell's army, a useless Medusa's head, less valuable than a handy six-pounder, and almost stopping all progress. For at about two miles beyond Centreville the turnpike crossed a steep ravine where a ramshackle wooden affair known as the "Suspension Bridge" carried it over Cub Run; and there the advance was nearly brought to a stop. It was no place for a 6000-pound gun. Finally, after mighty efforts and nearly breaking down the bridge, the monster was safely hauled up to the other side of the ravine.[2]

It must have been about sunrise (4.52 A.M.), when Schenck reached the junction of the Sudley Spring road. He had now, or perhaps a little earlier, deployed a half battalion as skirmishers, a proper precaution. Apparently

---

[1] Hains, "The First Gun at Bull Run," *Cosmopolitan*, August, 1911.

[2] For the delays of Schenck's brigade see the reports of Wilson and Fuller, O. R. Ser. I, vol. II, 362; 366.

when just past Cub Run, he had fortified his courage by throwing a few shells along the road in the direction of Stone Bridge.

Getting no response, Schenck resumed his march, and at six o'clock, having reached a point about a thousand yards from Stone Bridge, he deployed to the left of the road; Sherman's brigade, which did not leave Centreville till 3.30 A.M.,[1] coming up behind Schenck, deployed on the right. Presently, at 6.15 A.M.,[2] the Parrott gun opened fire again, sending shells along the Warrenton turnpike beyond Stone Bridge, but eliciting no reply from the Confederates who remained under cover and refused to unmask their guns.

Keyes' brigade, following Sherman's, was halted midway between the line Tyler had deployed and the Sudley Spring crossroads at a point where a road came up from Ball's Ford to join the Warrenton turnpike.[3] As Keyes cleared the junction of the Sudley Spring road, Hunter's advance turned into it, and Heintzelman's column, back at Centreville, was at last enabled to make a start.

Leaving Hunter and Heintzelman to make their long circuitous march to Sudley Spring, we can sum up in a few words the operations that were carried on meanwhile by the Federals at Stone Bridge and near Centreville.

---

[1] Kelly's report, O. R. Ser. I, vol. II, 371.

[2] New York *World*, July 23; Nott's relation, *Reb. Rec.* II, Doc. 92.

[3] There is now a road from this point to Poplar Ford.

During the three or four hours that Tyler was left to face the Confederates at Stone Bridge, he did little more than push his skirmishers and infantry gradually down to the stream, and intermittently direct his batteries against supposed Confederate positions on the farther bank. He did so little damage and exercised so little pressure that a few companies of infantry with a few guns were for some hours a sufficient protection for that part of the enemy's line.

At Centreville General Miles had been strengthened by Richardson's brigade of Tyler's division. Apparently his men were paraded at the same time as the other troops and had to wait patiently until daylight before moving. Blenker's brigade was then posted behind Centreville, two regiments facing east on either side of the Warrenton turnpike, another regiment facing south, and a fourth in reserve in the village. A half battalion was detached in observation along the Union Mills road. Intrenchments were thrown up across the turnpike, facing east, and the brigade batteries were placed along the front of the position.

Richardson's brigade advanced towards Mitchell's Ford, placed its guns along the ridge, deployed two regiments in support and kept two in reserve. Davies pushed on behind Richardson, coming into line on his left. The position of the troops and guns about 8 A.M. is more fully indicated on the sketch map.

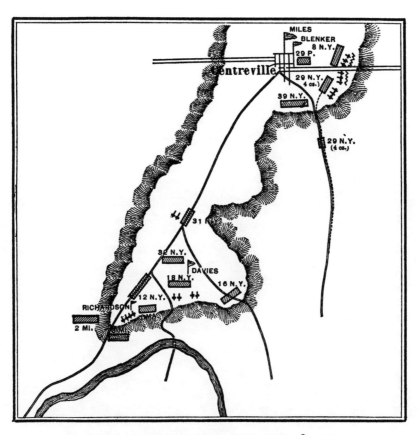

MILES AT CENTREVILLE, JULY 21ST, 8 A.M.

The curious disposition of Blenker's brigade at Centreville serves to bring out some of the fundamental weaknesses of McDowell's situation. In his effort at all costs to outflank the enemy he had had to swing so far to the northwest as practically to abandon his line of operations. His deficiency in mounted troops tended to the same result; for a few hundred sabres, with infantry supports, thrown out towards Sangster's and Union Mills, would have freed Blenker and given the Warrenton turnpike some protection to the east of Centreville. These facts were all the more serious in that McDowell was faced by a problem in the matter of reserve artillery ammunition: that for his flanking divisions had been left at Centreville under Miles' protection; he hoped to get it up along the Warrenton turnpike when Tyler should clear the way at Stone Bridge. But more important than this was the fact that there was a shortage, especially in the ammunition for the heavier guns.[1]

In the afternoon of the 19th, Lieutenant Hawkins, of the commissariat service, had been sent from Centreville to Fairfax Station to forward supplies.[2] On the 20th, he began to receive ammunition from Alexandria, the track being cleared to within a short distance of the station; but apparently he did not succeed in sending through

---

[1] There is little material available for working out the facts as to the ammunition supplies.

[2] Hawkins' interesting report is given in O. R. Ser. I, vol. II, 341.

any of this ammunition to the army. On the 21st, the
gap between him and Blenker at Centreville was always
at the mercy of any Confederate detachment.

Meanwhile, at about 8 A.M., Richardson and Davies
opened fire with their artillery, doing little damage, and
revealing by the slowness of their fire and its lack of
concentration that it was not to be taken seriously. In a
couple of hours the heavier guns had used up most of
their supply, and there was no reserve to fall back on.

It is time now we turned to the Confederate side.

SOUTH

During the night the Confederates had caught at more
than one point the rumbling of wheels and other noises
denoting the movement of McDowell's army. Here and
there a group of officers or of soldiers had guessed the
meaning correctly. But at headquarters there was no
definite information, nor any consequent modification of
plans. At about 4.30 A.M., Johnston was awakened to
find that nothing had been done and that he was required to sign Beauregard's unsatisfactory order. This
he did, and for the rest, on the inconclusive pretext that
he knew nothing of the ground, he and his staff refused
to act,[1] leaving all to Beauregard, — an extraordinary
attitude for a commander-in-chief.

---

[1] When, a good many years after the war, Johnston and Beauregard got
into a controversy as to their respective shares in the event, the latter did

Beauregard, meanwhile, sent out the order that was supposed to hurl the Confederates on to the Centreville ridge. Longstreet, at Blackburn's Ford, received it at five, just as Schenck with Tyler's advance was reaching the junction of the Sudley Spring road. Longstreet understood that the order was "preliminary," but got his troops over the run into the woods under the Centreville ridge, and, there lying close, awaited further instructions.[1] One of his volunteer aides, Colonel Terry, made his way to the left through the woods and succeeded in getting a view of the Warrenton road about three miles to the northwest, probably at about half-past six, and reported it full of troops marching west, — Hunter's or Heintzelman's column. This information was promptly sent back to Beauregard.

Farther to the left Bonham was on the alert. His officers had suspected McDowell's move during the night, and he himself, from the height behind Mitchell's Ford, caught sight of Tyler's troops on the Warrenton pike at dawn. He reported this to headquarters and held his command ready. No trace of his receiving orders to advance can be found, nor did his command make any forward move-

not hesitate to impute to Johnston that his attitude in the early stages of the battle was governed by pessimism as to the outcome and a desire to shift the responsibility on to Beauregard. This is difficult to believe, and does not agree with Johnston's signing of Beauregard's order of battle. The fact that the order was dictated to Major Whiting of Johnston's staff, which Beauregard emphasizes, does not seem important.

[1] Longstreet, *From Manassas to Appomattox*, 44.

ment during the entire morning. The only fair inference is that Bonham remained during that time in personal contact with Beauregard, who for some hours conducted operations from just back of Mitchell's Ford, and received instructions by word of mouth. Stretching this inference to its utmost one might conclude that Beauregard, from the moment that news reached him of McDowell's apparent extension westwards, which must have been just about the time when his order for a general advance was going out, weakened in his offensive intention, while not abandoning it. Possibly one or two copies of the order were actually withheld.[1] And yet McDowell's movement really emphasized the need for the Confederate offensive : the Federals were stretching northwest, the direction from which Patterson might be expected, and by stretching northwest were rendering more vulnerable their line of communications and the very positions which the strong Confederate right wing was best placed for attacking.

On the Confederate right were Jones, at McLean's Ford, and Ewell at Union Mills, with other troops in second line. Here is the account given by these two generals, in their reports,[2] of the orders that reached them from Beauregard. Ewell says : —

I first received orders to hold myself in readiness to advance at a moment's notice.

[1] There were vague stories of orders going astray.
[2] O. R. Ser. I, vol. II, 536–39.

This was presumably the general order, received about the same time as Longstreet had received it, say five o'clock.

I next received a copy of an order sent to General Jones and furnished me by him, in which it was stated I had been ordered at once to proceed to his support.

So far as Jones is concerned, nothing whatever is reported as happening before 7.10 A.M., making it possible that the general order never reached Jones at all.

At 7.10 A.M. the following order was received, viz: —

July 21, 1861.

BRIG.-GEN. D. R. JONES,
  Commanding Third Brigade:
 GENERAL: General Ewell has been ordered to take the offensive upon Centreville. You will follow the movement at once by attacking him in your front. Respectfully,

    G. T. BEAUREGARD,
    Brigadier-General, Commanding.

I immediately placed my brigade in readiness to advance, and dispatched a messenger to communicate with General Ewell, whose movement I was to follow. Not receiving a prompt reply I crossed McLean's Ford and took position with my artillery in battery on the Union Mills road, . . . I here awaited the advance of General Ewell for about two hours and a half at the end of which time I received a somewhat discretionary order . . . and a few minutes after the following positive order. . . .

10.30 A.M.

 GENERAL JONES: On account of the difficulties in our front it is thought preferable to countermand the advance of the right wing. Resume your former position.

    G. T. BEAUREGARD.

On this Jones recrossed McLean's Ford, and then received from Ewell what was presumably Beauregard's general order, on which Fitz Lee, his A.A.G., had indorsed : —

The general says this is the only order he has received. It implies he has to receive another. Send this to General Beauregard if you think proper.[1]

To add to this hopeless confusion, Ewell had meanwhile, in leisurely fashion, crossed Union Mills Ford, following Jones' previous movement across Bull Run, "but whilst so doing received an order to fall back to my former position, which I did. . . ."[2] The time was now about 11 to 11.30 A.M.

To make this record of bungling complete we may add Early's account of how, about an hour later, Beauregard's order to march in support of the left wing reached him : —

General Jones asked me if I had received an order from General Beauregard, directing that I should go to him with my brigade. Upon my stating that I had received no such order, he said that he had received a note from General Beauregard in which he was directed to send me to the General. The note, which was in the hands of one of Jones' staff officers, was sent for and shown to me. It was in pencil, and after giving brief directions for the withdrawal across the Run and stating the general purpose to go to the left where the heavy firing was, there was a direction at the foot in very nearly these words, — "Send Early to me." This information was given to me some time between 12 M. and 1 P.M. The note did not state to what point I was to go. . . . I . . . directed . . . Captain Gardner to ride to Mitchell's Ford and ascertain where General Beauregard was, as well as the route I was to pursue.[3]

[1] O. R. Ser. I, vol. II, 538. [2] Ewell's report, O. R. Ser. I, vol. II, 536.
[3] Early, *Autobiography*, 19.

With such a system of command, and such a method of writing orders, it was truly a wonder that the Confederates ever got any of their reinforcements into line.

Comment on the miscarriage of Beauregard's orders appears almost superfluous. It may best be summed up, perhaps, by saying that his staff arrangements were as crude as his orders. The offensive of the Confederates had now failed; it remains to be seen how they dealt with the developments that McDowell's flank march threatened.

The explanation of why Jones did not receive Beauregard's first orders is possibly to be found in Johnston's words, when he writes: " Soon after sunrise, and before the distribution of these orders could have been completed, a light cannonade was opened upon our troops at Stone Bridge." [1] This clearly refers to the shots fired by Schenck along the Warrenton turnpike shortly after he passed Cub Run at about 5 A.M. Half an hour later Evans signalled from Stone Bridge that the enemy was in sight and deploying on the opposite side of the run; and at 6.15 A.M., Tyler's artillery opened at Stone Bridge. This was the first sign of activity by the Federals since their repulse at Blackburn's Ford on the 18th; coming as it did with reports of movements of troops on the Warrenton turnpike, it probably made Beauregard

[1] Johnston, *Narrative*, 41.

hesitate for a moment whether or not to carry out his projected attack.

Johnston apparently first joined Beauregard soon after sunrise at the latter's headquarters which lay well back from Bull Run on the edge of the Manassas plateau. At about 8.30 A.M., however, we find the two generals, accompanied by their staffs, on the high land behind Mitchell's Ford, where it seems probable that General Bonham joined them. Meanwhile the continued strength displayed by McDowell in the direction of Stone Bridge had produced a modification in the Confederate arrangements. Jackson's brigade was ordered to move from between Manassas and Blackburn's Ford to an intermediate position between Bonham and Cocke; General Bee's brigade, lying farther west, was sent to Cocke at the Lewis house; and Colonel Wade Hampton, who had just arrived at the Junction after a thirty hours' journey from Richmond, was at once ordered with his legion to the same point.

This reinforcing of the centre and left was for the moment intended to coincide with an offensive on the right. This was the intention evidenced by Beauregard's dispatch to Jones at 7.10 A.M., already quoted.[1]

At nine o'clock, or perhaps a little later, Captain Alexander, Beauregard's able signal officer,[2] who was keep-

---

[1] Johnston in his *Narrative* repeatedly blames Beauregard for the staff failure to get the right wing attack delivered.

[2] The chief signal station was near Manassas Station, about two miles

ing his glass on the semaphore near the Van Pelt house, behind Stone Bridge, distinguished a considerable body of troops about two miles above the bridge. This he immediately reported to Beauregard, while he semaphored to Evans: "Look out for your left, you are turned." [1] Almost simultaneously with this signal, Evans received a scout's report that conveyed the same intelligence.

It was probably on receipt of Alexander's message, although it may have been previously, on the succession of reports as to the movement along the Warrenton road, that the order was issued for Jackson, Bee, and Hampton to move to the left. For about an hour more the Confederate generals awaited developments, and then came another message from Alexander reporting a heavy cloud of dust, from well back of the Confederate left, as though the Federal troops first reported had described a wide semicircle, or as though Patterson's columns were approaching from Aldie Gap. This seemed alarming, though, in truth, it was only Johnston's transport train nearing Gainesville on its way to Manassas.

Johnston, at first, was disinclined to believe that McDowell would venture on a wide turning movement; [2]

from the first position of Johnston and Beauregard. Alexander communicated with headquarters by couriers. In his *Memoirs*, and articles, he refers to the Van Pelt house as the Van Ness house.

[1] *South. Hist. Soc. Paps.* XVI, 94; Alexander, *Military Memoirs*, 30; reports of Beauregard and Johnston, O. R.

[2] Richmond *Dispatch*, July 29.

he was far more inclined to believe that the cloud of dust to the northwest might be caused by Patterson arriving from the Valley. In any case he was restless, and dissatisfied as to Beauregard's would-be offensive operation. He urged him to proceed to the left wing, but Beauregard for the moment insisted on carrying out his projected attack on the Centreville ridge.[1]

Presently a staff officer arrived at headquarters from

General Ewell informing me [Beauregard], to my profound disappointment, that my orders for his advance had miscarried, but that in consequence of a communication from General D. R. Jones he had just thrown his brigade across the stream at Union Mills. But in my judgment it was now too late for the effective execution of the contemplated movement . . . it became immediately necessary to depend on new combinations and other dispositions suited to the now pressing exigency. The movement of the right and centre . . . was at once countermanded with the sanction of General Johnston, and we arranged to meet the enemy on the field upon which he had chosen to give us battle.[2]

This statement of Beauregard glosses over some awkward facts. It is doubtless true that at some time between 10.30 A.M. and 11.30 A.M. he received information which showed that his orders had miscarried, but he should have known this much earlier. The fact undoubtedly was that the sound of cannonade and musketry could now be heard away to the left and was becoming more and more insistent, until at 11.30 A.M. Johnston could stand

---

[1] Alexander, *Military Memoirs*, 32.
[2] Beauregard's report, O. R. Ser. I, vol. II, 491.

it no longer. "The battle is there!" he said; "I am going!" With that he walked rapidly to his horse, jumped into the saddle, and rode away at a gallop followed by his staff.[1]

Probably at the moment that Johnston started for the point of danger, he instructed Beauregard to issue orders shifting a considerable part of the army to the left. How hastily and badly Beauregard did this has already appeared from Early's statement previously quoted. In addition to Early's brigade, Holmes' was ordered to the Lewis house, and the 2d and 8th South Carolina, with Kemper's section of artillery, were detached from Bonham and moved in the same direction. But before he followed Johnston to the left, Beauregard's fixed idea of operating against Centreville reasserted itself, and he again issued orders for the movement forward of Ewell, Jones, Longstreet, and Bonham; but this time the attack was not to be pushed home, it was to be merely a "demonstration" to amuse the enemy.[2] He then hurried off to overtake Johnston.

While the Confederate right, insufficiently organized and badly led, thus remained inert or making aimless movements, the left at Stone Bridge was threatened with

[1] Alexander, *Military Memoirs*, 34.

[2] Beauregard's report, O. R. Ser. i, vol. ii, 491. It would seem from Johnston's report, O. R. Ser. i, vol. ii, 475, that these dispositions were made, as has been suggested, after some assertion of authority on the part of Johnston.

disaster. Colonel Evans was in command at that point, with eleven hundred bayonets and two smoothbore six-pounders. His position lay about six hundred yards back of the river on a little hill over which the Warrenton turnpike ran, and where stood the Van Pelt [1] house. His infantry and guns were lying close under cover at this point, not replying to Tyler's cannonading, and watching the bridge, where a considerable obstacle had been formed during the few days preceding by a dense abatis about one hundred yards long.[2] Although it was reported at McDowell's headquarters that the bridge was mined, this was not the case. It does not appear that Beauregard had ever considered the question either of destroying or of fortifying the bridge. Evans' position was well chosen for a small post of observation and defence.

Schenck's thirty-pounder gave Evans plenty of warning, from about five o'clock, that an advance towards Stone Bridge was in progress; and when Schenck, and then Sherman, deployed, Evans sent word to headquarters. But he took care not to reply to the Federals' harmless fire, to a certain extent because his guns were considerably out-ranged by those of his opponents and were placed to command the bridge and not the country beyond.[3]

---

[1] Also referred to as the Van Ness or Van Vliet house.
[2] *South. Hist. Soc. Paps.* XXXII, 743; "Eppa Hunton at Bull Run."
[3] Sloan's report, O. R. Ser. I, vol. II, 560.

Evans soon realized that the movement in his front was merely a demonstration. After several hours' desultory fusillade in the woods along Bull Run, information reached him, as we have already seen, that the Federals were in large force on his left in the direction of Sudley Spring. He immediately gathered together the greater part of his command, and leaving three or four companies[1] at the Van Pelt house, he marched northwards with the 4th South Carolina, the 1st Louisiana, and Davidson's section of Latham's battery, to oppose the Federal flanking movement in that direction.

[1] It is variously stated.

VIII

McDOWELL TURNS THE CONFEDERATE LEFT

ALTHOUGH McDowell was unequal to the almost hope-less task which he had been set, although he blundered and weakly listened to bad advice, he deserves some de-gree of admiration for the real courage he displayed in attempting to carry out the mission that had been im-posed on him. He was not well at the time, sick indeed on the very night of the 20th to the 21st;[1] the weather had become oppressively hot, and he had at times to seek relief from the saddle by driving in a light carriage; yet his actions from the beginning to the end of the long, cruel day on which he lost the battle of Bull Run show that from the early hours of the morning till he dropped to sleep from exhaustion at Fairfax Court House some twenty hours later, he never did less than his best.[2]

McDowell followed his advance closely, and apparently joined Tyler's division opposite Stone Bridge a little be-

---

[1] *Report Cond. War*, II, 41; McDowell's evidence. He ate canned fruit on the evening of the 20th, and suffered a choleraic attack; Barrett Wendell, quoting Stedman, *Mass. Hist. Soc. Proc.* 3, II, 191.

[2] The only serious reflection made against McDowell in this sense is in the privately printed *Memoir* of Tyler, by Donald Mitchell, which con-vinces one of little more than that by the time McDowell had got back to Centreville he was extremely fatigued and dejected. This does not in itself invalidate what has been stated above.

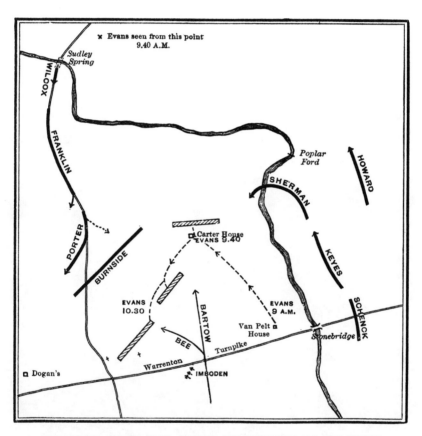

MCDOWELL OPENS THE ACTION BY SHIFTING TO HIS RIGHT

fore seven o'clock.[1] Leaving Centreville about four, he had at once discovered that the attacking column was not advancing and that the road was blocked. He made his way towards the Cub Run bridge, near which the last brigade of Tyler's division (Keyes') was still obstructing Hunter's advance. He ordered the regiments off the road and into the fields on the south side,[2] and then hurried on to get a view of the situation near Stone Bridge. He directed the artillery to search the Confederate position at various points, and as Evans remained obstinately silent, he concluded that the enemy's strength was towards Blackburn's Ford, as in truth it was, and that he was in danger of being attacked by his left. He then rode back to the junction of the Sudley Spring road and turned off.[3]

Howard's brigade of Heintzelman's division, the last in the flanking column, was now marching by. McDowell stopped to watch the brigade file past, and when it had cleared the Warrenton turnpike, he instructed Howard to halt and wait further orders.[4] McDowell's

---

[1] It is a fair inference from all the accounts that the two generals kept away from one another, and did not actually meet. McDowell probably rode from one point to another, keeping out of Tyler's way. See Tyler's *Memoir*, by Mitchell; Fry, *McDowell and Tyler;* and the official reports.

[2] Tyler claims to have given this order, but his evidence is very doubtful. *Rep. Cond. War*, ii; Tyler's evidence.

[3] This paragraph is largely a matter of deduction; see the reports of McDowell, Tyler, and Howard in O. R. Ser. i, vol. ii.

[4] Howard should have been placed under the orders of the nearest

object was to leave Howard within supporting distance
of Centreville in case of an emergency; but in the result
he merely weakened his flank attack. At this moment,
then, say half-past seven to eight, the Federal army presented a remarkable tactical disposition, being broken
into three marked groups: on the Centreville ridge,
three brigades; close to Stone Bridge, four brigades; on
the Sudley Spring road marching north, four brigades.

McDowell followed his flanking column, but did not
succeed in getting to its head until after Sudley Spring
was reached. Meanwhile Burnside, with the leading brigade, had slowly advanced. At first his march took him
through a difficult wood road, where it was necessary in
more than one place to effect repairs before the guns
could be got through. Had Burnside or his engineer
guides known it, a good track through the woods led to
a fordable and unguarded crossing of Bull Run at Poplar Ford, and another one by the Red House farm to
Sudley Spring at a saving of quite two miles. This ford
was indicated in McDowell's order as the "lower" ford;
but no one seemed able to find the way to it until later
in the day when Howard's brigade discovered it. So the
troops kept on northwards, a long, circuitous route.[1] Be-

divisional general, Tyler. He would in this case probably have followed
Sherman's movement and been of some use in the battle. Heintzelman
apparently gave Howard no orders; so that the brigade was virtually
detached from any divisional organization.

[1] But Barnard says that the engineer officers who guided the column

yond the woods, well to the north of Bull Run, open
country was found. The route now led them south and
a little west, until at half-past nine Sudley Spring was
reached, and the men were given a rest along the banks
of the stream.[1]

But reports of the Federal movement had already
reached Evans, and the Federal commanders from the
rising ground just north of Sudley Spring presently
caught sight to the south of them, a mile or more away,
near the Carter house, of Confederate troops coming into
position. Then presently these troops moved across farther west towards the Sudley Spring and Manassas road.
Burnside immediately advanced along the Manassas
road towards them. It was then, probably, about ten
o'clock. Before relating what followed, however, it will
be better to consider the ground for one moment, in connection with McDowell's order of the 20th. The immediate field of operations was roughly a triangle of which
the Warrenton turnpike was the base, Sudley Spring the

refused to turn off to the left because they thought this would bring them
under the fire of Confederate batteries on the farther bank of Bull Run.
O. R. Ser. I, vol. II, 331.

[1] Burnside reached Sudley Spring at 9.30; his head of column was engaged at 10.30. Franklin reached Sudley Spring at 11; and found Porter,
or the rear of Porter, still there. Willcox reached Sudley Spring at 12.30.
Each of these brigades stretched, therefore, over an hour of road, and, as
their rate of advance was at least more than two miles an hour and each
brigade averaged about 3000 men, it follows that every man took well
over a yard of road.

apex, Bull Run the east side, and the Manassas road the west side. From Sudley Spring due south to the crossing of the Manassas and Warrenton roads was about a mile and a half; to Stone Bridge across the Pittsylvania farm — hilly fields and woodlands — was almost two miles. From the crossing of the Manassas road to Stone Bridge was a little over a mile. How did McDowell's order fit this ground?

Hunter's division had been ordered to cross Bull Run "above the lower ford"; and Heintzelman's "at the lower ford," meaning presumably Poplar Ford. But, as already stated, the engineer officers who guided the columns did not succeed in discovering the road to this ford, so that Heintzelman followed Hunter all the way to Sudley Spring.

Once across Bull Run, what was the army to do? ". . . turning down to the left, descend the stream and clear away the enemy who may be guarding . . . the bridge. It [Hunter's division] will then bear off to the right to make room for the succeeding division." There is some ambiguity here as to the precise points of crossing; and there may be some confusion of thought as to the relation of Tyler's corps to the two others; but the general idea, however badly expressed, is clear beyond the possibility of mistake. Once over Bull Run the advance was to be left flank forward, following the stream down to the bridge, clearing the fords and linking the army up again; and when once the all-important bridge and Warrenton turnpike were reached, then the extension to the right might take place. As it happened, precisely the contrary was about to occur.

As Burnside crossed the ford and advanced along the Manassas road beyond, the Confederates were moving across his line of advance towards that road. For from the Pittsylvania or Carter house, Evans' direction was of necessity southwesterly if he was to prevent an advance along the Manassas road. He judiciously picked a position not across the road but slightly flanking it, with a wide zone of fire on its front and with its right resting in a belt of woods; there he awaited developments.

Hunter, with Burnside's brigade, Porter's following, marched straight on the enemy. He continued along the Manassas road, which was the obvious thing to do. When he reached a point within six or seven hundred yards from the Confederates he found that to the left of the road the ground was broken and wooded while to the right it was open farmland. Burnside's brigade was at this moment marching in column of route, the 2d Rhode Island leading, followed by the Rhode Island battery. Apparently an order had been given for skirmishers to be thrown out, but, in effect, there were only flankers on each side of the road.[1]

---

[1] For this, and the movements of the Rhode Island battery generally, see Monroe, *Rhode Island Artillery*.

The Confederates opened fire at about six hundred yards. Immediately, Hunter ordered the Rhode Island battery forward through a fringe of trees to the left of the road. The infantry apparently broke back at once. They were soon formed into line, however, on the right of the road, and without waiting for the deployment of Burnside's other regiments, Hunter pushed up the 2d Rhode Island diagonally across the road to support the guns. These had opened fire, but were in an obviously exposed situation, their safety being due, in fact, to the weakness of Evans' line. To the south and west of the point where Hunter had begun his deployment, open fields extended towards the Warrenton turnpike.

While getting the 2d Rhode Island into action, Hunter was shot down severely wounded, as was also its colonel, Slocum. The command of the division devolved on Porter, who was not yet at the front, so Burnside continued the work of getting his brigade engaged. This took time, and was at first a somewhat piecemeal affair; yet a line was formed, as shown in the diagram. Its right

2 howitz. -H-		+-+-+-+- R.I. Batt.	
2d N.H.	1st R.I.	71st N.Y.	2d R.I.

was near the Sudley Spring road, and it faced about southeast. Porter was now fast coming up behind, moving his own brigade forward under cover of Burnside's, which was exchanging volleys with Evans. Porter deployed his troops in the open ground to the right of the road, prolonging Burnside's right along a crest that ran southwest to the Dogan house. Thus began a general shift of the whole column towards the right, instead of towards the left, that was to continue through all the operations and that played an important part in the developments of the battle.

It was about this time that McDowell arrived on the scene. From Sudley Spring he had seen the dust clouds made by the troops that Johnston was hurrying to his menaced flank. He judged it necessary to quicken and strengthen his attack before the Confederates should have time to ward it off. He therefore sent orders to Howard to march on Sudley Spring, and to Tyler to press the attack at Stone Bridge; this order the latter in fact anticipated, as we shall presently see. McDowell then rapidly proceeded to the front, urging the troops of Franklin and Porter as he passed by them to quicken their march.[1] But the small Confederate force was well posted, and offered a remarkably stubborn resistance to the Federal advance. Even after Porter had prolonged Burnside to the southwest towards the Warrenton turnpike, Evans succeeded in holding on for a while. Presently reinforcements reached him under Bee, momentarily relieving the pressure.

[1] At eleven o'clock McDowell got prisoners from Johnston's corps and knew as a fact that he had to face the combined Confederate army. *Rep. Cond. War*, II, 40 ; McDowell's evidence.

The Federal infantry showed little inclination to move forward to the attack, which was not unnatural in view of their lack of training and of competent officers. The theory most acted on was that the troops should be saved when exposed to fire by having the men lie on the ground. This was good sense, but only up to a certain point; for the muzzle-loader is difficult to load in such a position, and if the troops are too constantly kept under cover they are quickly demoralized when exposed to direct fire.[1] It was probably the Federal preponderance in artillery that decided the issue, for the infantry was lying down most of the time, and when efforts were made to carry it forward, broke back; its musketry was probably ineffective. On the Federal line, after Griffin's battery, of Porter's brigade, came into action, were six thirteen-pounders and four ten-pounders all rifled, together with two twelve-pounders and two small howitzers; to this all the Confederates could at first oppose were two smooth-bore six-pounders and, after Bee came up, four more.

It was about a quarter past eleven when Porter came into action. Burnside's line was wavering badly at this moment, and Porter detached to his left Sykes' battalion of regulars to stiffen it and support the guns. At the same time Griffin's battery was coming into action

[1] Part of the zouave drill then taught was the acrobatic feat of rolling over on the back, placing the musket between the knees, and then loading it; a very unsafe performance it would seem! This was taught only to the so-called zouave organizations.

farther to the right, and poured in a very hot and effective fire, before which the Confederate line immediately showed symptoms of breaking up.

The fight was not yet over, for Bee had now arrived. He succeeded in maintaining the resistance for another half-hour or so before the end came.

But the Federal line kept extending. Franklin's brigade, of Heintzelman's corps, had followed the general movement by deploying still farther to the right and prolonging Porter's line. Rickett's battery was quickly to the front, and from a position to the right of the road not far from the Dogan farm played effectively on Evans and Bee.

The 1st Minnesota was detached to support Burnside's left, which was getting more and more shaky, and Franklin's two other regiments, the 5th and 11th Massachusetts, were hurried along the road and deployed into line near the Warrenton turnpike ; but they were immediately thrown into confusion on coming within the zone of fire of Imboden's battery on the Henry house plateau.[1]

Willcox, following Franklin, reached Sudley Spring about 12.30 P.M. and received orders to leave Arnold's battery there to cover the ford. This was done, and the 1st Michigan was detached in support. The 4th Michigan had stayed behind at Fairfax Court House, which left only the 11th (zouaves) and 38th New York with

[1] Supporting Bee from the Henry house hill.

which to continue the advance. With these two regiments, Willcox appears to have reached the crossing of the Warrenton and Manassas roads between 1.30 and 2 P.M., after the Confederate line had at last given away. He thus describes the situation at that moment : —

We . . . came upon the left of what I supposed to have been Franklin's line. . . . The troops on our left were engaged in a desultory fire with the enemy posted in the thicket and ravine across the Warrenton road, not far from the Robinson house.[1]

Ricketts meanwhile had moved to the Dogan house, overlooking the crossroads, whence he was throwing shells, none too effectively because of the distance, at any target he could find on the Henry house plateau. Franklin, following in support, eventually descended to the Warrenton turnpike, crossed Young's Branch and began to move up the hill on the farther side. The 2d New Hampshire, of Burnside's brigade, was moved up to support him ; and at about 2.30 P.M. he advanced to occupy the Henry house plateau.

Just as the Confederates under Evans and Bee, no longer able to withstand the superior Federal artillery, began to stream away to the rear, another body of Federal troops began to appear on the left; this was Sherman's brigade.

As soon as McDowell, after arriving at Sudley Spring, had realized the situation, he had sent Tyler an order to

---

[1] Wilcox's report, O. R. Ser. I, vol. II, 408.

press on against the enemy. A little previous to this, however, Sherman, from the right of his position, had observed to the north of him a horseman, doubtless one of Evans' scouts, riding down the hill on which stood the Red House farm and disappearing in the hollow. From this he concluded that there must be a ford, and, in fact, Poplar Ford lies just below the farm. When Tyler ordered him to cross Bull Run if possible, he promptly led his brigade off to his right where he hoped to find the ford indicated by the horseman. Once in the hollow, however, his soldiers soon worked their way down to the river bank, and there presently discovered a couple of fords about two hundred yards short of Poplar Ford and commenced to cross. It was probably assumed that the horseman had also passed at this point, though a staff or engineer officer pushing on another two hundred yards would have discovered the mistake. And the mistake had its importance, for where Sherman actually crossed it was found impossible to get over his brigade battery under Ayres, while at Poplar Ford there would have been not the least difficulty.[1] Ayres counter-marched and returned to the Warrenton turnpike, where he reported to Schenck near Stone Bridge.

[1] This account is based not merely on the documents but on a careful survey of the ground with my friend Major McAndrew, U.S.A. Not a doubt was left in our minds as to the point where Sherman crossed. Fry, *McDowell and Tyler*, 59, and Allen, *Hist. of 2d Wisconsin*, 385, appear to support this conclusion.

Just as Sherman was crossing Bull Run, Schenck pushed the bulk of his infantry half a mile or so downstream to a point near Lewis' Ford. A few well-aimed shots from the Confederate guns guarding the passage soon sent him back to the Warrenton turnpike near Stone Bridge, where, in fact, he remained until the end.

Sherman's leading regiment, the 69th New York, was thrown out into a skirmishing line as it neared the Carter house, and exchanged shots with some stragglers from Bee's command, already in retreat. In this desultory firing Lieutenant-Colonel Haggerty, of the 69th, was killed. The brigade was then halted while Sherman rode across to consult McDowell; Keyes meanwhile crossing and forming to the left of Sherman; with Keyes came Tyler. Presently Sherman returned and the advance was resumed.

By this time the first phase of the fight was over on the right. McDowell had had a success, but at a considerable cost. His advance had been delayed for two or three hours by a small detachment of the enemy; one of his brigades, Burnside's, was entirely used up. It fell to pieces, the men taking to the woods along the Sudley Spring road and playing no further part in the battle, with the exception of the 2d New Hampshire which kept its organization and presently resumed its advance. Burnside covered up the demoralization of his men under the plea that they had to replenish ammunition and re-

tired for that purpose, but he personally followed the 2d
New Hampshire and was in the fighting that took place
on the Henry hill.[1]

Even among the troops that had come less directly
under fire than Burnside's, disintegration set in during
the lull that followed the first engagement. Many of the
men believed a complete victory had been won. They
were hot, tired, thirsty. The company officers were incompetent and had little control. The result was that
many men dispersed, and some of them not to rally
again.[2]

It will be better not to attempt, until after we have
looked at the Confederate side, to do more than to indicate the general line of the Federal advance after the resistance of Evans and Bee had been overcome. It was
from the Carter house and along the Manassas road to
the line of the Warrenton turnpike. Two brigades were
on the left under Tyler; Porter's brigade formed the
centre; Heintzelman's two brigades formed the right and
were now farther south than the others, so that the whole
might roughly be described as an advance right wing
forward.

SOUTH

ON THE WARRENTON TURNPIKE. Evans states that
it was at nine o'clock that he marched from Stone Bridge

[1] Hayes, *Hist. 2d New Hampshire*, 32.
[2] King's address, *Papers Minnesota Command, Loyal Leg.* 6.

to oppose Hunter's advance. His scouts had informed
him that large bodies of the enemy were higher up Bull
Run, on the north side, and at the same time came a
message from Alexander's signal station to the same
effect. He immediately decided to shift the responsibility
for guarding Stone Bridge on to Cocke, whom he notified
that he was moving towards the enemy. He then started
for the Carter house, with eleven companies of infantry,
one troop of cavalry and two six-pounders. He left behind three companies and two six-pounders facing the
bridge from the Van Pelt house.

On arriving at the Carter house, Evans, with the enemy
now clearly in sight at Sudley Spring, deployed his
infantry. His position was well chosen for resisting an
attempt by the Federals to work down Bull Run and
uncover Stone Bridge. But presently, seeing or fearing
a movement along the Manassas road that would turn
his left, he decided to move over towards the road so as
to prevent the Federals from reaching the crossing of
the Warrenton turnpike, which seemed to be their objective. It was this change of position that virtually turned
McDowell's operation from an advance left flank forward
to one right flank forward.

Evans deployed for the second time along a ridge
stretching northeast from the intersection of the Sudley
Spring and Warrenton roads. His left was right over
the crossroads. His front commanded a zone of fire five to

six hundred yards wide, while on his right, where woods filled a hollow between his position and the Carter house, he placed the 1st Louisiana under Major Wheat, a little forward of his main line, which was held by Colonel Sloan with the 4th South Carolina. One of Davidson's guns was behind Sloan; the other was placed in advance and a little to the left enfilading a stretch of the Sudley Spring road.[1] When Burnside attempted to advance, Sloan poured in a heavy fire on him; Wheat counter-charged and broke the 27th New York,[2] and for a while Evans more than held his own. Presently, however, numbers began to tell.

Meanwhile Bee, following his orders from Beauregard, had marched to a point about three quarters of a mile west of Stone Bridge and just south of the Warrenton turnpike where a well-defined elevation, since generally known as the Henry house plateau, induced him to deploy his brigade for defensive purposes; he had about 2700 bayonets with four guns of Imboden's battery. He judged that Evans was beaten and that a new line must be established.

But Evans was too closely engaged to get clear away in good order. One of his staff officers rode up to Bee begging him to advance, and he decided to comply.

---

[1] This position, which does not accord with that generally given in the books, has been carefully reconstructed on the ground.

[2] Moved up from Porter to stiffen Burnside. Slocum, *Hist. of the 27th New York.*

Coming down from the Henry house plateau, he moved across the Warrenton turnpike, pushed Bartow to the right with the 7th and 8th Georgia towards the Carter house, and with the rest of his brigade faced to the left and stiffened Evans' weakening line. The move was risky, and Imboden was held back, taking position on the northwesterly point of the hill whence he fired across at Porter as the Federal right stretched farther and farther southwest towards the Dogan house.

Behind Bee, Hampton was marching along the Manassas road, and Jackson, from near Island Ford, had already started, not waiting for orders, to the sound of the guns; Holmes, Early, and Bonham's two regiments were also marching in the same direction; while Kirby Smith, so long delayed at Piedmont, was at last reaching the army, — his first train arriving at Manassas Junction a little after noon.

Bee's advance across the Warrenton turnpike was ill-timed. Had he waited a few minutes longer, Evans would have been dislodged and the occasion for advancing would have disappeared. Could he, on the other hand, have reached the scene half an hour earlier, he might have had time to settle down to an effective defence. As it was he arrived just at the moment when Evans was completely beaten, and when there was nothing left to do but to make the best of a bad job. Bee did this, prolonging the hopeless resistance for some

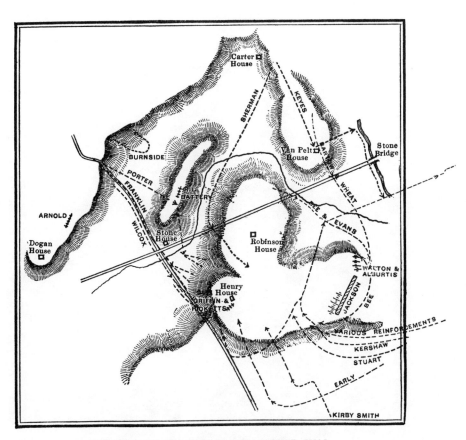

THE ATTACK ON THE HENRY HOUSE HILL

time; but he, too, at last had to yield to superior force. When it came to retreat, his troops, like all other troops engaged at Bull Run, had not enough cohesion to maintain their organization under fire in the open.

As the brigades of Bee and Evans broke up, they streamed away almost eastwards, for McDowell's batteries had been edging farther and farther to the right, and played on the retreating Confederates down on the turnpike which they soon reached, and for more than a mile along the·slopes of the Henry house plateau. Some of the fugitives kept along the turnpike or climbed up the hill and, under a constant fire, moved across the plateau to its descent on the east side; others kept in the hollow following Young's Branch, turning south beyond the Henry house plateau, thus rejoining the other broken commands.

It may be as well, before proceeding farther, to describe the ground towards which the conflict was now moving. From Stone Bridge the Warrenton turnpike ran about west, cutting at two points the S-like course of Young's Branch, a small stream of no importance save for the hollow it formed. Looking from north to south across the Warrenton turnpike the ground presented itself in the following way: For the first half-mile from Stone Bridge there was open rising ground back of the tree-fringed hollow in which Bull Run flowed. To the west of this the Henry house plateau jutted out sharply northwards, rising nearly a hundred feet above Young's Branch and in part timbered. Farther south, following Young's Branch, was a considerable ravine running up into the Henry house plateau. Between the ravine and Bull Run south of Young's Branch were wooded heights, close to Lewis' Ford, difficult to penetrate. The next half-mile of the Warrenton turnpike went up the projecting angle of the Henry house plateau, one hundred feet, and down again, Young's Branch circling nearly a quarter of a mile north and then joining the road again at a point just beyond which were the Stone house and the crossing of the Manassas–Sudley Spring road. Beyond this the Warrenton turnpike need not be followed in its westward course.

From Stone Bridge around by the Carter house to the Stone house, a well-marked semicircle of rising ground followed Young's Branch on the north; it was everywhere about thirty or forty feet lower than the Henry house plateau and was broken by several patches of woodland.

From its crossing with the Warrenton turnpike in the hollow of Young's Branch, the Manassas road, leading about south, rose gradually some seventy feet in two thirds of a mile diagonally across the western edge of the Henry house plateau; descending thence towards Manassas six miles or more away. West of the road at this point lay another hill of about the same height as the Henry house plateau, which was sometimes called Chinn's hill. This point in the Manassas road between the two hills was about three thousand yards as the crow flies southwest of Stone Bridge. The first two thousand yards of this line roughly coincided with the rear or southeasterly line of the Henry house plateau, and it was along that two thousand yards that the main Confederate line of battle was eventually formed, facing rather more west than north. We can now return to the retreat of Evans' and Bee's brigades with better understanding.

No effort of their officers could hold up the broken troops as they fled over the Henry house plateau or along the hollow until they neared or reached the protection of the ravine at the southeasterly corner. Even there the few field officers left had their hands full to restore order. The Confederates, like their opponents, had paid the price always exacted of an insufficiently prepared army. The officers had had to expose themselves continuously. The 4th Alabama had lost all its field officers. Of the colonels, Sloan, Wheat, Gardner, and Jones had been severely wounded. Bee had exposed his life freely, and was now working desperately to rally the fugitives. It was at this moment, as he rode up and down trying to re-form his men near the head of the ravine behind the Robinson house, that he caught sight to the left of a long line of Confederate infantry in position

across the plateau, with their general, cool and determined, pacing his horse slowly along their front. It was
Jackson's brigade, standing as firm as a stone wall.[1]

[1] The "stone wall" story was apparently first printed four days after the
battle in the form which has been generally followed since. The quotation
is from the Charleston *Mercury*, July 25, 1861 (special correspondence from
Richmond): —

GEN. BERNARD E. BEE

The name of this officer deserves a place in the highest niche of fame. He
displayed a gallantry that scarcely has a parallel in history. The brunt of
the morning's battle was sustained by his command until past two o'clock.
Overwhelmed by superior numbers and compelled to yield before a fire
that swept everything before it, Gen. Bee rode up and down his lines, encouraging his troops, by everything that was dear to them, to stand up
and repel the tide which threatened them with destruction. At last his
own brigade dwindled to a mere handful, with every field officer killed or
disabled. He rode up to Gen. Jackson and said: "General, they are beat-
ing us back." The reply was: "Sir, we'll give them the bayonet."

Gen. Bee immediately rallied the remnant of his brigade, and his last
words to them were: "There is Jackson standing like a stone wall. Let us
determine to die here and we will conquer!" —

On the face of it this account has no character of authenticity, and the
words ascribed to Bee smack less of the battlefield than of the editorial
sanctum. This account of the Charleston *Mercury* was reproduced at the
time by a number of Southern papers, and by several pamphlets. After
them came the historians, and without exhausting the list, the following
may be mentioned as giving the same story, with or without slight variations: M. Addey, *Life of General T. J. Jackson*, New York, 1863; "Ex-
Cadet," *Life of Thomas J. Jackson*, Richmond, 1864; "A Virginian," *Life
of Stonewall Jackson*, New York, 1864; R. L. Dabney, *Life and Camps of
Jackson*, New York, 1866; J. E. Cooke, *Stonewall Jackson*, New York, 1866;
S. N. Randolph, *Life of General T. J. Jackson*, Philadelphia, 1876; Dr.
McGuire, "General Jackson," *South. Hist. Soc. Paps.* XIX, 307. Mrs. Jackson in her biography of her husband, Colonel Henderson in his well-known
life, and other writers merely echo the formulas of these early biographers.

General D. H. Hill, though not going into any precise details, rejected

HEADQUARTERS. Meanwhile Johnston and Beauregard had left their first position in rear of Bonham, under circumstances already noted. Just before doing so, about eleven o'clock, Johnston discovered that trees were being felled along the Federal front on the Centreville ridge, evidently for abatis, and this confirmed his opinion that nothing serious was intended by McDowell on that side. It was clearly up towards Stone Bridge that the battle was to be fought, and as Johnston galloped towards the Lewis house, he turned Pendleton and Alburtis with their batteries [1] in the same direction, ordered Cocke to detach the 8th and 49th Virginia towards Stone

the whole story as fabulous (see an article in the *Century*, February, 1896). But this is unconvincing because it was undoubtedly the case that immediately after Bull Run Jackson was known by his famous sobriquet. It seems inherently probable that something was said by somebody, during or immediately after the battle, that likened Jackson or his men or both to a stone wall. Alexander (*Military Memoirs*, 36) relates that as he rode over the Henry house plateau on the evening of the battle with Johnston, that general, pointing to what had been Jackson's position, said: "Preston's regiment stood there like a stone wall." This remark may have been the origin of the story long current about Bee. Two other variants may be added to the accepted story: Conrad, a combatant at Manassas, gives the words: "Close up, men, and stand your ground. Colonel Jackson with five regiments of Virginia troops is standing behind us like a stone wall and will support you" ("First Battle of Manassas," *South. Hist. Soc. Paps.* XIX, 901); Robbins, a major in the 4th Alabama, writing in 1891, declares that he heard Bee say: "Yonder stands Jackson like a stone wall. Let us go to his assistance." (*South. Hist. Soc. Paps.* XIX, 164; another account by J. Q. Jones in the same volume hardly deserves notice.)

[1] Pendleton's battery was actually commanded by Brockenbrough, the former acting as chief of artillery. Imboden, *Battles and Leaders*, I, 235.

Bridge, sent back officers to hasten on the troops already marching, and an order to Ewell to move to the threatened point with his whole brigade.

Johnston, followed by Beauregard, apparently arrived at the eastern edge of the Henry house plateau about half-past twelve, just as Bee's and Evans' broken troops reached the same point. Evans' two regiments were disbanded beyond hope of retrievement. Bee's were almost in as bad a plight. Johnston himself took an active part in re-forming the men; he carried forward the flag of the 4th Alabama, made a few of the men rally, and appointed Colonel Gist, of his staff, to command them. About four companies of disorganized men were beaten together and placed under Colonel Thomas, Johnston's chief ordnance officer, who was killed at their head a little later.[1]

After the first flurry was over and the retreating troops had been partly rallied, Beauregard pressed Johnston to be assigned to the command of the wing there facing the Federal advance, and after a discussion Johnston consented to this and rode back to the Lewis house where he would be better placed for controlling the army as a whole. He was still so anxious about the situation of his left wing that on arriving there his first instinct was to

[1] Johnston, *Narrative*, 48, 49. He says that the four companies under Thomas was the largest of the bodies of reorganized troops. But it is clear, though the direct evidence is lacking, that Bartow succeeded in rallying one if not both of the Georgia regiments.

order Cocke with the remainder of his brigade to Beauregard's assistance ; but on looking over the ground with Cocke he decided that troops must be left to guard Ball's Ford and Lewis' Ford, against which Schenck had already made a demonstration earlier in the day.

Let us now examine more closely the situation of the Confederates at the moment when Beauregard took command of what may be described as the left wing of the army.

Evans and Bee had held their positions just long enough to enable Wade Hampton and Jackson to reach the Henry house plateau. Hampton received orders at Manassas Junction to move in the direction of Stone Bridge. He accordingly marched towards Lewis' house, and when near there learnt that the enemy was approaching. The sound of Evans' and Burnside's guns was presently heard, and Hampton moved straight in that direction. This took him across the Henry house plateau diagonally, and he appears to have reached the western edge of it at the precise moment when Evans and Bee were breaking back, and when the Federal troops were beginning to show in pursuit on the hillsides beyond Young's Branch. Hampton threw himself into the breach. He moved to the Robinson house, just north of which the turnpike crosses the plateau, and from there checked the pursuit of Bee and Evans and covered the ravine in which their troops were in part re-formed. He was exposed to a galling fire, losing his lieutenant-colonel, Johnson, and presently fell back a couple of hundred yards towards the ravine, where he was presently supported by the re-formed troops that Bee and Johnston led forward to his assistance.

Jackson came up immediately behind Hampton and by the same route. But instead of crossing the plateau he stopped short at the point where it began to dip northwesterly. There was an irregular belt of trees in undulating ground where he deployed his brigade in the order shown.[1] He was joined by Imboden's battery as it retreated, leaving behind one of its guns disabled on the edge of the plateau. Jackson placed Imboden, with his brigade battery, Stannard's, in front of his centre, where Pendleton on arriving also formed Brockenbrough with his four guns; Pendleton taking command of the whole. Alburtis unlimbered to the right. Imboden, however, soon went back to the rear, having exhausted his ammunition.[2] Jackson's line faced a little north of west,

---

[1] This order is variously given. The positions of the 5th on the right and of the 33d on the left, with the guns massed about in front of the centre, seem most certain.

	Brockenbrough, 4 guns	Stannard, 4 guns	Imboden, 3 guns		Alburtis, 4 guns
33d Virg.	2d Virg.	4th Virg.	27th Virg.	5th Virg.	

[2] Imboden, *Battles and Leaders*, I, 235.

towards the crossing of the Warrenton and Manassas roads.[1]

The deployment of Jackson's brigade came in the nick of time and was extremely well judged. He avoided the mistake of attempting to hold the plateau from the edge nearest to the enemy where their batteries would have had an easy target; he preferred to take up a position partly sheltered and to attack which his opponents would have to cross a fire-swept zone; the issue justified him.

Jackson's left was about three or four hundred yards short of the Manassas road, and as the Federals now held this road as far as its crossing with the Warrenton turnpike, there was evident danger of his being outflanked. This was to prove a critical point, and

[1] The diagram below represents roughly a section of the Henry house

plateau at the chief point of conflict. Jackson's infantry was at *A*; his guns and gunners could just get protection from a slight swell of ground at *B*. At *C*, in a saucer-like fold southeast of the Henry house, were the Federal batteries, and just behind them at *D* was the edge of the plateau lined by the Federal infantry. From *A* to *D* was about three hundred yards. The Federal guns were firing over the heads of the Confederates, their shells apparently bursting a considerable distance behind Jackson's line, or burying themselves in the ground in front of it. (Conrad's statement that the fire must have been ineffective because uncut fuses were found on the ground hardly affects the issue. *South. Hist. Soc. Paps.* xix, 89.) The Confederate guns were similarly firing over the heads of the Federals. But the use of canister on either side would create a zone that infantry could not easily move in.

Beauregard at once began strengthening it. He sent
Bee to take command, with the 4th Alabama and 7th
Georgia, with which he prolonged Jackson's left just
in time to face Heintzelman's advance. Then Johnston
sent the 49th Virginia from Cocke, and Beauregard the
2d Mississippi; at 2.30 P.M. the 6th North Carolina,
a strong regiment with 634 bayonets, came up from
Manassas Junction.[1]

On the right Hampton, unable to withstand the fire
of the Federal batteries, presently fell back across the
ravine to a spur of the plateau prolonging Jackson's position and was there supported by the 8th Virginia, the
first of Cocke's regiments to reach the scene. But the
Federal batteries now changed position and began to
play against Jackson, so that from this moment pressure
towards the ravine relaxed, the Confederate right was
no longer threatened, and later it became possible to
shift Hampton's legion across behind Jackson to support
the hard-pressed left.

We have already seen that Jackson had massed in his
front three of the five batteries of the army of the Shenandoah. Of the others, Beckham's was soon to come into
action with Stuart's cavalry on the extreme left, while
that of Alburtis, which we have seen ordered forward by

[1] It does not seem possible to accept the statement in Colonel Peters'
relation that the 1st Maryland fought at this point. There is no corrobo-
ration, and the regiment was undoubtedly with Ewell. *South. Hist. Soc.
Paps.* XXXIV, 170.

Johnston, appears to have reached a position on the Henry house plateau to the right of Jackson, from where it was shifted still farther towards the right, whence it apparently swept the turnpike just beyond the Robinson house. Of Beauregard's guns, Rogers' battery [1] was guarding Lewis' Ford with the support of Cocke, whose numbers gradually dwindled as his regiments were moved by Johnston to the left, so that by three o'clock only one company of the 19th Virginia remained in support of these guns. Walton, with three smooth and two rifled six-pounders, was sent to the scene early. At 8.30 A.M. he was at the Lewis house, whence he detached his two rifled guns to the spurs overlooking Stone Bridge, whence later they played effectively against the advance of Keyes. The three others moved to the right of Jackson on the Henry house plateau, thus concentrating eighteen guns on the main line of battle, to be reduced presently by Imboden taking three to the rear, and increased later by six more, Beckham's and Kemper's. This preponderance of artillery proved a considerable factor in the result. And it should be kept in mind that so long as the artillery was being used at short ranges on the Henry house plateau, the Confederate smoothbores were just as effective as the long ranging rifled pieces of the Federals.

[1] Now commanded by Heaton. Imboden, *Battles and Leaders*, I, 235.

IX

THE FIGHT AT THE HENRY HOUSE

NORTH

AT the very moment that Bee and Evans gave way under the fire of the Federal batteries, Burnside's men were apparently done with. They made no attempt at pursuit, but on the contrary fell back ; Burnside's official euphemism runs : —

> I withdrew my brigade into the woods in rear of the line for the purpose of supplying the troops with ammunition. . . . The 2d New Hampshire . . . was sent forward to assist one of Colonel Heintzelman's brigades, at that time three quarters of a mile distant.

Porter, on Burnside's right, had been less exposed and had done better. Two of his regiments, however, had broken, the 14th New York and 8th New York Militia. The former was apparently rallied ; the latter took little part in the subsequent proceedings and presumably went to replenish ammunition along with Burnside's men in the woods. But as the Confederates fell back to the hollow of Young's Branch and up on to the Henry house plateau, Porter followed, until he reached the rising ground where Evans had formed his line. To his right Heintzelman's infantry was working down towards the Warrenton turnpike ; to his left Sherman was closing in towards him and in the direction of the apex of the Henry house plateau. Griffin's and Ricketts' guns on the right continued firing on the retreating Confederates, sweeping them off the plateau towards the ravine, and driving Imboden's guns back towards Jackson.

Farther to the left, Keyes, following Sherman, was diverging towards Bull Run, opening an ugly gap between the main part of the Federal line and Stone Bridge. Neither Sherman nor Keyes had any guns, nor could any reach them from across the run until Keyes should clear a way for Schenck to cross the bridge. The artillery, therefore, was, for practical purposes, concentrated on McDowell's right.

McDowell's situation at this juncture was far from good. The configuration of the ground and the Confederate dispositions had constantly deflected him towards his right along the Manassas road to the west of the wedgelike point of the Henry house plateau. He was fast tending to face backwards towards Centreville, and the constant and rapid weakening of his numbers from the difficulty of keeping the men with the colors made it doubtful whether his long curving line could be maintained without breaking. He had little choice but to strike as quickly as he could at the Confederate forces on the Henry house hill, and this he set about doing after a pause made inevitable by the fatigue and disorder of his troops. But the infantry had already revealed its lack of offensive power, while the disorder of the men and lack of a proper system of command made it difficult to handle them. McDowell therefore decided to continue the attack by throwing forward his artillery on to the plateau and by edging around the enemy's position towards the right.

There was much to justify McDowell's decision. His infantry was clearly not to be relied on for a frontal attack, and might therefore prove most useful in outflanking the enemy. His regular batteries had proved their quality and seemed to give promise that they could break down the enemy's line. And yet the decision proved fatal. The ground was not known. The enemy's line was not located. The risk of the guns being lost for want of support was fairly obvious. Jackson had not disclosed the position either of his infantry or of his artillery. The edge of the plateau was well forward of the Federal line, and there was no certainty of what support the infantry would be able to give. Yet McDowell ordered his guns forward, — " the fatal blunder of the day." [1]

Of the four batteries with McDowell, we can first dispose of the Rhode Island. It did not follow the retrograde movement of Burnside's brigade, but apparently moved forward under McDowell's orders to a position immediately northeast of the crossroads, whence it be-

[1] Imboden, *Battles and Leaders*, I, 234.

gan firing over the depression of Young's Branch at the Henry house plateau. One gun, however, had been disabled; another gun soon used up its ammunition and was sent back to the rear; and of the four remaining, two moved to the right and took position near the Dogan house. The two that remained were eventually ordered by Governor Sprague of Rhode Island to cross Young's Branch and take position on the Henry house plateau. This they did at the moment when the Federal army had just begun its retreat, so that they played no part in the struggle at that point.[1]

It was Griffin's and Ricketts' batteries that were chosen to deal the blow; and McDowell apparently instructed Major Barry to direct the movement in person.[2] Barry rode over to Griffin, — the two officers were not on good terms personally, — and ordered him to limber up and move to the Henry house plateau. Griffin objected. "I hesitated . . . because I had no support."[3] He even argued the case, having no confidence in the infantry, and believing the position he was being sent to far too advanced. But Barry was positive, and Griffin, leaving a disabled gun behind, started for a point to the right of the Henry house in column of pieces. Porter, who saw

[1] Monroe, *Rhode Island Artillery*, 19. This points to defective organization in the matter of reserve artillery ammunition. The intervention of Governor Sprague is too characteristic to require comment.

[2] O. R. Ser. I, vol. II, 346; *Rep. Cond. War*, II, 143.

[3] *Rep. Cond. War*, II, 168; Griffin's evidence.

his brigade battery going forward, became very anxious when it started up the hillside ; after the action he began to reprimand Griffin until it was explained that he had acted by superior order.[1]

The order to Ricketts did not come through Barry, but was delivered by Lieutenant Kingsbury, McDowell's A.D.C. According to one rather doubtful witness McDowell himself rode up at this moment, and on Ricketts' querying : " By whose orders am I to go there ? " the general replied : " By mine, sir." [2] On this the battery moved forward, climbed the plateau, not without difficulty, went over the crest and unlimbered just beyond, a little to the left and in advance of Griffin. The two batteries were well sheltered by a depression of the ground, but were for the moment without support. McDowell, who was constantly changing position,[3] and therefore not keeping in close touch with his divisional commanders, went up the hill immediately after the batteries and climbed to the roof of the Henry house where he stayed for a few minutes studying the battlefield.[4] At his feet were the eleven powerful guns of Griffin and Ricketts firing rapidly, while in front and to his left, among the undulations and patches of pine and scrub, he could have seen nothing much beyond the

[1] *Rep. Cond. War*, II, 172; Griffin's evidence.
[2] Barrett, *What I saw at Bull Run*, 18.
[3] Barrett, *What I saw at Bull Run*, 18.
[4] Fry, *Battles and Leaders*, I, 188.

flash of Pendleton's guns replying vigorously. To his right the ground became denser and the hidden Confederate line was nearer and nearer as it stretched out towards the Manassas road, out of sight beyond the trees. It was there that the crisis of the battle was to arise, but McDowell could not guess it. Now let us turn to the infantry that was to make secure the risky position into which Griffin and Ricketts had been sent.

Willcox had already been ordered to push along the Manassas road and then to oblique up the slopes of the Henry house plateau to his left. Franklin followed Willcox, and his regiments were pushed up the hill to the left at intervals. Behind Griffin and a little to his left, the 11th New York took cover under the crest ; farther along, still under the crest, were other regiments, the 5th and 11th Massachusetts, the 14th New York, the Marines.

All this infantry came up rather badly and irregularly ; the supports forming from the left slowly towards the right ; but the batteries held their own, though with some difficulty, for about half an hour. Then, less than two hundred yards to the right of the guns, a body of infantry appeared which Griffin quickly decided to face and meet with canister ; but Barry at once declared that it was a supporting regiment and must not be fired on. There was much confusion all through the battle owing to the fact that there were some blue uniforms among the Confederates, while on the Federal side many regiments wore gray; with no wind stirring, the flags were mostly undistinguishable.

As a matter of fact it was Cumming's 33d Virginia that had advanced through the scrub and outflanked the Federal guns. Their colonel spoke to his men, brought them on a few more yards, and then poured in a terrible volley. "It seemed as though every man and horse of that battery just laid right down and died right off. . . . The destruction of the battery was so complete that the marines and zouaves seemed to be struck with such astonishment, such consternation, that they could not do anything." [1] What they did do, we shall see presently; but first it will be better to turn to the other sections of McDowell's line.

On the left Tyler, with Keyes' brigade, diverging steadily from Sherman and bearing towards Stone Bridge, came to the little height on which stood Van Pelt's house, six hundred yards from the stream and just north of the Warrenton road. This had been Evans' original position and it was still held by some small Confederate detachments that promptly opened fire. Keyes, with no guns to help him, made headway very slowly; but he succeeded in pushing his infantry up to the Van Pelt house. There, however, it at once came under fire of the Confederate guns farther back towards the Lewis house. Keyes thereupon obliqued rapidly to the left and

[1] *Rep. Cond. War*, II, 216; Averell's evidence.

got his troops under the wooded bank of Bull Run. Along this he now cautiously pushed his way towards Stone Bridge.[1]

Sherman bore away somewhat to the right, coming down the declivity from the Carter house to Young's Branch at the apex of the Henry house plateau. He formed the 13th New York in column by divisions, and behind it deployed his three other regiments in line. In this formation, apparently, he held on until he crossed Young's Branch and rose the hill, inclining still farther to the right and so reaching the Warrenton turnpike at its descent from the plateau westwards. Sherman says, and this seems to fix his position : " At the point where this road crossed the ridge to our left front, the ground was swept by a most severe fire of artillery, rifles, and musketry. . . ." [2] Sherman did not attempt, therefore, to maintain contact with Keyes, or even to gain the plateau at the apex where the Warrenton turnpike crossed it, but bore over towards McDowell and advanced from his shelter by once more inclining to the right in the direction of the Henry house, reaching the plateau well to the left of Ricketts' battery.

The situation may be described in a general way as follows : From where Sherman had brought his brigade

---

[1] There is a humorous contemporary account of this skirmish called *Wooden Nutmegs*, by " Frinkle Fry."

[2] O. R. Ser. I, vol. II, 369.

on the Warrenton turnpike to a point on the Manassas road seven hundred yards south of the crossroads, the whole attacking line of McDowell was concentrated within less than three quarters of a mile, with Griffin's and Ricketts' batteries thrown forward towards its centre, and the Rhode Island battery and Arnold's, — ordered up from Sudley Spring, — in support behind Young's Branch. Burnside's brigade was out of action ; Howard's was now coming up from the rear. Of Porter's, most remained on the north side of Young's Branch, the rest went forward to Sherman's right. Willcox and Franklin were farther to the right. The whole of this force was facing almost east. Beyond Sherman's left there was a gap a mile wide. For Keyes, as we have seen, was sheltering under the bank of Bull Run, while Schenck was still on the other side of Stone Bridge. The adjustment was bad and the reverse of what McDowell had contemplated.

It is difficult, really impossible, to give a co-ordinated and chronological account of McDowell's efforts to gain possession of the Henry house plateau. Clearly the first real attack was the throwing forward of Griffin's and Ricketts' batteries. For the rest it will be clearest, perhaps, neglecting for a while Keyes and Schenck at Stone Bridge, to follow the movement point by point from Sherman towards the right.

Sherman's attack consisted in a sending-up of his

regiments one at a time beyond the crest on to the plateau. The direction of this attack was from between the Robinson and Henry houses to about the centre or right of Jackson. Of Sherman's four strong regiments some did better than others, but none was firm enough to stand long against the musketry and grape that Jackson and the batteries to his right dealt out to them. One after the other was beaten and came back in disorder. After all four had been punished, and this consumed some time, Sherman succeeded in forming the remnants into a brigade line under shelter of the crest. But by this time the battle was nearly over, and there was no offensive vigor left in the troops.[1]

McDowell, on leaving the Henry house, appears to have been near Porter's brigade for a while, and was not far behind Sherman when that general advanced to the attack. Soon after this, and just before Griffin and Ricketts were disabled, he moved across to the Manassas road to supervise operations towards the right. He had already pushed forward in that direction the 14th and

---

[1] Sherman's attack was made on an order from McDowell delivered by Major Wadsworth, of his staff. What the terms of the order were is not known. The 13th New York was the first regiment sent up. Then followed the 2d Wisconsin, which succeeded in advancing some distance. It was driven back, re-formed, and driven back again, in much confusion, heightened by the fact that Sherman's other regiments fired into it, taking it for Confederate because of its gray uniform. The New York 79th, and then the New York 69th, were in turn sent in to continue this piecemeal attack.

27th New York and the battalion of marines, all from
Porter's brigade. The 1st Michigan was also reaching
the scene now from Sudley Spring, with Arnold's battery, which was left near the Dogan house and thence
fired over the hollow towards Jackson's left and centre.[1]

It was while McDowell was just below the plateau behind the guns that the fatal charge of the 33d Virginia
took place. The batteries, as we have seen, were put out
of action at a single volley. And now the struggle at
this point was to resolve itself into who should obtain
possession of the disabled guns. General Heintzelman
was on the spot and began a series of efforts to regain
control of the guns. First he got the zouaves over the
crest where the Virginians faced them at comparatively
short range, perhaps two hundred yards. The red-
trowsered New York firemen advanced twenty yards
and fired, as did their opponents, "and both parties
broke and ran." [2]

At the first fire they broke, and the greater portion fled to the rear,
keeping up a desultory firing over the heads of their comrades in front.
At the same moment they were charged by a company of Secession
cavalry on their rear. . . . I then led up the Minnesota regiment

[1] The position taken up by Arnold is difficult to fix. He says that he was
ordered up to the support of Ricketts and that he took position eight hundred yards from the enemy. Accepting his estimate of the distance, — for
an artillery officer should be a good witness on such a point, — this
suggests that from the Dogan house he was firing across at the space between Jackson's left and Ricketts' and Griffin's guns. O. R. Ser. I, vol. II,
416.

[2] *Rep. Cond. War.* II, 30; Heintzelman's evidence.

which was also repulsed, but retired in tolerably good order. . . . Next was led forward the 1st Michigan which was also repulsed and retired in considerable confusion.[1]

Then the 14th New York was brought up.

Soon after the firing commenced the regiment broke and ran — says Heintzelman.— The want of discipline in these regiments was so great that the most of the men would run from fifty to several hundred yards to the rear and continue to fire — fortunately for the braver ones very high in the air — compelling those in front to retreat. During this time Ricketts' battery had been taken and retaken three times by us, but was finally lost.[2]

As Heintzelman, like Sherman, used up his regiments one by one in his unavailing effort to recover the guns and to press on against the Confederate left, many of the men as they disbanded passed into the woods on the right along the Manassas road, where some of the troops, notably the 1st Michigan, rallied and did well; a considerable but confused struggle took place at that point which can be best related later from the Confederate side.

A great many of our regiments, — says an eyewitness, — turned right off the field as they delivered their fire, turning even as they delivered their volleys. They did not go off in any system at all, but went right off as a crowd would walking the street. . . .[3]

[1] O. R. Ser. I, vol. II, 403.

[2] O. R. Ser. I, vol. II, 403. Many claims are put forward in contemporary accounts that this or that regiment captured or re-captured the guns. They were certainly put out of action by the 33d Virginia, and after that were several times in the temporary possession of advancing Federals or advancing Confederates. They remained, however, where they had been unlimbered until the close of the action when, of course, they were in Confederate hands.

[3] *Rep. Cond. War.* II, 170; Griffin's evidence.

And in general they moved to the woods about the Manassas road and beyond it.

In the valley below, McDowell, Barry, and other officers struggled hard to rally the men, seized flags and bore them forward, and with little result.[1] Farther up the slope and to the right men were edging away from Jackson's front to the woods lying between the Henry house and the Chinn hill.

Franklin, meanwhile, with the 5th and 11th Massachusetts, a little to the left and nearer Sherman, was doing his best to drive these regiments up to the enemy. On several occasions he got them over the crest to deliver their fire, but they would not remain to protect or to drag away Ricketts' guns.[2] Their officers could do little with them.[3]

For two hours, more or less, this struggle continued. There was no wind, it was intensely hot, and the sulphurous smoke hung heavy on the ground. The exhaustion of the Northern troops was extreme. Thirsty, weary, and discouraged men were moving to the rear in increasing numbers. The turn of the tide had come, and the Confederates were now about to assume the offensive. While reinforcements were coming up on their

[1] *Rep. Cond. War*, II, 147; Barry's evidence.

[2] *Rep. Cond. War*, II, 34; Franklin's evidence.

[3] The regimental histories contain accounts that may, after careful comparison with the official reports, especially Franklin's, be dismissed as purely fantastic.

extreme left, Jackson's infantry advanced towards the Henry house "in large force with heavy and well-aimed volleys."[1] The Massachusetts regiments melted rapidly away. For a while the 1st Minnesota stood its ground; "friends and foes were for a time confounded";[2] and then presently it followed the general movement backwards.

Through a great stream of stragglers setting back from the battlefield towards Sudley Spring, panting from their forced marching, Howard's troops were just arriving. Instead of being used, as they should have been, to cover the retreat of what was clearly a defeated army, they were sent straight up the contested hill where the disabled Federal guns fatally drew every effort; McDowell went up with them.[3] It would appear that Howard did a little better than most of the brigade commanders. He succeeded in deploying two lines, the 4th Maine and 2d Vermont in the first, the 3d and 5th Maine in the second.

On rising the hill Howard met Lieutenant Kirby, "with his face covered with blood, on a horse that had

[1] Franklin's report, O. R. Ser. I, vol. II, 406.

[2] O. R. Ser. I, vol. II, 406.

[3] Fry, *Battles and Leaders*, I, 190. Bicknell (*Hist. of the 5th Maine*, 58) gives the following account of Howard's march: "Unaccustomed to such severe marches, suffering intensely from thirst and heat, pressed on at as rapid a rate as possible, our thinning ranks began to show the effects of overexertion. Men seemed to fall in squads by the roadside, some sunstruck, some bleeding at nose, mouth, ears."

been shot through the nose." [1] He was the only officer
not killed or disabled of Ricketts' battery, and was bringing off a caisson, all that was saved. The troops advanced into the fire zone, to find the Confederate infantry facing them within two hundred yards of the
crest. Howard claims that his men stood their ground
while they fired twenty to thirty rounds. He quickly
brought up the second line to strengthen the first. But
with no artillery, no supports, a victorious enemy to face,
and McDowell's army streaming away on all sides, it is
not surprising that before many minutes had passed his
brigade also broke up and joined the procession of
fugitives. And at that moment the Federal right was
already turned by the advance of two fresh Confederate
brigades, Kirby Smith's and Early's.

Napoleon once remarked to Chaptal : " After fighting
for six hours a soldier will seize on any pretext to quit, if
it can be done honorably ; and the appearance of a reserve is almost always a sufficient reason."

SOUTH

On the Confederate side we have to trace the phases
of a defensive action for the space of about two hours,
during which reinforcements were marching, to play an
important part when at last the moment came for taking
the offensive.

[1] O. R. Ser. I, vol. II, 418.

On the morning of the 21st, Stuart was stationed, with his three hundred sabres, between the Lewis house and Manassas; and it does not appear that he received any orders changing his position. Stuart, however, moved up to the Lewis house, possibly at the sound of the cannon of the first engagement, and there Johnston met him after he had left Beauregard in charge on the Henry house hill. Apparently Johnston first thought that he could take advantage of McDowell's overextension by attempting to counterattack him through Ball's Ford, coming out on the Warrenton turnpike midway between Centreville and Stone Bridge. But the pressure on the Henry house plateau was too great to allow of any counterstroke for the moment. Presently Johnston turned Stuart westward to cover the Confederate left, whence Jackson had already called for his assistance. On his way Stuart fell in with Beckham's battery of Johnston's corps, and kept it with him during his further movements. He reached the end of Jackson's line close to the Manassas road just as the 11th New York had exchanged volleys with the 33d Virginia, and he charged it in its retreat. A confused struggle ensued of which both sides claimed to have had the best. Stuart withdrew, however, and moved away farther still to the left.

Jackson's brigade, stiffened by Pendleton's strong battery and resolutely commanded, was standing the Federal shock well. The perfectly timed advance of the 33d

Virginia, which put the Federal batteries out of action, relieved the pressure immensely. Now that the guns were
silenced it was possible for Jackson to attempt the occasional advance of his infantry for a counterstroke, a
manœuvre he appears to have several times indulged
in.[1] But beyond Jackson the situation was more difficult.

To the left, as the Federals extended away from
Griffin's guns towards their right, the few weak units
that Bee at first ranged in line were hard put to it to
withstand the pressure of Heintzelman. Bee and Bartow
did their best to keep their men up to the work, and both
paid for it with their lives. The 4th Alabama melted
entirely away. The Georgians and Mississippians were
not much better off. The 18th Virginia was moved
around from the right, and only just succeeded in closing
up the gaps. Had the Federals been able to deploy a
whole brigade in line, instead of sending a succession
of regiments to the attack, or had they moved directly
along the Manassas road, they must have overlapped
and swept away the Confederate left.

On the right, Radford's cavalry, the 30th Virginia,
was early up in support, and Beauregard placed it in
reserve of his right, notwithstanding Jackson's demand
that it should be sent to him. But the 2d and 8th South
Carolina, of Bonham's brigade, with Kemper's two guns,
arriving at about 3.30 P.M., were thrown in at the critical

---

[1] This is a doubtful statement; but probabilities point that way.

point on the left and helped to continue the struggle. They soon found themselves engaged with a part of the New York zouaves that had rallied.

At the ravine Beauregard was in the thick of the fight, and had a horse killed under him. Yet the pressure here was on the whole far less severe. Alburtis' battery, with Walton's five guns and Heaton's section, made up a strong line of artillery on this wing; these pieces played mostly on Sherman's advance and swept the northern end of the plateau. Cocke's brigade was gradually sent in by Johnston, as we have seen. The 18th Virginia, which had been stationed in front of Ball's Ford, was withdrawn across the run at two o'clock, and about half an hour later was sent across to the left to help resist Heintzelman's attack; it reached there just in time to throw back the advance of the 14th New York. The 28th followed the 18th, arriving too late to take any very active part in the engagement.

As the battle progressed the pressure had become more marked on the Confederate left, less marked on the Confederate right. For east of Sherman the gap in the Federal line remained unfilled, and at Stone Bridge, Tyler, with Keyes' brigade, still hugged the bank of Bull Run, and Schenck remained a fixture beyond the bridge, while the guns from the Lewis house hill easily checked the Federals farther south. The general effect of this distribution of pressure was that the Confederate line tended to slue around until it faced almost due west.

From the Lewis house, Johnston could see in the direction of Manassas clouds of dust that indicated the advance of his reinforcements, of which Kirby Smith's and Early's brigades were to arrive in time to play a part in the battle. There was a momentary alarm on a false report — and false reports were continuous — that the approaching troops belonged to the enemy;[1] but this presently proved untrue, and Johnston, who realized how bad the situation was on his left, now rode across from the Lewis house to take his position behind the threatened point and to dispose the reinforcements to best advantage. It was time they arrived. General Bee had been killed early, and after him Colonel Bartow, Colonel Thomas, and Colonel Jones. The thinnest of lines remained, while the woods were full of Federal troops and an ever-increasing current of stragglers, just as with the Federals, was flowing away to the rear.

But the Federal line was spent and could not be reinforced with fresh troops, while Kirby Smith was just

---

[1] At 1.15 P.M. Alexander sent the following alarming message to headquarters from his observation post near the Junction: "Large reinforcements are pushing towards the enemy crossing Bull Run far above Stone Bridge. The column of dust . . . is going straight towards Manassas Junction. . . . Another column is visible in the far distance near Paris." Alexander, *Military Memoirs*, 41. He might almost have added that he could see General Patterson riding at the head of the column! As a matter of fact it was Johnston's baggage train arriving from the Shenandoah.

reaching the scene. His brigade had been detrained as rapidly as possible at Manassas Junction between twelve and one o'clock, and had then pushed along the Sudley Spring road. It reached the scene of action about half-past three, and Johnston personally directed its deployment to the left of the road and ordered Kirby Smith to advance towards Chinn's hill.

It is difficult to state what Federal troops were in position on McDowell's extreme right at this moment. Fractions of the regiments of Franklin, Willcox, and Porter, which Heintzelman had unsuccessfully sent up against the Confederate left, had been rallied below the crest and formed into a line extending farther westwards. There was a Federal line facing Kirby Smith as he deployed, but it offered little resistance, though the first shots fired resulted in his being severely wounded and handing over the command to Colonel Elzey. That officer continued to advance steadily through the woods on the left of the road pushing back such bodies of Federals as appeared in his front.

Meanwhile Early had come up, first to the Lewis house, then along the rear of the fighting line, picking up the 19th Virginia of Cocke's brigade, and moving towards the Manassas road. Johnston directed him to cross that road behind Kirby Smith and to deploy farther to the left in the pastures of the Chinn farm. Early soon established contact with Elzey's advance, while beyond him he found Stuart and Beckham. As Elzey and then Early came into action, Stuart shifted farther along until he found a good position for Beckham's battery, and opened fire in reverse on McDowell's right.

It was just previously to this that Jackson assumed the offensive. To his left the Confederate battalions were nearly spent. He judged that the crisis of the battle was reached and that a strong push might drive either side off the field. He ordered the 4th and 27th Virginia to charge. With loud yells — Ha ! ha ! ha ! ha ! — the Confederates advanced. Wade Hampton and the 5th Virginia on the right moved towards Ricketts' and Griffin's guns. Beauregard sent orders for all the troops to come forward. And before this movement the Federals at last broke up. Howard staved off defeat for a few minutes. Sykes' battalion of regulars came bravely and steadily up among the broken regiments towards Chinn's hill, where the 1st Michigan and other troops were still holding on under Willcox.[1] But nothing now could serve to rally the broken army, and all Sykes could do was to retard the advance of Elzey and Early, while Stuart and Beckham continued to overlap his flank and to force him back.

McDowell and his officers made desperate efforts to

---

[1] Willcox had his horse shot under him; then his arm was wounded, his A.D.C., Captain Withington, being killed as he was binding it up. Finally he was captured with a small party of the 1st Michigan.

re-establish their broken line beyond Young's Branch between the Dogan house and the Carter house. But Pendleton galloped his guns to the northern edge of the Henry house plateau whence he opened a brisk fire, and the two fresh brigades with Stuart's cavalry kept steadily pushing up towards Sudley Spring. The Federals drew off a few of their guns ; a few regiments attempted to re-form north of Young's Branch, but soon broke ; Sykes, however, kept his formation and left the field in good order with the support of Arnold's battery, which helped to cover the retreat. The defeated troops moved at a walk — for there was apparently little or no running — towards the fords, some for Poplar Ford, others for Sudley Spring. From these points they made their way along the road they had travelled in the morning, or across country, circling around to the Warrenton turnpike at points near Centreville. McDowell hurried around to Stone Bridge in time to give orders for saving Tyler's thirty-pounder.[1] Sherman, some minutes later, found the Confederate cavalry already near Cub Run bridge and had to turn back and make a detour around to the north.

As soon as Johnston judged that McDowell was beaten, he sent orders for Radford with the 30th Virginia Cavalry to cross at Ball's Ford and strike the retreating enemy on the Warrenton road near Cub Run. Kershaw, with Bonham's two regiments and Kemper's

[1] Hains, "The First Gun at Bull Run," *Cosmopolitan*, August, 1911.

guns, had arrived so late on the Henry house plateau as to be very lightly engaged. Still ready for action he moved [1] to near the Robinson house, whence, under Jackson's orders, Kemper shelled the retreating troops towards Stone Bridge. He then resumed the advance, with Kershaw's infantry, towards Stone Bridge, found the abatis cut through, and continued along the Warrenton turnpike. He reached the rise above Cub Run about half an hour later than Radford, say at about six, and there saw immediately before him a stream of Federals pouring along the Sudley Spring road and turning into the Warrenton turnpike. He promptly shelled them, sending the stream of fugitives back north, to find their way through the fields and woods around to Centreville. There had already been a stampede along the Warrenton turnpike between Stone Bridge and Cub Run bridge. The attack of Radford, followed by that of Kershaw, continued this stampede along towards Centreville. But Radford was weak in numbers and not overbold. Kershaw was held up by orders from Beauregard first to use caution, and later to stop the pursuit.[2] This attack, however, following Radford's, created a jam on Cub Run bridge, which broke down, thus preventing the Federals

---

[1] "During the action . . . Kershaw received no orders and saw none of our generals, but fought it out on his own plan. . . ." Charleston *Mercury*, July 29.

[2] First order carried by Alexander, "to advance very carefully and not to attack"; second order by Ferguson. Alexander, *Military Memoirs*, 45.

from drawing off the guns that had reached this point. The unfortunate thirty-pounder stuck in the ford.

THE FEDERALS AT STONE BRIDGE

We have neglected, so far, to follow out the not very important movements of Keyes and of Schenck immediately preceding the break-up of McDowell's army.

At Stone Bridge, Captain Alexander, of McDowell's staff, succeeded in clearing a way through the abatis at about the moment when, over a mile to the west, Howard was nearing the scene of action. Tyler was on the west bank near the bridge; just south of him was Keyes skirmishing with the enemy; and to the east, across Bull Run, Schenck still lay. At this moment the prospect was none too reassuring. Keyes' position was false and dangerous, and the farther he advanced the more he widened the gap between Sherman and himself. However urgent it might be to establish a connection with McDowell along the Warrenton turnpike, it looked a risky step to order Schenck across for that purpose. And so Tyler, instead of acting as a connecting link and instead of creating a useful diversion, simply remained inactive and awaited developments. He did not have to wait long.

Already Tyler could see to the west of him streams of disbanded men crossing Young's Branch and going back up the slopes to the north. Some of these, though probably a small proportion only, worked their way around to the Warrenton turnpike so as to cross Bull Run at Stone Bridge. Presently their numbers began to increase rapidly, and it became clear that McDowell was in full retreat. Tyler now ordered Keyes back to the bridge, crossing himself to look after Schenck.

Apparently it never occurred to Tyler or to his subordinates that, with the main part of the defeated army retreating by the fords above Stone Bridge, it was their business to attempt to hold that point so as to protect the retreat and form a screen behind which the disbanded troops might reach Centreville. As it was, Schenck apparently ordered his brigade back to Centreville without awaiting orders as soon as he perceived the symptoms of retreat, and Tyler ordered back such guns as he happened to see. But before the retirement could be effected, the Confederates were on them.

Jackson had promptly ordered Kemper's battery to the apex of the Henry house hill, whence he opened fire along the turnpike eastward. Other guns joined in from near the Lewis house, including Walker's rifled pieces of Holmes' brigade which had just come up. Radford's cavalry, moving with great rapidity, soon struck Schenck in flank near Cub Run bridge. Although Schenck, deploying two companies of the 2d Ohio, for the moment held Radford back, yet he did not retain the position, but, unmindful of the troops in his rear, continued the retreat, which rapidly became disordered, to Centreville.

Radford's attack, together with the searching of the turnpike by the Confederate shells, resulted in a stampede. In this were involved Schenck's brigade, Keyes' brigade, a number of fugitives from Sherman, and other troops that had crossed Bull Run close to Stone Bridge or that had moved very fast around from Sudley Spring, and, together with these, troops, civilians, sight-seers, transport wagons, politicians, and journalists. The panic spurred them the whole four miles from Stone Bridge to Centreville, notwithstanding the utmost efforts made by a few brave men to stop the rout, among whom must be specially mentioned Captain Alexander, Colonel Speidel, and the Hon. Elihu Washburne.[1]

This rout of a fraction of McDowell's forces along the road from Stone Bridge to Centreville was far less excusable than the breaking-up of Heintzelman's and Porter's troops. The latter had accomplished a very hard day's work and had for some time faced a hot fire, while the losses and labors of Schenck and Keyes had been comparatively light. The stampede brought out, inevitably, the worst side of human nature. The newspapers, so indulgent for the logrolling, moral cowardice and ineptitude of politicians, were severe enough on the

[1] Of Illinois, afterwards Minister to France. New York *World*, July the 23d.

demoralized mob of exhausted, undisciplined men, who were after all merely seeking safety by the only obvious method they knew. "All sense of manhood," said the New York *Tribune*, "seemed to be forgotten . . . the sentiment of shame had gone. . . . All was lost to the American army even its honor."[1] Leaving rhetoric and coming to fact, it does not appear that the rout was marked by much loss of life, but the jam at the bridge at Cub Run prevented the escape of the Rhode Island guns, together with those of Arnold and Carlisle.[2]

[1] July the 26th.

[2] The number of guns lost at this point is variously stated and impossible to fix. Probably four of Carlisle's, the thirty-pounder Parrott, five of the Rhode Island battery and four of Arnold's were in the number. It is possible, though unlikely, that one or two of Griffin's and Ricketts' guns were got back as far as this, and the same remark applies to the howitzers of the 71st New York. The loss at this point may fairly be put down at fourteen guns, and possibly one or two more.

X

AT CENTREVILLE, AND BACK TO WASHINGTON

NORTH

WE left Davies and Richardson keeping up a mild cannonade from the height near Blackburn's Ford, with Blenker behind them, snugly ensconced in Centreville. At about half-past ten or eleven, under the direction of Lieutenant Prime, of the Engineers, acting under instructions from McDowell, intrenchments and abatis were begun, and the Confederates, as we have seen, concluded from this that no offensive was to be looked for at this point.

Until four o'clock nothing of moment occurred. Then came a Confederate movement in the hollow on Davies' front, which was greeted with a prolonged fire of artillery from Hunt's and Edwards' guns under which the enemy retired without effecting anything; Davies suffering no losses. It was at about the same time that the first information was reaching General Miles at Centreville that things were not progressing as they should beyond Stone Bridge.

It is not possible to identify which was the first message Miles received. But the written documents that have been preserved, telling part of the story, are perhaps worth setting out. They may tentatively be fixed as having been sent from a little before 4 P.M. until 5.45. Here, then, is a telegraphic dispatch of Miles to Washington sent off from Centreville, on receiving a note from McDowell's chief of staff, sent from the field: —

COLONEL TOWNSEND: —

Captain Fry writes to me to say — Telegraph to Washington: — *Send on immediately all the troops that can be spared.* — Colonel Hunter has just arrived badly wounded.

D. S. MILES, Colonel.[1]

Immediately afterwards followed another dispatch : —

CENTREVILLE, July 21 — 4 P.M.

ADJUTANT-GENERAL THOMAS: —

General McDowell wishes all the troops that can be sent to come here without delay. He has ordered the reserve now here under Colonel Miles to advance to the bridge over Bull Run, on the Warrenton road, having driven the enemy before him. Colonel Miles is now about three or four miles from here directing the operations near Blackburn's Ford, and in his absence I communicate.

G. H. MENDELL. . . .

McDowell's order was, in fact, that one of Miles' brigades should be moved to the junction of the Warrenton and Sudley Spring roads, just beyond the Cub Run bridge, to protect the retreat by covering that point;[2] this order was entirely reasonable, but could not have been executed even had Miles made the attempt owing to the stream of fugitives that already blocked the turn-

---

[1] O. R. Ser. I, vol. II, 747. According to Barnard, Fry's note to Miles was written on his own responsibility.

[2] McDowell's report, O. R. Ser. I, vol. II, 321.

pike and made any advance in the opposite direction impossible. Miles did issue an order, which was delivered by Lieutenant Prime, for Blenker's brigade to move to Stone Bridge; but Blenker did not get more than half a mile west of Centreville.[1]

McDowell left the field about 4.40 P.M., and reached Centreville an hour later. We find him at 5.45 P.M., telegraphing as follows to Colonel Townsend at Washington : —

CENTREVILLE, July 21, 1861 — 5.45 P.M.

We passed Bull Run. Engaged the enemy, who, it seems, had just been reinforced by General Johnston. We drove them for several hours, and finally routed them. They rallied and repulsed us, but only to give us again the victory, which seemed complete. But our men, exhausted with fatigue and thirst and confused by firing into each other, were attacked by the enemy's reserves, and driven from the position which we had gained, overlooking Manassas. After this the men could not be rallied, but slowly left the field. In the meantime the enemy outflanked Richardson at Blackburn's Ford, and we have now to hold Centreville till our men can get behind it. Miles' division is holding the town. It is reported Colonel Cameron is killed, Hunter and Heintzelman wounded, neither dangerously.[2]

Miles, meanwhile, had after a fashion been attempting to carry out orders. He had brought Blenker's brigade from the east to the west of Centreville, where it deployed across the Warrenton turnpike. He then galloped to the brigades at the south end of the ridge. Without reflection as to any offensive movement the Confederates might

[1] Prime's report, O. R. Ser. I, vol. II, 335.
[2] O. R. Ser. I, vol. II, 316.

attempt from Blackburn's or Mitchell's Ford, he ordered
Richardson and Davies to march in to Centreville at
once, thus leaving the enemy an opportunity of striking
at the army's line of retreat. Galloping here and there,
confused and irregular in his instructions, he soon came
into open conflict with his subordinates. The fact was
that Miles was drunk. Richardson's account of the incident runs as follows: —

> I . . . found this regiment [3d Michigan] deployed in line of battle
> and in another position. I inquired of Colonel Stevens the reason
> of their position being altered. He told me that Colonel Miles had
> directed this movement. I asked him why. Colonel Stevens replied —
> "I do not know, but we have no confidence in Colonel Miles." — I in-
> quired the reason, and Colonel Stevens replied, — "Because Colonel
> Miles is drunk." — That closed the conversation. . . . I then reported
> to Captain Alexander . . . that I could not carry out General Mc-
> Dowell's orders as long as I was interfered with by a drunken man.[1]

McDowell had now reached Centreville, as we have
seen, and was much alarmed to find that Miles had
withdrawn the two brigades from the fords. He rode
up to Richardson and exclaimed: "Great God, Colonel
Richardson, why did n't you hold on to the position at
Blackburn's Ford?"[2]

McDowell worked desperately to rally the troops. At
first he appears to have hoped that he might establish
the army at Centreville. But Tyler had done nothing to

[1] O. R. Ser. I, vol. II, 376. His evidence before the Congressional Committee is even more specific, and was supported by that of other officers.

[2] *Rep. Cond. War*, II, 26; Richardson's evidence.

cover the Warrenton turnpike; panic prevailed from Stone Bridge to Centreville, and even beyond; and it was clear that the most that could be hoped for was to protect some part of the army during its retreat. Miles was relieved from command; McDowell assumed direct control of the brigades at Centreville, and personally placed Richardson's in position across the ridge south of the village to meet any possible advance of the Confederates.[1]

By half-past seven the stream of fugitives had passed through Centreville, where Blenker, Richardson, and Davies, together with three regiments that had come up from Runyon,[2] stood awaiting an attack.

There was now no alternative for McDowell: he could only order a retreat back to Washington. His own report states:—

The condition of our artillery and its ammunition, and the want of food for the men who had generally abandoned or thrown away all that had been issued the day before, and the utter disorganization and consequent demoralization of the mass of the army, seemed to all who were near enough to be consulted, division and brigade commanders and staff, to admit of no alternative but to fall back.

He left for Fairfax Court House in the course of the evening, and from there wrote to Townsend the two following dispatches:—

---

[1] Richardson, on a narrow front, formed a double line, placing regiments ployed in column of divisions closed in mass, in the intervals of the deployed regiments of the first line.

[2] 1st and 2d New Jersey, that had passed through Vienna, and the de Kalb regiment.

FAIRFAX COURT HOUSE, July 21, 1861.

The men having thrown away their haversacks in the battle and left them behind, they are without food; have eaten nothing since breakfast. We are without artillery ammunition. The larger part of the men are a confused mob, entirely demoralized. It was the opinion of all the commanders that no stand could be made this side of the Potomac. We will, however, make the attempt at Fairfax Court House. From a prisoner we learn that 20,000 from Johnston joined last night, and they march on us to-night.

IRVIN McDOWELL.

A few hours later he wrote : —

Many of the volunteers did not wait for authority to proceed to the Potomac, but left on their own decision. They are now pouring through this place in a state of utter disorganization. They could not be prepared for action by to-morrow morning even were they willing. I learn from prisoners that we are to be pressed here to-night and to-morrow morning, as the enemy's force is very large and they are elated. I think we heard cannon on our rear guard. I think now, as all of my commanders thought at Centreville, there is no alternative but to fall back to the Potomac, and I shall proceed to do so with as much regularity as possible.

IRVIN McDOWELL.[1]

The retirement was, in fact, continuous from the Henry house plateau back to the Potomac, and no efforts of any general could have stayed it. Richardson's brigade, bringing up the rear, left Centreville at 2.30 in the morning of the 22d, and that night all of the Federal troops were back in the positions from which they had started on the 16th.

Before dealing with the army's losses and attempting

[1] O. R. Ser. I, vol. II, 316.

a critique of its operations, we must return to the Confederate side and trace the movements of the victorious army, and especially of its right wing which we have lost sight of since the morning.

SOUTH

Let us turn to the right wing and see what happened to Ewell's, Longstreet's, Bonham's, and Jones' brigades, while the battle on the Henry house plateau was raging.

Twice in the course of the morning had Ewell taken his brigade over Bull Run at Union Mills Ford, each time to be recalled. On his second return, as previously stated, he was ordered to the support of the left.

There appears to have been considerable delay about the delivery of this order, and for the rest it is as well to give Ewell's own account: —

I deem it proper to state that the courier said he had been accompanied by an aide-de-camp whose horse had given out before reaching me. I countermarched and marched at once to headquarters in the field, remained in reserve at that point until ordered back to Union Mills, which I reached after a long and fatiguing march that same night.[1]

This statement is a little difficult to interpret, but it would seem that by "headquarters in the field" Ewell meant Johnston's actual position during most of the afternoon, near the Lewis house. Ewell reached that point between 5 and 6 P.M., after Holmes' brigade; he was ordered back to Union Mills Ford, nearly at once,

[1] O. R. Ser. I, vol. II, 537.

on a false report of a Federal counterstroke at Blackburn's Ford, having played no part in the operations.

We left Bonham's brigade at Mitchell's Ford, just as Kemper's battery and two regiments of infantry were being detached from it towards the left under Kershaw. From that moment till nearly five o'clock in the afternoon Bonham remained under cover within his lines at Mitchell's Ford where Richardson's guns kept him under an intermittent but harmless fire. Farther downstream Longstreet crossed and recrossed Blackburn's Ford four times in the course of the day, as conflicting instructions reached him. He received orders from Johnston about five, as did Bonham, to advance on Centreville and intercept the retreating Federals.

From about three o'clock of the afternoon Johnston had last assumed the functions of general-in-chief. From that moment he in fact directed the Confederate army, although its deficient organization largely neutralized his action. We have seen his move to the left wing and his disposition of Kirby Smith and Early on that wing as they arrived just in time to play an effective part. As soon as Johnston was assured of victory he appears to have returned to the Lewis house, directing Radford to move over Ball's Ford towards the Warrenton turnpike and sending orders to Bonham and Longstreet to strike at Centreville.

This last order was feebly executed; Bonham in particular showing extreme timidity. Advancing at the very instant when Miles' ill-judged retirement gave the Confederates a splendid opportunity of seizing the ridge and pressing right in on Centreville, Bonham, and in less degree Longstreet, felt their way so slowly that McDowell had time to rectify Miles' mistake and to deploy Richardson across the ridge while the Confederates were still a mile or more from the village. Bonham was to the left, Longstreet to the right; it was now past seven; their artillery was just in position; they were within cannon shot of Centreville, and about to launch their attack. In plain sight, along the turnpike, the routed troops were still pouring. But at this juncture Bonham's courage oozed out, and, unfortunately for the Confederates, he was the senior officer.

As the guns were about to open, — says Longstreet, — there came a message that the enemy instead of being in a precipitate retreat was marching around to attack the Confederate right. With this report came orders, or reports of orders, for the brigades to return to their positions behind the Run. I denounced the report as absurd, claimed to know a retreat such as was before me, and ordered that the batteries open fire, when Major Whiting, of General Johnston's staff, rising in his stirrups, said:

— "in the name of General Johnston I order that the batteries shall not open." —

I inquired, — "Did General Johnston send you to communicate that order?" —

Whiting replied, — "No; but I take the responsibility to give it.—"

I claimed the privilege of responsibility under the circumstances, and when in the act of renewing the order to fire, General Bonham rode to my side and asked that the batteries should not open. As the ranking officer present this settled the question.[1]

Even if we discount Longstreet's statement, it is evident that the Confederates had a wonderful opportunity to strike the retreating army a heavy flank blow at Centreville. But just as Miles had blundered in withdrawing Richardson and Davies, so did the Confederates blunder in not pushing in vigorously when their opponents had presented them with such an opportunity. Even so, when Bonham at last was ready to open fire, it was probably too late to effect anything, as the bulk of the retreating troops had already filed through the village. Presently, with darkness coming on, Bonham decided he must go back to Bull Run to water his troops, and so the Confederates marched down the hill again, having accomplished nothing.

Beyond Longstreet, at McLean's Ford, was the brigade of D. R. Jones, whose crossings and recrossings of Bull Run we have already followed up to the moment when, late in the forenoon, an order was once more sent that he should cross Bull Run and advance towards the Centreville ridge, connecting on his left with Longstreet and on his right with Ewell; this order probably reached Jones between twelve and one.

I recrossed the ford, — says Jones, — my men much fatigued by the morning's march, many just convalescing from the measles, and re-

[1] Longstreet, *From Manassas to Appomattox*, 52. See also Johnston's *Narrative*, 53.

traced my route to the position I had occupied in the morning, and thence endeavored to communicate with General Ewell.[1]

By this time, however, Ewell was toiling westwards towards Stone Bridge, a fact of which, in the absence of a divisional staff to co-ordinate the movements of these brigades, Jones knew nothing. He appears to have spent some time attempting to link up on either side; finally he decided to push on by himself. Taking no measures for locating the enemy, he came out under the ridge close to where Davies' brigade was posted at about four o'clock and was received by a galling fire of artillery. His regiments, except the 5th North Carolina, were broken, and finding no support at hand, he decided to fall back towards McLean's Ford. Jones took no further part in the operations.

When Bonham and Whiting had overruled Longstreet and fallen back from in front of Centreville, they had imagined that the mass of men they could see in the distance moving along the Warrenton road represented not a rout but a strong column advancing — backwards — to attack the Confederate centre; this intelligence they sent back to Johnston. Two brigades not yet in action, Holmes' and Ewell's, were then just coming to hand at the Lewis house, and might well have been employed in pressing after the enemy along the Warrenton road, together with Kershaw. Johnston, however, accepted Bonham's report at its face value and grossly misjudged

[1] O. R. Ser. I, vol. II, 538.

the situation. He at once ordered Ewell, as we have seen, back to Union Mills Ford. Walker's battery of Holmes' brigade arrived in time to unlimber and send a few shells after the fugitives along the pike; but the infantry was held back near Ball's Ford.

Farther to the left pursuit was not practicable. Stuart, with less than three hundred sabres, did all that so small a force could accomplish, and kept up the chase to a point a mile or two beyond Sudley Spring.

I followed with the cavalry, — he says, — as rapidly as possible, but was so much encumbered with prisoners, whom I sent back as fast as possible to the infantry, that my command was soon too much reduced to encounter any odds, but I nevertheless followed our success until I reached a point twelve miles from Manassas, when, by sending back so many detachments with prisoners, I had but a squad left. The rear of the enemy was protected by a squadron of cavalry and some artillery. We cut off a great many squads, many of whom fired on us as we approached. . . . I have no idea how many prisoners were taken.[1]

Of the infantry brigades Early's seems to have marched farthest in pursuit; at nightfall it bivouacked at a point between the Carter house and Sudley Spring. Behind, at the Henry house plateau, lay the bulk of the victorious troops, exhausted, confused, disorganized; many of the regiments had lost all formation. Jackson was given general command of all infantry and artillery at this point, but did not, in fact could not, make any attempt at pursuit. On the Warrenton road there was only Radford to press the retreating Federals, Kershaw

[1] O. R. Ser. I, vol. II, 483.

having been held back by Beauregard, and when, after his first check, he eventually moved towards Centreville after sundown, a volley or two from Blenker's troops sent him back again.

Summing up what the Confederates did, then, in the way of an immediate counter-attack and pursuit of their defeated opponents, it may be said that towards Sudley Spring, Stuart and Early did about all that could be done; towards Stone Bridge, the Confederates were too far spent and in confusion to accomplish much; towards Centreville, they failed very badly, and that mostly for lack of organization and proper staff work.

Immediate pursuit, however, was not the only question. Should the victorious army follow up its success on the morrow? That was the anxious problem that the Confederate leaders had to solve on the night of the battle.

As the last shots were being fired, Jefferson Davis reached Manassas Junction, and thence rode to the battlefield.[1] He remained at headquarters until the morning of the 23d, but it does not appear that he interfered in any way with Johnston's decisions. The latter says, referring to the clamor of the Southern press against him for not following up his success : —

My failure to capture Washington received strong and general condemnation. Many erroneously attributed it to the President's prohibition; but he gave no orders, and expressed neither wish nor opinion

[1] Johnston's statement is specific and entirely credible, as to the battle being over when Davis reached the field. *Narrative*, 54.

on the subject that ever came to my knowledge. Considering the rela-
tive strength of the belligerents on the field the Southern people could
not reasonably have expected greater results from their victory. . . .
All the military conditions we knew forbade an attempt on Washington. The Confederate army was more disorganized by victory than
that of the United States by defeat. . . . Many [volunteers] in ignorance of their army obligations left the army. . . . Besides this the
reasons for the course condemned by the non-combatant military
critics were: —

The unfitness of our raw troops for marching or assailing intrenchments.

The want of the necessary supplies of food and ammunition and
means of transporting them. Until near the 10th of August we never
had rations for more than two days, and sometimes none; nor half
enough ammunition for a battle.

The fortifications upon which skilful engineers . . . had been engaged
since April, manned by at least fifty thousand Federal troops . . .

The Potomac, a mile wide, bearing United States vessels-of-war, the
heavy guns of which commanded the wooden bridges and southern
shore.[1]

There is only one possible answer to Johnston's argument. It is true that his army lacked numbers, cohesion,
mobility, organization, food, and ammunition. But his
opponents, though better off in some respects, were worse
off in others, while a moral difference had been established between the two armies which to the mind of
one of the Confederate commanders might be decisively
increased by a bold offensive — "Give me ten thousand
fresh troops and I would be in Washington to-morrow,"
Stonewall Jackson is reported to have said on the night
of the battle.

[1] Johnston, *Narrative*, 59-61.

That Jackson said this, or that there was even a remote chance of success for a direct advance on Washington, may be doubted. If he did say it, one may surmise that he meant ten thousand well-supplied, well-organized, and well-commanded troops, which would rob his utterance of any immediate significance. Taking the Confederate army as it actually was, it could not have accomplished the march within twenty-four hours, especially as a heavy rainstorm came on that night. Nor had it sufficient weight of artillery to force a crossing of the Potomac against even a half-hearted resistance. The real question is whether an advance through Leesburg and Frederick, or, aiming at Patterson, through Harper's Ferry into Maryland, might not have succeeded. A move towards Baltimore might have led to the abandonment of Washington and the placing of the Confederate boundary along the Maryland–Pennsylvania line. This is the only case that seems arguable ; but even that does not seem strong. The verdict must be, without qualification, that Johnston was right in his decision, — and that the Confederate army was not fit to take up the offensive.

There was a midnight conference at Beauregard's headquarters between the two generals and the President of the Confederate States. None would take the responsibility of an advance on Washington. Presently a report came in. One of Beauregard's staff had reached Centreville, which was deserted. On this Davis drew up an instruction ordering a pursuit; but before he had finished, it came out that the officer was a well-known character known as "Crazy" Hill. Everything looked too uncertain; everybody was exhausted; sheets of rain were falling; and Davis reluctantly decided that all had been done that could be done.[1]

[1] Davis, *Rise and Fall of the Confederacy,* 352; Roman, *Beauregard,* 114.

XI

STATISTICS

NORTH

McDowell's official report shows a total of 481 killed, 1011 wounded, and 1216 missing for the battle of Bull Run;[1] but these figures require some correction and,

[1] O. R. Ser. I, vol. II, 327.

	Killed		Wounded		Missing		Remarks
	Officers	Enlisted men	Officers	Enlisted men	Officers	Enlisted men	
General Staff....................	1	—	—	—	—	—	
First Division, General Tyler.....	—	—	—	—	—.	—	
First Brigade, Colonel Keyes...	—	19	4	46	5	149	Eighteen others slightly wounded.
Second Brigade, General Schenck	3	16	—	15	1	15	
Third Brigade, Colonel Sherman	3	117	15	193	13	240	
Fourth Brigade, Colonel Richardson....................	—	—	—	—	—	—	Not engaged; guarding Blackburn's Ford.
Total, First Division........	6	152	19	254	19	404	
Second Division, Colonel Hunter..	—	—	—	—	—	—	
First Brigade, Colonel Porter...	1	83	9	139	9	236	Four surgeons missing.
Second Brigade, Colonel Burnside.....................	5	35	3	85	2	59	Five surgeons missing.
Total, Second Division......	6	118	12	224	11	295	
Third Division, Colonel Heintzelman, Division Headquarters..	—	—	1	—	—	—	
First Brigade, Colonel Franklin.	3	68	13	183	4	22	
Second Brigade, Colonel Willcox	1	70	11	161	—	186	
Third Brigade, Colonel Howard	2	48	7	108	6	174	
Total, Third Division.......	6	186	32	452	10	382	

even corrected, cannot be made to tally altogether
with those of the Confederates. By comparing Mc-
Dowell's reports with those of his subordinates[1] the
corrected number would be 491 killed, 1072 wounded,

	Killed		Wounded		Missing		Remarks
	Officers	Enlisted men	Officers	Enlisted men	Officers	Enlisted men	
Fourth Division, General Runyon	—	—	—	—	—	—	In reserve on the Potomac.
Fifth Division, Colonel Miles.....	—	—	—	—	—	—	
First Brigade, Colonel Blenker.	—	6	—	16	—	94	
Second Brigade, Colonel Davies.	—	—	1	1	—	1	
Total, Fifth Division........	—	6	1	17	—	95	
Grand Total...........	19	462	64	947	40	1176	

JAMES A. FRY,
Assistant Adjutant-General.

[1] In Schenck's brigade the losses of the 1st and 2d Ohio in killed and
wounded are apparently omitted, adding 2 killed and 6 wounded to the
total; while in the 2d New York, a very poor and demoralized regiment,
the missing should apparently be 141. In Sherman's, 11 reported "killed
and missing" from the 2d U.S. Artillery, Company E, and 1 killed from
Company M, are omitted from the total, and for statistical purposes will be
averaged as 6 killed, 6 missing (for these two brigades see the official reports
of Tyler's division). In Porter's brigade, the aggregates in the divisional
returns give 80 killed, 174 wounded, and 228 missing; which gives 4 less
killed, 26 more wounded, and 8 less missing; while in Burnside's, the differences are 10 more killed, 35 more wounded, 62 more missing, but with
no report from the 71st New York. In Franklin's brigade, according to
Heintzelman's report, the variations are 4 less killed, 7 less wounded, 72
more missing; in Willcox's, 10 officers missing do not figure in McDowell's
report; in Howard's, 1 more wounded and 342 more missing have to
be added. In Miles' division, 2 more missing must be added. The sum
of these differences would add 10 killed, 61 wounded and 624 missing to
McDowell's total, without any allowance for missing returns.

and 1040 missing, with some returns actually lacking. This difference in reality amounts to little. Allowing for slight variations and errors, it may be said that some of the missing should presumably figure as dead, so that it would be quite safe to say that the loss in that respect was something over 500. The number of missing is, on the other hand, more properly to be reduced than increased, were it not for the prisoners claimed by the Confederates. For there was little chance of actual desertion until the men could get to Washington; and some of the regimental returns were made so soon after the battle that the men had not yet had time to return to their colors.[1] The discrepancy as to missing arises from lack of or from incomplete returns. Summing up, then, it is safe to say that McDowell lost about 500 killed, 1000 wounded, and between 1500 and 1800 missing.

The distribution of these losses is of much interest.

Several brigades were virtually not in action. At Blackburn's Ford, Davies reported only two wounded, and Richardson no casualties at all.[2] Blenker, at Centreville, or on the retreat, had only 6 killed and 16 wounded, but missed 94 men. In other words, the three brigades near Centreville were practically not under fire.

---

[1] A very suggestive report on this question of the missing is that of Major Reynolds, commanding the Marine battalion. O. R. Ser. 1, vol. II, 392.

[2] It is possible that this is owing to an omission; yet the loss, if any, must have been trifling.

At Stone Bridge Schenck reported 21 killed and 21 wounded, the latter figure being apparently incomplete; 19 of the killed were in the 2d New York, and this represents a demonstration made in the morning, about eleven o'clock, toward Lewis' Ford that was checked by the Confederate artillery beyond Bull Run. The 1st and 2d Ohio each had only one man killed, from which it may be fairly inferred that their deployment to check Radford's advance on the Cub Run bridge was not a very serious affair, and that they were quickly on the way to Centreville again. On the whole Schenck's brigade saw hardly any fighting.

Keyes did little more. The 2d Maine was in the lead when the Van Pelt house was taken, and lost 13 killed. The 1st, 2d, and 3d Connecticut together had 6 killed as their total for the day. They proved adepts at taking cover.

The six brigades that fought on the Sudley Spring road and the Henry house hill were, in fact, the only part of McDowell's army seriously engaged, and even among these considerable variations will be found. So far as statistics go, it was Sherman's brigade that did the hardest fighting; and in that brigade the 13th New York suffered appreciably less than the others. The 69th and 79th New York, two very strong regiments, had respectively 38 and 32 killed, with 59 and 51 wounded. The 69th is stated to have gone into action 1000 strong; assuming 900 to have been present when it deployed on

the Henry house plateau, its loss in killed and wounded
would be nearly 11 per cent; the 79th may be placed on a
similar level, and the 2d Wisconsin not very far behind.

In Burnside's brigade of Hunter's division, the report
of the 71st New York, a poor regiment that seems to
have broken up completely, is missing. The three other
regiments had 9, 13, and 24 killed. We may assume
that these losses were mostly sustained in the attack on
Evans, and in any case the impression is strengthened
that this brigade would have done little but for the artillery support which it received. The 2d Rhode Island
had decidedly the best record, most killed and wounded,
least missing. In Porter's brigade, the 14th (Brooklyn)
and 27th New York incurred the heaviest losses. Sykes'
battalion of regulars, which retired steadily and in good
order from the field, had only 10 killed and 20 wounded;
so that it is not its well-ordered retirement that gives
cause for surprise, but rather that it was not better employed. Who knows that the superior discipline of this
regiment, with its complement of regular officers, would
not have pierced the Confederate line where the Zouaves
or the Highlanders failed? Save for the steadying of
Burnside's line at a critical moment in the morning, the
Federal commanders failed to turn to advantage their
one valuable unit of infantry. The marines were raw recruits, enlisted on the 1st of July[1] and they made no better

---

[1] They should never have been sent to the front.

showing than many of the volunteer regiments, which was not surprising. The 8th New York militia had but 8 killed and 17 wounded, no officers figuring in the list.

Turning to Heintzelman, the record presents some very uneven results. In Franklin's brigade the 1st Minnesota suffered heavier loss in killed or wounded than any other Federal regiment in the field, 42 killed and 108 wounded; a record all the more notable and honorable in that the missing numbered not more than 30. But his other two regiments, the 5th and 11th Massachusetts, were not good, and only had 13 killed between them, which confirms what is said of them earlier. In Willcox's brigade the statistics show something very similar. The 11th New York had 48 killed and 75 wounded; twice as many killed as the rest of the brigade; the 1st Michigan [1] and 38th New York apparently did little fighting. Howard's shows results ranging from 5 killed, 8 wounded, and 74 missing for the 3d Maine, to 26 killed, 46 wounded, and 121 missing for the 4th Maine.

Although the loss in officers was little out of proportion, yet it must not be forgotten that only a very few of those officers were of the regular army, as the volunteer regiments were officered almost exclusively by civilians. Bearing this in mind, the statistics confirm what all other evidence tends to show, that the regular officers

[1] Detached for a while at Sudley Spring, and one of the last regiments to maintain the struggle.

displayed the utmost courage and suffered heavily in consequence. Among the killed and wounded, almost all of them West Pointers, were the following officers holding the rank of colonel or lieutenant-colonel : Haggerty, Cameron, Ballou, and Slocum (2d Rhode Island), killed, and Wood, Marston, Farnham, Lawrence, Slocum (27th New York), Hunter, Heintzelman, and Willcox, wounded.

The loss in artillery was officially returned as follows : [1]

| Batteries | Commanders | Guns lost | | | Remarks |
		Rifled	Smoothbore	Total	
1st U.S. Artillery, Company G; two 20-pounder Parrotts, one 30-pounder Parrott..........................	Lieutenant Edwards	1	–	1	20-pounders saved.
1st U.S. Artillery, Company I; six 10-pounder Parrotts	Captain Ricketts	6	–	6	None saved.
2d U.S. Artillery, Company D.......	Captain Arnold	2	2	4	None saved.
2d U.S. Artillery, Company E; two 13-pounder James, two 6-pounders (old), two 12-pounder howitzers..........	Captain Carlisle	2	2	4	Two 6-pounders saved.
5th U.S. Artillery, Company D ; two 10-pounder Parrotts, two 6-pounders (old), two 12-pounder howitzers.....	Captain Griffin	1	4	5	One 10-pounder saved.
Rhode Island battery, six 13-pounder James	Colonel Monroe	5	–	5	One saved.
Total lost......................	....	17	8	25	

To this list should be added, however, the two small howitzers of the 71st New York, bringing the total up to twenty-seven guns.

Of the missing, the Confederates claimed over 1400 as prisoners.

[1] O. R. Ser. I. vol. II, 328.

BULL RUN

SOUTH

On the Southern side the statistics are far more defective. The total of casualties shown by the Official Records[1] is 387 killed, 1582 wounded, and 13 missing; which might be described as about equal, save in the matter of missing, to McDowell's.

FIRST CORPS

(Confederate statistics, from O. R. Ser. I, vol. II, 510. The column "Aggregate" has been omitted. It will be noticed that for the Second Corps there are no returns for artillery or cavalry: i.e., for Stuart and Pendleton.)

Command	Killed Officers	Killed Enlisted men	Wounded Officers	Wounded Enlisted men	Missing Officers	Missing Enlisted men
Infantry —						
1st Louisiana Battalion	—	8	5	33	—	2
7th Louisiana	—	3	—	23	—	—
13th Mississippi	—	—	—	6	—	—
17th Mississippi	—	2	—	9	—	—
18th Mississippi	2	6	2	28	—	—
5th North Carolina	—	1	—	3	—	—
2d South Carolina	—	5	6	37	—	—
4th South Carolina	1	10	9	70	—	6
5th South Carolina	—	3	—	23	—	—
8th South Carolina	—	5	3	20	—	—
Hampton Legion	—	19	—	100	—	2
1st Virginia	—	—	—	6	—	—
7th Virginia	—	9	1	37	—	—
8th Virginia	—	6	—	23	—	1
17th Virginia	—	1	—	3	—	—
18th Virginia	—	6	1	12	—	—
19th Virginia	—	1	—	4	—	1
28th Virginia	—	—	—	9	—	—
49th Virginia	1	9	1	29	—	—
Artillery —						
Alexander's Light Artillery	—	1	—	2	—	—
Latham's	—	—	—	1	—	—
Loudoun	—	—	—	3	—	—
Washington	—	1	—	2	—	—
Cavalry —						
30th Virginia	2	3	—	4	—	—
Hanover	—	—	1	3	—	—
Total	6	99	29	490	—	12

[1] In the Official Records, Ser. I, vol. II, 570, is a statement headed "No.

SECOND CORPS

Command	Killed		Wounded		Missing	
	Officers	Enlisted men	Officers	Enlisted men	Officers	Enlisted men
Infantry —						
4th Alabama..............................	4	36	6	151	—	—
7th Georgia	1	18	12	122	—	—
8th Georgia..............................	3	38	6	153	—	—
1st Maryland.............................	—	1	—	5	—	—
2d Mississippi	4	21	3	79	1	—
11th Mississippi	—	7	—	21	—	—
6th North Carolina......................	1	22	4	46	—	—
3d Tennessee............................	—	1	—	3	—	—
2d Virginia.............................	3	15	3	69	—	—
4th Virginia	1	30	—	100	—	—
5th Virginia............................	—	6	—	47	—	—
10th Virginia...........................	—	6	—	10	—	—
27th Virginia	1	18	—	122	—	—
33d Virginia...........	1	44	—	101	—	—
Total..............................	19	263	34	1029	1	—
Grand Total......................	25	362	63	1519	1	12

These figures are both incomplete and incorrect, and require some adjustments.[1] It would be fair to say that

121. Casualties in the Army of the Potomac (Confederate) July 21, 1861." A footnote adds: "Compiled from the several reports and returns. . . ." This is one of the numerous examples of improper editing with which these costly volumes abound. Is this, as on its face it appears to be, the text of an original document, or is it not? Or is it merely a compilation from certain unspecified originals made by the editors?

[1] The reports of Jackson and his colonels as to casualties are not to be found; so, at least, it is stated at the foot of page 482 in O. R. Ser. 1, vol. 11; but in his report on the battle he says that his brigade lost 11 officers killed, 22 wounded, 100 enlisted men killed and 346 wounded, which is quite unlike the official figure. (See previous note.) The discrepancies in the number of men wounded are perhaps not important; but as to the officers killed and wounded Jackson's statement is, on the face of it, far the more probable, and the official compilation may be set down as incomplete.

In Stuart's report he alludes to his having 10 men killed; these do not figure in the official compilation.

Johnston, in his report, gives the grand total as, killed 378, wounded the Confederate figures of killed and wounded should be taken as an understatement on much the same scale as that of the Federals. It is not profitable to attempt any nearer approximation to the actual total.

Coming now to what the casualties show in relation to the fighting, it may first of all be pointed out that the three brigades of the army of the Shenandoah suffered more than two thirds of the total losses, and that of these three Bee's was the most severely, Kirby Smith's the least, cut up.

The part that Kirby Smith's brigade played was important because of the direction in which his advance was made; but the statistics reveal clearly that he met with little resistance. Two of the three regiments he actually brought into action lost each of them only one man killed; the 10th Virginia had 6 killed and 10 wounded; yet this regiment was in second line as the brigade was first deployed, which points to the loss being incurred during the pursuit, — perhaps when Arnold unlimbered near Sudley Spring and fired a few rounds.

1489, missing 30; while Beauregard makes it 369 and 1483, omitting mention of any missing.

The report of the 30th Virginia, giving the names of men killed, adds two privates to the official total. In D. R. Jones' brigade there are two or three trifling rectifications of the same sort to be made.

An editor's footnote in the Official Records states that the loss of the 18th Virginia was 5 killed, 16 wounded, 1 missing; it is officially given as 6 killed, 13 wounded.

Jackson's brigade suffered much more heavily. The 33d Virginia on his left, the regiment that charged Griffin and Ricketts and put their guns out of action, lost 45 killed and 101 wounded, out of less than 500 men. This was very severe, and tends to show how nearly spent the Confederate left must have been at the close of the fighting. The 2d Virginia, next in line from the left, also suffered severely, 18 killed, 77 wounded; the 4th Virginia even more, 31 killed and 100 wounded. The 27th Virginia lost 19 killed and 122 wounded; but the 5th Virginia, on the right of the line, came off lightly with 6 killed and 10 wounded. Jackson himself gives 100 killed and 368 wounded (the official figures are a little higher) [1] as his total loss, which was nearly 20 per cent of his numbers.

While Jackson averaged a loss of 112 killed and wounded per regiment, with Bee the figure rose to 164. All his regiments returned heavy casualties, from the 8th Georgia with 41 killed and 159 wounded to the 2d Mississippi with 25 killed and 82 wounded. The 11th Mississippi had only two companies present but lost 7 killed and 21 wounded. But it should be remembered that Bee's losses were accompanied by the complete breaking up of his brigade; while Jackson's brigade retained its organization at the close of the battle.

Turning now to Beauregard's troops, Evans and

[1] See note above.

Cocke bore the brunt of the fighting; but the former, with about 1100 bayonets, lost less heavily than might be supposed: the 4th S. Carolina had 11 killed and 79 wounded, the 1st Louisiana, 8 killed and 38 wounded. Cocke's five regiments were all eventually drawn into the fighting: the 49th Virginia, with 10 killed and 30 wounded, out of only 210 present, suffered most and the 28th Virginia, with 9 wounded and no killed, suffered least. Bonham's two regiments that went to Jackson's left and eventually pursued as far as Cub Run, the 2d and 8th South Carolina, lost respectively 5 killed, 43 wounded, and 5 killed, 23 wounded.

Hampton's Legion lost nearly 20 per cent, 19 killed and 100 wounded, and the 6th North Carolina, 23 killed and 50 wounded, a less proportion. Early's brigade, which got in on Kirby Smith's left at the very end of the action and turned McDowell's line, had, in 3 regiments, 12 killed and 67 wounded, most of these probably in the pursuit, which tends to show that the account of his brigade's operations given by Early in his "Memoirs" is exaggerated.

The brigades of Bonham (save for Kershaw's two regiments), Longstreet, Ewell, and Holmes were not engaged. That of Jones moved across Davies' front in the afternoon and suffered, in a few minutes, a loss of 14 killed and 62 wounded.

On the whole it may be said that the brigades of Bee

and Jackson did the bulk of the fighting on the Confederate side and suffered really heavy losses ; they received good support from several individual units ; while the brigades of Kirby Smith and Early, while they came in for no heavy fighting, played a great part tactically. The trifling loss of the Confederate artillery deserves no special note.[1]

The Confederate loss in field officers was exceedingly heavy. Of the three brigade commanders of Johnston's corps, General Bee was killed ; while Jackson and Kirby Smith were wounded, the latter severely. Among the colonels and lieutenant-colonels, Johnson, Thomas, Bartow, Fisher, and Jones were killed or mortally wounded ; Wheat, Gardner, Law, W. Smith, and Wade Hampton were wounded.

There is a slight discrepancy in the Confederate accounts of their captures. Johnston and Beauregard both claim 28 guns. Captain Alexander, the staff officer specially charged with reporting on this matter, makes it 27, but his statement contains obvious inaccuracies, though his total is probably correct.[2] Beauregard makes the

---

[1] One gets the impression that owing to the inferior calibre of their guns the Confederate artillery men were very careful to get cover, and reserved their fire as much as possible. At the short range which the configuration of the Henry house plateau gave, the smoothbore six-pounders were probably quite as effective as the more powerful Federal guns. It seems that wherever the ground had a slight up grade the Federal shells dug in on striking, thus getting small results.

[2] O. R. Ser. I, vol. II, 571.

total of prisoners, including one brigade commander, Willcox, and two colonels, 1460; Alexander reports 1421.

NUMBERS ENGAGED

The question of the numbers engaged must, in the nature of things, be resolved in a tentative manner. Making allowance for desertion, for troops left behind in camp,[1] for those who fell out by the way (one regiment was left at Fairfax Court House), it is doubtful whether McDowell disposed of any more than 27,000 men at Centreville on the 20th; while on the morning of the 21st, when the Pennsylvanians and New Yorkers left him, he lost about another 700 or 800 men.[2] Of his total, the three brigades near Centreville would account for 7000 and Schenck at Stone Bridge for about 2200, leaving about 17,000 men that crossed Bull Run.[3] Of these again, Keyes and Howard played no real part in the crisis of the battle, and it was probably less than 13,000 men — Sherman, Burnside, Porter, Willcox, and Franklin — that did the fighting from Sudley Spring to the Henry house.

[1] The 2d Wisconsin left 100 men behind. Allen, *Hist. of the 2d Wisconsin*, 379.

[2] Livermore, *Numbers and Losses*, I, 76, makes a rough calculation, by deducting three per cent from McDowell's return, and gives the effective total as 28,452; but this figure is much too high.

[3] McDowell, in his report, states that 18,000 crossed Bull Run, but he probably did not make sufficient allowance for the great wastage of his army. It is quite possible that the actual figure was even less than the 17,000 given in the text.

The Confederate figures are not so easy to establish. Beauregard, without counting a force of militia in the fortifications at Manassas which played no part, but adding Hunton, Holmes, Hampton, and the 6th North Carolina, had a little over 24,000 men, from which it might be fair to deduct 1000 for sick and missing, leaving 23,000 present for duty. Of these the following were actually used on the left: Kershaw's detachment from Bonham's brigade, say 1250; the Fifth Brigade, Cocke, including Hunton, 3000; the Sixth Brigade, Early, 1700; [1] the Seventh Brigade, Evans, 1100; making in all, of Beauregard's corps actually engaged, 7050 men. In addition, it may be recalled that Jones' brigade, with probably about 2000 present, was under fire near the Centreville ridge; while Hampton, and Fisher with the 6th North Carolina, might account for 1100 more between them. The remaining 13,000 men of Beauregard either arrived too late at the scene of action or were guarding the fords and uselessly demonstrating towards Centreville.

. The three brigades of Johnston's corps present totalled 7593,[2] of which Kirby Smith lost 550 by leaving the 13th Virginia behind at Manassas; so that the total may be placed at about 7000.[3]

[1] Allowing for various changes, and counting the 19th Virginia with Cocke.

[2] Johnston in his report gives nearly a thousand more, but apparently counted in the 6th North Carolina and perhaps some other units.

[3] Livermore, in his *Numbers and Losses*, takes the Confederates at the highest figures, making no deduction as he does for the Federals.

From these figures the reader can deduce his own conclusions as to when, where, and in what degree the preponderance of numbers inclined first to one side then to another. We must examine now what skill the generals displayed in utilizing their numbers, and other matters that belong to the field of tactics and of strategy.

XII

CONCLUSION

A CURIOUS thing about McDowell's enterprise at Bull Run is that one may fairly say that it was foreordained to failure, and yet conclude that it came within inches of success. Wholly untrained in the higher branches of the military art, he was compelled, by the force of circumstances, to operate with an army that was entirely unfit for active campaigning; but he had an opponent no better than himself, and the chief difference between two armies that both lacked the distinctive qualities of a field force resolved itself into that which lay between the disadvantage of the offensive and the benefit of the defensive.

In some ways McDowell did better than his critics have allowed. To move such an army at all, to get it concentrated at Centreville, to throw a wing of 17,000 men over Bull Run, meant much hard work and hard driving. And yet, as we have seen, all this fell entirely short of what was needed for success. Rapidity of action was essential, and at no moment, at no point, did McDowell show any tendency of the sort, — rather the contrary.

It is perhaps fairer to emphasize that McDowell had had no training or experience in the difficult art of generalship, than to say that he displayed no sign of possessing military qualities. It was certainly not easy for a junior officer in a military service that gave neither practical nor theoretical training to its higher ranks, when suddenly promoted to the command of an army to assume all the superiority and decision, to display all the science, that such a function demands. It is not surprising that he took too much advice, and deferred too much to the views of subordinates whose judgments, on the whole, do not appear to have been as good as his own.

In bringing his troops into contact with the enemy McDowell showed little tactical sense. His order of the 20th of July showed gross inability to handle marching arrangements. But he did better than his opponents in utilizing a considerable part of his forces for delivering his blow. His employment both of his guns and of his infantry was far from good. Griffin's and Ricketts' batteries were recklessly exposed; his infantry brigades were allowed to become mere supports for the artillery, and to go into action as strings of regiments employed one at a time. For these failings, the configuration of the ground, the superior tactics of the Confederates, the general lack of ability of McDowell's subordinates, the want of a proper system of command, and the general ignorance of staff work, were in part responsible.

Several of the Federal commanders ascribed their ill

success to what they believed to be the inferiority of their musketry. Thus Franklin says : —

It is my firm belief that a great deal of the misfortune of the day at Bull Run is due to the fact that the troops knew very little of the principles and practice of firing. In every case I believe that the firing of the rebels was better than ours.[1]

The truth appears to be this. The Federal infantry as it advanced was too carefully nursed by its officers; as soon as it reached the fire zone it was ordered to lie down and keep covered while the artillery did the work. So long as the artillery was successful in breaking down resistance the plan succeeded, but when the infantry was called on — after the hard day's work and much lying out of sight of the enemy in the sun — to advance into the open, firing at the enemy's line at short range, it jibbed away, fired wildly, and eventually broke.

Far more important than this was the complete and miserable failure of the regimental officers. Quite one half of McDowell's regiments were good stuff so far as the men went; all they needed was to be led and commanded. McDowell himself relates that on the field disorganized bodies of soldiers called to him asking to be led.[2] Colonel Biddle, speaking of the volunteers after their return to camp, says: "They had a perfect dread of going into battle with their officers, and

[1] O. R. Ser. 1, vol. 11, 407.
[2] *Rep. Cond. War*, 1, 132; McDowell's evidence.

they wanted to go back and enter into new organizations." [1]

If the regimental officers were for the most part worse
than useless, the field and staff officers were not much
better, though in a different way. The West-Pointers
were fearless enough, and fit to lead any troops into
battle; but they had no more knowledge of the art
of high command than the regimental officers had of
the art of company leading. This subject has already
been dealt with. Suffice it to say that on the field the
confusion of orders and of organization was almost complete. Everybody gave orders, and nobody gave orders.
McDowell's staff in large part disintegrated. No one
knew what to do, where to find headquarters. At the
moment when the attack on the Henry house plateau
began, Averell says: "this feeling was uppermost: want
of orders." [2] Later, even civilians like Governor Sprague
took it on themselves to order troops about.

It was the rout of the army back to Centreville and
Washington that attracted most attention at the time.
On the whole that was a mere incident of a not abnormal
character when all the facts of the case are considered.
That rout really began when, on the advance, the columns
were kept standing long hours in the sun and the officers
proved unable to prevent their men from going off into
the woods after blackberries; or when the Pennsylvania

---

[1] *Rep. Cond. War*, II, 198.   [2] *Rep. Cond. War*, II, 215.

and New York troops were allowed shamefully to abandon the army, with hardly a word of reproof, at the moment of battle; or even when Lincoln proclaimed that only the common soldier could be trusted and his officer was a leader not entitled to confidence. The rout at Stone Bridge was good newspaper copy, and little more.

It should be added that McDowell showed his even, steady bravery, in that disheartening hour. He continued to do all that was in him to the bitter end. At Young's Branch, at Centreville, and again at Fairfax Court House, he did his best to turn the stream of fugitives, he continued to take every measure he could to fulfil his duty as a soldier; from that high and honorable standard he never for a moment wavered. And his report is on the whole a straightforward and honest confession of failure, very little colored or distorted in an endeavor to evade responsibility.

On the Southern side the superiority of Johnston's corps in leadership, organization, and mobility stands out conspicuously. Bee got much out of his troops. Jackson showed the highest tactical ability, and great firmness of character, in the way he chose his position and handled his infantry and guns together on the Henry house plateau; he earned and he deserved the honors of the day. Johnston himself showed too much diffidence till about twelve o'clock, and it was not till about 2.30 or 3 P.M. that he really assumed control of operations. He displayed courage and at times judgment. Yet on the whole his conduct in the battle was far less creditable to him than the degree of organization and fighting quality he had succeeded in imparting to his little army, and the way in which he brought it from the Valley to Manassas.

Beauregard's errors, and his lack of the logic, system, and clearness of vision which are called for in the higher command of armies, have already been sufficiently emphasized. It is doubtful whether he did any one single thing that helped to bring success to the Confederate arms on the 21st of July, while his blunders would require a lengthy enumeration.

The defensive was assuredly a great advantage to the Confederate commanders. When their turn came to take the offensive on the Henry hill, — and they timed the moment skilfully, — their opponents were spent. Beauregard's orders and staff work certainly give one the impression that a Confederate offensive towards Centreville would probably have been marked by even less cohesion than McDowell's movement was. For although the Federal general failed to keep his brigades marching by the left after they passed Sudley Spring, he did at all events keep them together and strike a concerted blow. The movements of Ewell, Jones, and Longstreet do not suggest that Beauregard could have done as much.

Johnston himself wrote as follows : —

A large proportion of it [Beauregard's army] was not engaged in the battle. This was a great fault on my part. When Bee's and Jackson's brigades were ordered to the vicinity of the Stone Bridge, those of Holmes and Early should have been moved to the left also, and placed in the interval on Bonham's left — if not then, certainly at nine o'clock, when a Federal column was seen turning our left; and, when it seemed certain that General McDowell's great effort was to be made there. Bonham's, Longstreet's, Jones', and Ewell's brigades, leaving a few regiments and their cavalry to impose on Miles' division, should have been hurried to the left to join in the battle. If the tactics of the Federals had been equal to their strategy we should have been beaten. If, instead of being brought into action in detail,[1] their troops had been formed in two lines with a proper reserve, and had assailed Bee and Jackson in that order, the two Southern brigades must have been swept from the field in a few minutes, or enveloped. General McDowell would have made such a formation, probably, had he not greatly underestimated the strength of his enemy.[2]

The subsequent action of the Confederate authorities contains an official verdict on the generals. J. E. Johnston was left in charge of the main Confederate army at Manassas. Jackson was promoted to an independent command in the Shenandoah; while Beauregard was sent out West and placed under A. S. Johnston, with whom in the following year he fought the battle of Shiloh against Grant.

At Washington the scenes that followed the battle

[1] Perhaps Johnston does not make sufficient allowance for the configuration of the ground, and for the positions of Pendleton's and Walton's guns.

[2] Johnston, *Narrative*, 56. McDowell did not deploy a proper line of battle to attack the Henry house plateau for the much simpler reason that his army was far too confused in its mechanism when that stage was reached to make orders of that kind effective. The most he could do was to trust to his brigadiers to deploy.

were disheartening for the Federal cause. The city openly avowed its satisfaction at the Confederate victory. The volunteers showed up badly after their defeat. Discipline was at an end; drunkenness and disorder of the worst kind reigned supreme. The gravest anxiety prevailed, and a change of commanders was decided on that brought McClellan to Washington. Whether McClellan was any better than McDowell may be doubted, but at all events from that moment it was recognized by the Administration that the military problem was one for experts, and could not be solved by a handful of improperly organized three months' volunteers.

THE END

APPENDIX

APPENDIX

BIBLIOGRAPHY OF BOOKS AND MAPS

THE material for studying Bull Run has mostly been printed, and manuscripts are now difficult to find. I was long in hopes of getting access to some papers left by General McDowell which are said to contain information of importance as to his relations with the authorities at Washington; unfortunately I was unable to persuade those who have charge of them to let me see them.

OFFICIAL AND DOCUMENTARY

Over one hundred reports of the officers who took part in the operations, together with other documents, have been printed in the Official Records; this constitutes one of the two fundamental sources for the facts. But the editing of the Records has been so defective that the counsel of perfection would be to reject the printed form and go back to the manuscripts themselves. This has not been done in the present case, but it is not believed that any substantial inaccuracy is likely to have resulted. The Official Records are quoted all through: *O. R.* Less bulky and detailed, but more precise and valuable for establishing the facts dealt with, is the evidence given before the Congressional Committee on the Conduct of the War; their report is quoted: *Rep. Cond. War.* Within the same category, though of less importance, may be reckoned the collection of documents known as the Rebellion Record (quoted *Reb. Rec.*). The correspondence of Lincoln is strikingly poor for this period. Among other documents, the only other worth special mention is the Report of the Secretary of War (Confederate), of December 14, 1861. The newspapers are so inaccurate, and have so little knowledge of the nature of military affairs, that they are almost valueless. I have made a few unimportant quotations from articles reprinted in the Rebellion Records. In more important matters, such as the origin of the "Stonewall" story, the original newspaper files have been searched.

RELATIONS OF CONTEMPORARIES WRITTEN AT THE TIME

Among these, that of Doctor Russell, *My Diary North and South* (London, 1863), is probably the best known. It is vivid and informing, but the author did not actually reach the field and see the fighting. Warder and Catlett's *Battle of Young's Branch* (Richmond, 1862) is obviously a compilation from the accounts of eyewitnesses; it is particularly good for following individual regiments. Patterson's *Narrative of the Campaign in the Valley of the Shenandoah* (Philadelphia, 1862) adds little to our knowledge, and can only be read with his evidence before the Congressional Committee; while Major, later General, Barnard's *The C.S.A. and the Battle of Bull Run* (New York, 1862) is a pretentious and not trustworthy revamping of published reports and accounts. A more picturesque note is struck by an "English Combatant," in his *Battlefields of the South* (New York, 1864).

ACCOUNTS BY CONTEMPORARIES WRITTEN IN AFTER
YEARS

Chief and best among these is undoubtedly Johnston's *Narrative* (New York, 1874), which is able, clear, and probably written on the copies of the original documents which he had preserved. Three other Southern generals have given us more or less good accounts: Alexander, in his *Military Memoirs* (New York, 1907); Longstreet, in his *From Manassas to Appomattox* (Philadelphia, 1896); and Early in his *Memoirs* (Philadelphia, 1912). Of some importance, also, are Jefferson Davis' *Rise and Fall of the Confederacy* (New York, 1881); J. D. Imboden's *Incidents of the First Bull Run* in the Century Company's *Battles and Leaders*; the *Memoirs* of General Sherman (New York, 1875); various repetitious contributions of Beauregard, chief of which are his *Commentary on the Campaign and Battle of Manassas* (New York, 1891) and *The First Battle of Bull Run*, in *Battles and Leaders*, the latter containing a résumé of his preceding statements. Beauregard's attacks on Johnston were met by the latter in his *Responsibilities of the First Bull Run*, also in *Battles and Leaders*, which is not nearly as convincing as his *Narrative* and official reports. Controversy was not confined to the Southern side; Donald Mitchell's untrustworthy *Memoir of Tyler* (privately printed) was met by Fry's reply, *McDowell and Tyler* (New York, 1884); the same author contributed a fair article, on *McDowell's Advance to Bull Run*, to the *Battles and Leaders* series. Among many lesser contributions I note Townsend's *Anecdotes of the Civil War* (New York, 1884) and Wilkeson's *Recollections of a Private* (New York, 1887). Regimental histories and similar works will be noticed later.

HISTORIES AND BIOGRAPHIES

A long list of such books could be compiled, but it is not my purpose to inflate this enumeration for no useful purpose. Few general historians of the epoch show any understanding of military problems; most of them, indeed, show a depressing inability, almost unwillingness, to make the necessary effort. The Comte de Paris and J. C. Ropes have written the best known histories of the war, and the latter has a few clear and good pages on Bull Run. Nicolay's *Outbreak of the Rebellion* is not good, but has its uses; Roman's *Military Operations of General Beauregard* (New York, 1884) is voluminous and valuable on the personal and political side, but is very poor for military affairs. A number of biographies of Jackson are indicated in the footnote concerning the origin of his sobriquet; that of Colonel Henderson is by far the best.

REGIMENTAL HISTORIES AND PAPERS

The material of this description is most discouraging, almost valueless. The most conspicuous quality of the regimental annalist is always loyalty, — that is, loyalty to his regiment, not to truth. Every regiment that has a record is a regiment of heroes, a somewhat startling, in fact quite unbelievable fact, for the dispassionate investigator. Book after book and paper after paper, addressed to "old comrades," have been turned over without adding much to my store of information. Cudworth's *History of the 1st Massachusetts* is far less depressing than the fantastic records of the 5th and 11th Regiments of the same State. Allen's *2d Wisconsin at Bull Run*, Monroe's *Rhode Island Artil-*

lery at Bull Run, H. F. Lyster's "Bull Run," *Michigan Commandery Loyal Legion, Papers*, vol. I, King's "Address," *Minnesota Commandery Loyal Legion*, Ser. 6, all contain snippets of information. In a better class are Bicknell's *History of the 5th Maine;* Hayne's *History of the 2d New Hampshire;* Todd's *79th Highlanders;* Slocum's *History of the 27th New York;* and Woodbury's two books on the 1st and 2d Rhode Island. Less good are J. E. Smith's *A Famous Battery*, — a deceptive title, for it refers to the 8th New York; Whittemore's *History of the 71st New York;* and Curtin's *From Bull Run to Chancellorsville*, which is the history of the 16th New York. On the Southern side there is almost nothing, and I note that the series of the Military Historical Society of Massachusetts is unusually poor on the present subject.

The papers published by the Southern Historical Society are very similar to the above in general character, but far more voluminous and therefore useful.

An occasional reference has been given to a magazine article in the footnotes; and one may mention, in addition, W. Nowell, "The 1st Battle of Bull Run," *Infantry Journal*, VI, 7; and T. O. Murphy, "Some Mistakes in Organization," *Infantry Journal*, VI, 217.

MAPS

Military maps, especially those that indicate the position of troops, are evidence of the same general character as books. The number of contemporary maps of Bull Run is very large, as the newspapers and speculative printers furnished the public demand for such things with extraordinary, but for the most part misguided, energy. Such productions do not require cataloguing, and but few of them find place in the following list, which contains chiefly contemporary maps that have some value as historical evidence.

1. Map of northeastern Virginia and vicinity of Washington. Compiled by the engineer officers of McDowell's staff in the fall of 1861 and corrected down to August, 1862. O. R. Atlas, vol. I, plate VII. This map is in part reproduced in the end papers of this volume. It seems almost certain that McDowell used it during the operations. In that connection it is not unimportant to note that

it is inaccurate in delineating the ground at Blackburn's and Mitchell's fords.

2. Plan of the battlefield at Bull Run, July 21st, 1861. By Captain A. W. Whipple, of McDowell's staff, and assistants. O. R. Atlas, vol. I, plate III, 1. Good for the Federal movements in the morning; incorrect for the Confederate positions. There is a good reproduction of this map in Barnard's *C.S.A. and Bull Run.*

3. Map of the battlefields of Manassas. By Lieutenant W. G. Atkinson, of Beauregard's staff. O. R. Atlas, vol. I, plate III, 2. Presented by Beauregard to the city of New Orleans. Extremely good both for topography and movements of troops, and for the field of operations about the Henry house plateau.

4. Reconnaissance of the battlefield at Bull Run. By Lieutenant Henry L. Abbot, March 14, 1862. O. R. Atlas, vol. I, plate V, 7. Excellent for the topography of the Henry house plateau and ground near by. A better version of this map, more detailed, appears in Barnard, *C.S.A. and Bull Run.*

5. Battlefield of Young's Branch, or Manassas Plains. By Major Michler (?). O. R. Atlas, vol. I, plate V, 1. Good for topography and position of Confederate troops; untrustworthy for Federal positions.

6. Map of the ground of occupation and defence of the Division of the U.S. Army in Virginia in command of Brig.-Gen. Irvin McDowell. By H. C. Whiting; field work done in June and July, 1861. O. R. Atlas, vol. I, plate VI, 1. Good for the Federal fortifications on both sides of the Potomac.

7. Map of the battlefield near the Henry house in Warder and Catlett's *Battle of Young's Branch.* (Richmond, 1862.) A very useful map for position of Confederate regiments.

8. Map of the battlefield of Bull Run. By Solomon Bamberger; in Barnard's *C.S.A. and Bull Run.* A curious map reproduced from a Richmond publication.

9. Topographical map of Bull Run. By Captain Harris and J. Grant. Made for Beauregard and reproduced by the Century Company in *Battles and Leaders,* vol. I. Good for the topography of the Henry house plateau and neighborhood.

10. Map of the battlefield of Bull Run; compiled from maps accompanying the reports of Generals McDowell and Beauregard. (Washington, 1877.) An excellent map, of which the Military Historical Society of Massachusetts has a copy.

11. Plan of the battle of Bull Run. By Captain Mitchell, 1st Virginia. (White, Richmond.) Inaccurate.

12. Map of the seat of war. By V. P. Corbett. (Washington.) Inaccurate.

13. Volume of lithographed maps from an original of McDowell's used at the trial of FitzJohn Porter, and preserved by the Military Historical Society of Massachusetts. These maps refer to the Second Manassas, but are excellent for the topography of Bull Run.

14. Military map showing the works erected at Manassas Junction. By Colonel Thomas H. Williamson. (Richmond, 1861.) Not very important. There is a copy in the Confederate Museum at Richmond.

INDEX

INDEX